BEYOND GATSBY

Contemporary American Literature
Series Editor: Bob Batchelor

Gatsby: The Cultural History of the Great American Novel, by Bob Batchelor, 2013.

Michael Chabon's America: Magical Words, Secret Worlds, and Sacred Spaces, edited by Jesse Kavadlo and Bob Batchelor, 2014.

Hypermasculinities in the Contemporary Novel: Cormac McCarthy, Toni Morrison, and James Baldwin, by Josef Benson, 2014.

Stephen King's Contemporary Classics: Reflections on the Modern Master of Horror, edited by Philip L. Simpson and Patrick McAleer, 2015.

Beyond Gatsby: How Fitzgerald, Hemingway, and Writers of the 1920s Shaped American Culture, by Robert McParland, 2015.

BEYOND GATSBY

How Fitzgerald, Hemingway, and Writers of the 1920s Shaped American Culture

Robert McParland

ROWMAN & LITTLEFIELD
Lanham • Boulder • New York • London

Published by Rowman & Littlefield
A wholly owned subsidary of The Rowman & Littlefield Publishing Group,
Inc.
4501 Forbes Boulevard, Suite 200, Lanham, Maryland 20706
www.rowman.com

Unit A, Whitacre Mews, 26-34 Stannary Street, London SE11 4AB

British Library Cataloguing in Publication Information Available

Library of Congress Cataloging-in-Publication Data

McParland, Robert.
Beyond Gatsby : how Fitzgerald, Hemingway, and writers of the 1920s shaped American culture /
Robert McParland.
pages cm. – (Contemporary American literature)
Includes bibliographical references and index.
ISBN 978-1-4422-4708-6 (cloth : alk. paper) – ISBN 978-1-4422-4709-3 (ebook)
1. American fiction–20th century–History and criticism. 2. Popular culture–United
States–History–20th century. I. Title.
PS369.M37 2015
813'.5209–dc23
2014042912

∞ ™ The paper used in this publication meets the minimum requirements of
American National Standard for Information Sciences Permanence of Paper
for Printed Library Materials, ANSI/NISO Z39.48-1992.

Printed in the United States of America

To my parents, Joan and Robert G. McParland

CONTENTS

PREFACE

Nearly one hundred years ago, F. Scott Fitzgerald's *This Side of Paradise* (1920) heralded a new era. A new generation appeared in its pages: one with a zest for life in a changing America. It also marked the beginning of a decade in which writers would change the face of American fiction and shape the American imagination. The first printing of 3,000 copies of Fitzgerald's novel about college life, published March 26, 1920, sold out in three days. With a subsequent printing, sales quickly reached 20,000 copies. Fitzgerald soon sold nine short stories to magazines, including his first to the *Saturday Evening Post*. Some 50,000 copies of *This Side of Paradise* had been sold by the end of 1922. Clearly, something about the novel had caught the spirit of the times. It seemed as if a new adventure had begun.

Fitzgerald cast images of the 1920s that became central to how the era is seen and interpreted. Youthful and energetic, he provided the picture of his age that we most remember. He set the tone and offered the image that the "Roaring Twenties" constituted a glamorous time of jazz, dancing flappers, and ecstatic spontaneity. His short story collection *Flappers and Philosophers* supports this image. *The Beautiful and Damned*, appearing in early 1922, reached sales of 40,000 to 50,000 copies. *The Great Gatsby* (1925), with a 20,780-copy first printing, was less successful commercially. Yet, it is the most enduring of his works and the chief source of our popular images of the period he called the "jazz age."

The extravagant parties in *The Great Gatsby* make for intriguing imagery and symbols on the page and splashy effects on the movie screen; however, the lights and glamour of Jay Gatsby's parties only offer a partial picture of a broader and more complex social phenomenon. Certainly, the image that the Roaring Twenties was entirely a matter of exuberance, dancing, and drinking has to be qualified. The literature of the 1920s provides a crucial reference point to help us understand the American dream. These stories reveal the hopes and concerns that people held and the changes that were in process in the America they knew. Perhaps in response to the Great War, Prohibition, and the Victorian age, the new generation depicted by Fitzgerald did indulge, but any period is more complex and varied than this.

While there were fads and frenetic flappers, the roar of motors of cars and airplanes, and the blare of jazz horns, there were lives that were modest and staid, as well as those that were indulgent and wild. Some may have danced through a time of spectacle and decadence. Others looked to the notion of a "lost generation" that Hemingway inscribed in an epigraph to his first novel, *The Sun Also Rises* (1926). That generation brought startlingly novel voices to American literature, including those of F. Scott Fitzgerald, Ernest Hemingway, and William Faulkner. The 1920s brought social critiques from Sinclair Lewis and John Dos Passos, and reflections on American culture from Willa Cather and the writers of the Harlem Renaissance. In the craft and innovations of these writers, something new, something vital, perceptive, and lasting, was emerging.

This book explores this crucial turning point in American literary history and assesses the literary landscape that the reading audience responded to. Nearly one hundred years later, the cultural milieu of the 1920s is not our own; however, the imagery, issues, and concerns of the 1920s still speak to us. Film has recently given us Leonardo DiCaprio in *The Great Gatsby*. Television has given us *Boardwalk Empire* and *Downton Abbey*. Yet, even clearer images of the 1920s and their continuing relevance can be found in the literature of that time. Some of that literature is of a lasting quality, addressing what is universal in human life and cultural experience. As Bob Batchelor observes, "Literature and literary figures can be used to establish context in debates that seem far removed from the era in which the work appeared."[1]

This volume is about the contexts that the novels of the 1920s offer for our present debates. It is about the cultural responses that they engendered in their own time. It is also about the wonder of reading and imagination, and the continuing relevance of stories written nearly one hundred years ago. The focus on American writers of that era is intended to provide a better understanding of the continuing value of the classic works of American fiction. The dynamic relationship between America's major authors and their readers is investigated to highlight the ongoing relevance of reading and thinking about the issues in our own lives. This study looks at how that "one bright book of life," as D. H. Lawrence called the novel in the 1920s, shaped the modern American imagination.[2] Narratives offer us ways of organizing life. They create a space in which we might think about our lives and feel along with characters who suggest the experience of other people's lives. Stories help us put ourselves "in another person's shoes." That empathy is strikingly important in the debates of today's global environment.

The importance of reading persists throughout the generations. Readers in the 1920s were captivated by the novels discussed here. Revisiting them, we have some control with regard to how we imagine and construct this experience. When we watch television or film, the physical image and voice of a character are given to us. So is a particular angle of vision and the pace at which the story moves. When we read, we can adjust that pace by reading faster or slower. We can close the book and put it aside. We can also imagine a character based on the description the writer gives us. We can imagine the setting that character is in and hear that character's voice.

The novels of the 1920s still spark the imagination. While our era is, in many respects, quite different from the 1920s, the thought, styles, and voices of that period remain something more than quaint nostalgia. By taking classic 1920s novels off the shelves, we are not merely dusting off old relics. Many stories of the 1920s address the human condition, and with them we may also look at our own time, as if in a historical mirror. A novel may continue to have life and relevance beyond its time, long after its moment of popular consumption. Indeed, some novels that were less than popular during their time—James Joyce's *Ulysses*, William Faulkner's *The Sound and the Fury*, or F. Scott Fitzgerald's *The Great Gatsby*—have grown in stature throughout the years. Characters in 1920s fiction presented sharp images of their time.

These novels not only portrayed life, for some readers they provided markers of how to negotiate life. They helped people find meaning in the disparate chaos of the modern world. Oftentimes something about these characters transcended their era. In that sense, they are relevant to us today.

Books continue to be part of America's national psyche. Some years ago, political scientist Benedict Anderson theorized that the exchange of print culture fostered what he called "imagined community." We will never meet everyone in a broad, expansive nation like the United States, but we may imagine our connection through shared media. Such awareness that others are reading some of the same books and periodicals, Anderson believed, has supported the development of nations. This awareness might be defined as a public consciousness informed by commonly shared news and media, collective memory, and archetypes.

To explore American consciousness, we turn to the texts of the 1920s for their cultural relevance. A goal of this study is to encourage further inquiry into how readers assimilated these works and how these books affected and connected people. American fiction provided readers with familiar narratives and common characters, images that people shared culturally. Mass media emerged from this distribution network, and these stories became part of the common language of American culture. They reflected human aspirations, brought readers imaginatively to new places, and prompted reflection on values.

Media globalization, digital technologies, and electronic texts have become part of a world of changing reading habits. We live in an information age filled with a plethora of facts. So why do we read fiction? Robert Penn Warren once simply said, "because we like it." Fiction, "as an image of life," he told the readers of the *Saturday Evening Post* in 1986, "stimulates our interest in life." It is, he said, "life in motion."[3] A novel can dissect or disclose the world. It might even create a public conversation, as occurred with Sinclair Lewis's *Main Street* (1920) and *Babbitt* (1922). A novel may reveal life in its aesthetic form and characters, enabling us to enter other lives and situations.

The novel is also a cultural marker, one that records a slice of experience and may help us think about our world, our nation, and people's lives in different ways. With books like Sherwood Anderson's *Winesberg, Ohio*, James Joyce's *Portrait of the Artist* and *Ulysses*, and D. H. Lawrence's *Women in Love*, "you tear the masks from off your fellows," wrote Louis Kantor in 1922.[4] "It can help you not to be dead in life," D. H. Lawrence writes of the novel. Characteristically, he emphasizes "aliveness" and he says that a good novel could "make the whole man alive tremble." A person ought to be fully alive, he insists, not "like a pianoforte with half the notes mute."[5]

Many people in our time have held that something important happens when we read good fiction. Gordon Hunter has spoken of "how the talk about books becomes the sound of culture conversing with itself."[6] Elizabeth Long observes that reading fiction "sharpens social skills, expands perspective, and augments the ability to empathize."[7] In his *New York Review of Books* blog (March 26, 2012), Tim Parks writes that a historically dense and complex story provides a sense of the unique individual beneath "surface transformations," "dilemmas," and "conversations."[8]

Novels are like windows into national consciousness. American fiction assists us in discovering "Americanness," for these novels are, in a variety of ways, representative of this. When political scientist Michael J. Sandel argues in *Democracy's Discontent* that we should "not become storyless," he underscores the insight that stories are central to our lives and the life of our communities.[9] They embody past and present, reflect culture and individual effort, and present and illuminate ideas. In the 1920s, the novel helped some people make sense of their surroundings. They might also help us make further sense of ours.

To read a novel from the 1920s may require some patience. It is a bit like yoga, as Susan Shillinglaw suggests in her study of John Steinbeck: It forces a person to be deliberate.[10] Yoga forces one to focus on each muscle and one's breathing. To read is to set aside that high speed Internet connection and slow down; however, the time spent in these imagined worlds may help us better understand the themes and issues of American culture then as now. This book takes the view that we might more fully comprehend our national character by looking back at the 1920s through these stories. Significant American writers emerged in the 1920s. Such voices as those of Ernest Hemingway, F. Scott Fitzgerald, William Faulkner, Willa Cather, and the writers of the Harlem Renaissance have contributed to our cultural consciousness and shaping the American imagination and the American dream in the present.

The American novel will be our focus. Drama and poetry are considered here only in passing, although they too were vital features of the literary landscape. Poets of the 1920s, from Robert Frost, Wallace Stevens, and Carl Sandburg to Marianne Moore, Hart Crane, and Ezra Pound, are mentioned briefly. The sustained attention their poetic contributions to 1920s culture merits would comprise another study. T. S. Eliot's *The Waste Land* is presented only as a suggestive figure representing the times or one way of viewing the postwar early 1920s. There is no attempt made to analyze Eliot's poem. It serves as a marker of the period.

The novel is presented here as reflective of American culture. This study is concerned with how critics and readers received major American novelists in their own time and how they made a lasting impact on American literary culture. The stories of these writers ought not be seen as merely mimetic of that 1920s culture. Rather, they are complex, imaginative works that are given to audiences of readers, including us, who may interpret them in a myriad of ways.

These writers merit our close attention. Yet, it would also be interesting to know more about their readers and begin to find those readers across region, race, gender, and class. In this respect, we might discover how the novels of the 1920s were received by readers other than professional critics. I gesture toward this project here, but it is one that will take further efforts amongst cultural historians of reading and literature to accomplish.

Attention here primarily focuses upon novels and novelists who have endured into our own time—at least for some readers. They have received critical regard and been valued by many readers outside the literary establishment. Such novels have staying power beyond their milieu, not only when they have been made into feature films or have been taught as required texts in classrooms. They endure—at least in reputation, if not also in actual readership—because they have compelling characters and touch on universal themes. They are stories that may still enable readers today to understand their world—or wonder at it.

* * *

One hundred years ago, World War I drew the attention of Americans overseas. As a spokesman for a generation of postwar youth, F. Scott Fitzgerald suggested what it meant to be alive in the 1920s. In his lyrical fiction, he examined what it meant to dance the Charleston, deal with Prohibition, listen to jazz, or ride a trolley. He and his contemporaries wrote stories that still speak to us about the courage of characters, their aspirations, and the efforts of their lives. As a result, novels like *The Great Gatsby*, or Ernest Hemingway's *The Sun Also Rises*, or Theodore Dreiser's *An American Tragedy* continue to be significant. From a variety of viewpoints, these novels repeatedly address the American dream or the hopes of modern people wrestling with the human condition. They also remind us that fiction and the culture from which it emerges are inseparable. These novels help us to study the past so that we might better know the present.

Today we might download Hemingway's *A Farewell to Arms* or Cather's *One of Ours* onto our Kindle or read Lewis's *Babbitt* on an iPad. One might have a DVD of the film version of Edith Wharton's *The Age of Innocence* or see Leonardo DiCaprio star as Jay Gatsby in Baz Luhrmann's film and then turn to the book as a listener of Nick Carraway's narrative read by an actor on CD. In the 1920s, readers held these books in their hands; they turned the pages of the physical book: paper, ink letters, the heft of a hardcover, and pages perfect bound. We may wonder how they entered the fictional dream, that willing suspension of disbelief that allows a reader to feel the atmosphere of another place, the wonder of words, the design and pattern of images and story in an imaginative encounter. People clearly took the time to reflect on books. Sometimes they saw themselves or their society reflected in them.

Our world has changed since the 1920s and so has the reputation of many writers of that time. We may seldom read Nobel Prize–winning author Sinclair Lewis these days, except, perhaps, in school. Yet, in today's political rhetoric we hear about "Main Street," as well as Wall Street. Babbitt, Lewis's famous character, serves as an archetype of a superficial, provincial man of limited scope and taste, whose self-worth is attached to his purchase of the latest electronic gadget or Xbox video game. On the evening news, one might hear about questionable Elmer Gantry figures: evangelical charlatans or clerical pedophiles whose hypocrisy casts clouds over organized religion but cannot undermine the faithfulness and good works of devoted clergy that go on each day. The 1920s produced the sounds and images of the jazz age, which still cling to the air of modern America. They were in the Harlem Renaissance, its assertion of a dream deferred, a black arts movement revived during the 1960s and later. The 1920s saw the first works of Hemingway, whose image of stoicism and athleticism blended with the World War II image of masculinity, the Marlboro man, and John Wayne films of the 1950s and 1960s.

The 1920s changed American culture, and the classic novels of the decade seem to have declared that American literature had finally arrived on the world stage, with its own voice, style, and subject matter. The American novel engaged in and encouraged critical thinking about society. It sought the American vernacular. As we look back from a point in time nearly one hundred years afterward, we do so living in a context that developed from those times. Novels and the humanities continue to be significant—indeed necessary—for modern society. To read the American classic novels of the 1920s is not merely to engage in an act of nostalgia; it is to discover America and an era's search for meaning through a variety of stories and literary forms. It is to recognize that elements of that past are reflected in our present time. Just as the Homeric epics bound together Greek society or Native American tales illuminated the life of indigenous cultures, the stories of America recall and illustrate the American dream. They provide clues to our dreams, struggles, and expectations, for they are the myths of our possibility. Our stories are an important part of who we are.

The classic novel of the 1920s continues to speak to our contemporary society and remind us of the creative energy of our predecessors. A novel, while it may imagine a life, is never as rich as the story of any single human life. Each of our ancestors lived a unique life and had his or her own story. Yet, the fictional imagination can give us a window to their lives and lasting contributions to the human enterprise. The best stories endure, with their archetypal heroes, like the rocky faces of Mount Rushmore. Human emotions live on, generation after generation, and the best writers feel them and craftily grasp them like fireflies caught in a child's hand on a warm summer evening.

We may ask what it means for a novel to enter the cultural mindset of the nation. Readers interpreted these novels differently as they brought their lives and concerns into their reading. Still, they also knew that other people were reading these same novels, that they were part of a conversation in the imagined community just as much as the Super Bowl or televised Academy Awards shows may be today. Novels written in the 1920s participated in culture, and they were read by people who did not have television to fill their leisure hours.

Several novels of the 1920s interrogated American culture. The American dream of the characters in some of these stories intersected with readers' sense of America and the narrative of their own lives. They could see that the rags-to-riches Horatio Alger myth was not effective in the life of Dreiser's Clyde Griffiths in *An American Tragedy*. Nor was the small town of Sherwood Anderson's *Winesberg, Ohio* a community. Soldiers like Hemingway's Harold Krebs returned from war with posttraumatic stress disorder, although it was then called "shell shock," and they felt they had no one they could talk to about what they were going through.

We might ask whether this is any different from the experiences of today's veterans of the Iraq and Afghanistan conflicts. When George Babbitt is reduced to the acquisition of trinkets and boosterism, one can imagine him standing in line at Target, Walmart, or Best Buy in quest of a digital device. In the 1920s, he desired toasters and esteemed Warren Harding; today he buys iPads and reveres Bill Gates. He fills material needs and social needs for belonging, as one might see in Abraham Maslow's hierarchy of needs, without aspiring to self-actualization and social contribution.

These novels of the 1920s continue to offer us predicaments that are relevant to our own time. Like Dreiser's Clyde Griffiths, young men are still allured by the lights of the city, gaudy hotels, and dreams of business success. The young man from a small town who desires a society girl from the bright lights and big city acutely feels Gatsby's longing for Daisy, beset as he is by social stratification. Lewis's Carol Kennicott still comes from a little town and has the desire to reshape society. Perhaps America has changed enough that this woman, unlike Carol, can now do so. Today from Nebraska come those like Cather's Claude Wheeler, a young man who sought to grow; he has felt a sense of responsibility to the land and nation, and he goes off to defend America's liberties on the field of war. Like the young reporter George Willard in *Winesberg, Ohio*, the rookie broadcast news reporter of modern times is sent out to some godforsaken locale in the rain to cover a story. She discovers people with shattered lives or distorted dreams who need to tell their stories. Like Sherwood Anderson's character, she becomes a listener and an interpreter.

Through novels, readers of the 1920s were interpreting themselves. They were looking at where life was going during a time of precipitous change. For some readers, such novels were not only a means of escape or solace, they were cultural signposts. A reader might use them to interpret the nation or local society. The 1920s saw the rise of consumer culture and abandonment of Victorian notions of thrift. Advertisements began to saturate American culture, as they do now. They appeared in the front and back pages of books, in magazines and newspapers, on billboards, and in store windows. This world of signs and images promised health, beauty, love, and economic advancement. It prodded consumers to purchase items on credit. The green light of Jay Gatsby's dreams flickered across the water. The magic glittering balls of hotel chandeliers lured Clyde Griffiths, and bright ads for new toasters enticed Babbitt. Novels from the 1920s satirized a new world, sending out warnings about the Siren's tempting call. Images came from the movies as well: Mae West was a shrewd and tantalizing Circe figure. Buster Keaton was a comic figure baffled by modernity. Charlie Chaplin was a sympathetic tramp with a bowler hat and little mustache, satirizing modern times. Novels and their film versions influenced how people saw the world and thought about America—about love and belonging, wealth and power, and dreams and ideals. Novels offered insights, as well as entertainment. They were mirrors of culture, refracting that bit of light and the images they portrayed. Read in many different ways by their readers, they participated in the cultural work of making America.

INTRODUCTION

The 1920s

Some critics have called the 1920s a golden age of American literature. The 1920s, the "jazz age," saw a new generation of writers beginning to appear that would change the direction of American writing. Following World War I, these writers shared a new world with their readers. Some believed that a coherent order of civilization had been lost to the war. Postwar disillusionment was a reality for many of America's expatriates. The themes of the wasteland and the lost generation are often repeated by critics. Yet, this does not seem to have characterized the tone of the nation in 1920 or afterward. The 1920s that is evoked in much popular culture is ebullient: It is the "Roaring Twenties," a time of prosperity and glamour. Before we begin investigating the literature and writers of this period, let us take a look at the cultural atmosphere.

The carpe diem spirit of the times was observed by Frederick Lewis Allen, who attributes some of the "eat, drink, and be merry for tomorrow we die spirit" to World War I.[1] In the September 1920 installment of *Atlantic Monthly*, John F. Carter writes, "The older generation had certainly pretty well ruined this world before passing it on to us."[2] Walter Lippmann comments that what most distinguished the new generation was their disillusionment with their own rebellion.[3] A sense of disillusionment hung in the air alongside that *Gatsby* image that looms large in our way of looking at the 1920s.

In our time, it seems that flappers, bootleggers, and Al Capone have taken on new life. A recent biography of Calvin Coolidge, HBO's *Boardwalk Empire*, the BBC show *Downton Abbey*, and Baz Luhrmann's film *The Great Gatsby* have once again turned our attention to the 1920s. Reading the novels of that time period provides us with a way of looking at our own lives and our own time in the mirror of the past. The classic novels—those of Sinclair Lewis, Willa Cather, and John Dos Passos, as well as Ernest Hemingway's *The Sun Also Rises*, F. Scott Fitzgerald's *The Great Gatsby*, and William Faulkner's *The Sound and the Fury*—not only mark prodigious advances in American fiction, they show us the wonder, struggle, and promise of the American dream.

The Great Gatsby films of 1974 and 2013 have kept Fitzgerald's novel and characters in public awareness, as Bob Batchelor demonstrates in *Gatsby: The Cultural History of the Great American Novel* (2014). Meanwhile, film has made Gatsby more concrete than the elusive and mysterious figure of Fitzgerald's novel. Thinking of the character, one tends to see Robert Redford or Leonardo DiCaprio. Nick Carraway's first-person point of view and limited knowledge cannot be easily reproduced.

In the 1974 film, romantic scenes occur between Gatsby and Daisy that Nick could not possibly know of personally. His narrative is a work of interpretation and not entirely reliable. For example, he begins in the novel by insisting that his father told him never to judge and then proceeds to spend the rest of the narrative judging everything and everyone. We begin our acquaintance with Gatsby by being told by Nick that he turned out all right in the end, suggesting that the best way for us to grasp Fitzgerald's creative vision is to read his novel.

LITERARY CHARACTERS AND CULTURAL DREAMS

Few characters in literature attain the mythic or iconic status to which Gatsby has risen throughout the years; however, the 1920s developed numerous archetypal heroes and antiheroes. The audience knew the soldier returning from the front and the financier seeking power and fortune. It responded to Lewis's image of Babbitt, striving within his locale, and his controversial Elmer Gantry, who became the image of a hypocritical preacher out to bilk his congregation. The Hemingway masculine image also had considerable force in twentieth-century America. Stoic and a man of few words, he exemplified the tough-guy image of noir detective fiction and the resolve of John Wayne, *Gunsmoke*, and the Marlboro Man. The fiction of the 1920s instigated these characters and images.

When the automobile rolled out of Ford's dreams, World War I came to an end and the bright lights began to come on as soldiers returned home, and the sky was filled with the possibilities of thrilling flight, the conditions became ripe for the age of jazz, flappers, and novelty. The 1920s brought mass-media culture to America. Radio, film, and advertising influenced how people thought of themselves and their world. Popular culture introduced such fads as crossword puzzles, Mah-Jong, and the Charleston. Images of pop stars and heroes appeared, from singer Rudy Vallee and actress Clara Bow to pilot Charles Lindbergh. It was an exciting time in American literature and a pivotal period in modern American history; it was a time of new technologies and rapid change, much like today. Of course, the "Roaring Twenties" is a convenient label for the spirit of the times that characterize this period. The trends of the 1920s began at an earlier time and continued for a few years thereafter.

Changes in writing and reading were afoot in the 1910s with modernism, and they were heightened by the war, as Gertrude Stein then noticed and many critics since have pointed out. Features of the decade continued into the early 1930s, despite the widespread effects of the Great Depression. Still, to say "Roaring Twenties" is to point to a period of American life characterized by rapid change and creativity that remains quite relevant in modern times, for this time period generated, in literature and the arts, media and popular culture, the beginnings of what America has since become.

To speak of the 1920s also reminds us that writers and their readers live in history, in a place and time. With this comes what Malcolm Bradbury calls the "communal consciousness of a generation."[4] In the 1920s, that consciousness included an awareness that change was in the air. It was a more hopeful age for American women, for women's suffrage had emerged after the war, in an amendment ratified and completed on August 18. Flappers wore thin dresses with short sleeves or sleeveless dresses that revealed their bare shoulders. Their legs were visible to the knee; some women wore their stockings rolled up. Some of the girls smoked and drank liquor. Short, bobbed hair, shorter skits, and slender figures were the rage. When young women went out on dates, the automobile increased freedom and motion across a greater geographical range. As the 1920s proceeded, more cars were produced with closed tops. According to Allen, there were 6,771,000 cars on the road before 1920 and 23,121,000 by 1929.[5] Roads now crisscrossed the nation. There were garages, like the one run by Wilson in *The Great Gatsby*. There were rest stops, restaurants, camping sites, and hot dog stands.

Movies, radio, and mass-circulation magazines created popular culture, as skyscrapers, airplanes, automobiles, retail chains, and a culture of credit was changing the social landscape of America. In *Only Yesterday*, Allen calls it a time of transformation. Women had been given the right to vote. Prohibition made liquor illegal—a law resisted by many. Shared public events arrived with the advent of radio, with the first radio broadcast taking place in East Pittsburgh on November 2, 1920. During the winter of 1921–1922, writes Allen, the world was suddenly filled with the sounds of the radio. From 1922 to 1929, radio sales increased from 60,000,000 to 842,548,000.[6] The radio cabinet became a proud feature in living rooms, and rooftops were dotted with antennae. Radio advertising became big business. By 1930, radio broadcasting had become a "billion-dollar industry."[7] George W. Gray estimates that the number of radio stations grew from 508 in 1922 to more than 700 in 1926. He also points to the rise of radio advertising and the income that the National Broadcasting Company (NBC) derived from it, including some $150 million in 1929. His article enumerates the commercial possibilities of radio, citing the success of toothpaste sales.[8]

This was an age of advertising and salesmanship, marketing an abundance of commodities. Allen notes the appearance of "cigarettes, refrigerators, telephones, chemical preparations (especially cosmetics), and electrical devices."[9] Advertising had turned into a $3 billion business by 1929.[10] The craft of catching the American public's attention became a profession. Radio was enlisted to promote products, and sponsors targeted ads for items that seemed appropriate for the show's content. This advertising was soon the financial backing for radio broadcasts. Media, advertising, and the popular arts fueled popular culture. Meanwhile, American business, largely unaffected by the Great War, grew in leaps and bounds during those years when Lewis's Babbitt sought gadgets and new toasters. The economy received a boost in the "prosperity years" of the mid-1920s. Allen points out that American employees increased their purchasing power at a rate of more than 2 percent annually.[11] Consumers were increasingly buying on credit. In Allen's view, what many wanted was "to be young and desirable, to be rich, to keep up with the Joneses."[12]

Keeping up materially was accompanied by the need to keep up with the new pace of life in America's cities. In the 1920s, America's youth experienced a decade that was driven by the clock, the appearance of the wristwatch, the pulse of time. In poetry, T. S. Eliot presented J. Alfred Prufrock's insistence that "there will be time," as his days elapsed in convention and inaction, "measured with coffee spoons." In Eliot's *The Waste Land* (1922), there is the phrase "hurry up please it's time." American life sped up in the 1920s. Allen observed the disillusionment of youth and says that the "decade was unhappy."[13] Recalling this time, Ann Douglas adds that it "was the most theatrical generation" in American history.[14] Yet, it was also a time of Eliot's "The Hollow Men" (1925), in which the ash heaps of *Gatsby* recall Eliot's *The Waste Land* and Fitzgerald's *The Beautiful and Damned*.

AMERICAN CITIES AND NEW VOICES

American cities grew rapidly between 1900 and 1930, largely because of immigration. In the 1920s, Chicago was a thriving city of industry, one beset by the legendary crimes of Al Capone. New York City developed the look it still has today through the steady construction of skyscrapers, highways, bridges, subways, tunnels, commercial offices, and apartment housing. The Chrysler Building, Chanin Building, Daily New Building, Bank of Manhattan Trust, and Empire State Building were constructed during this time. The Holland Tunnel was finished in 1927, followed by the George Washington Bridge in 1931. New York emerged as a center for finance, as well as for radio networks, record labels, theater, and publishing. The garment industry thrived there. Industries were also centered in other major cities, namely automobile manufacture in Detroit, steel manufacturing in Pittsburgh, and meatpacking and shipping in Chicago.

The black arts movement in Harlem emerged with the voices of Langston Hughes, Zora Neale Hurston, Jessie Fauset, Jean Toomer, and others. They spoke of the creative spirit of African Americans and addressed a wasteland of racial inequality with vibrant imagination and determination. The Harlem Renaissance set its vitality against the challenges of urban life, which were compounded by socioeconomic need and the broader reality of racial prejudice in America. The vitality that arose in Harlem has to be set within the larger framework of America. Harlem was transformed by the arrival of African Americans from other regions of the country and the world. Zora Neale Hurston came from Alabama. Claude McKay arrived from the Caribbean. Jean Toomer was the mulatto son of an upper class family in Washington, DC. He traveled to Wisconsin to study agriculture and then to Massachusetts and other states before arriving in New York. Langston Hughes was born in Joplin, Missouri, and grew up in Lawrence, Kansas. Scholar William Edward Burhardt (W. E. B.) Du Bois spent his early years in Massachusetts and attended Harvard University. Jessie Fauset was the daughter of an African Methodist Episcopal minister in Camden, New Jersey.

The world of Harlem was one that was familiar with adversity. In theory, black Americans were free. In practice, they were frequently shut out. Some found Harlem to be a locale where they might develop a private life, a sense of freedom and connection with others. From that culture, sentiment, and state of mind emerged art, music, and literature. The Harlem Renaissance is considered by some to be one creative moment in a process that is ever at work in modern times.

NEWS OF THE 1920S

Newspapers carried the national news to readers throughout the country. Along with books and radio, newspapers continued to be one of the binding forces of the imagined community of America. They reported that in Chicago, a legendary crime wave had begun with the actions of the notorious Al Capone, the poster child of bootlegging during Prohibition. The news declared that radicalism was in the air. On September 16, a bomb exploded in New York across from the J. P. Morgan firm's offices in front of the Assay Office. In April 1920, two men shot a paymaster and a guard carrying the payroll of a shoe factory. Police arrested two Italian radicals and charged them with the crime. Sacco and Vanzetti were tried before Judge Webster Thayer, and a jury found them guilty. During the next several months, the radical press of France, Italy, and Spain publicized the case. Doubts were raised about the guilt of the convicted men. Appeals delayed the death sentence for seven years.

After World War I, the United States retreated from world affairs in a decade of isolationism. The U.S. Senate defeated the bill to join the League of Nations. Domestic affairs captured the attention of America's readers, and newspapers had much to report. In 1923, the Harding administration was unsettled by the Teapot Dome Scandal, in which Secretary of the Interior Albert B. Fall was implicated, along with Harry F. Sinclair of the Mammoth Oil Company and Edward F. Doheny of the Pan-American Company. Corruption in the Veteran's Bureau administration would land Charles R. Forbes in jail in 1926, for fraud. Attorney General Harry Daugherty was brought to trial in 1927, for influence peddling, but the indictment against him was dismissed. He did not take the stand in the trial. Accounting records had been conveniently burned. There were claims that he received kickbacks from bootleggers, who sought federal protection.[15] President Warren G. Harding did not live to see this. In the summer of 1923, he visited Alaska. He returned to San Francisco after ptomaine poisoning and developed pneumonia and died on August 2.

When in public, Calvin Coolidge, Harding's successor, was "as silent as a cake of ice."[16] The new president represented a steady work ethic. He said little that was striking or new and repeated maxims of diligence and piety. Quiet as a Vermont snowfall, he was not the sort of man that one would find today on a late night talk show with Jimmy Fallon. Allen describes him as "pale and diffident" and says that he was as cool as ice.[17]

In contrast with the laconic president, boisterous sensationalism and novelty drew public interest during these years: the wonder of Lindbergh's transatlantic flight and the stirring ticker-tape parade that celebrated the hero's return, the intensity of murder trials, Jack Dempsey's boxing and Babe Ruth's home runs, mahjong and crossword puzzles. Mass media began to come into its own with national advertising, publicity, product sales, the emergence of radio, tabloid newspapers, mass-circulation magazines, and fewer major newspapers with larger circulations. Radio broadcasters and press agents, as well as film stars and syndicated columnists, appealed to the public imagination, and America's novelists explored the pulse of contemporary society in fiction.

THE SEARCH FOR RENEWAL

In the wake of World War I, American society turned to sensation and the creation of celebrities and heroes. Among the most sensational events of the decade was Charles Lindbergh's transatlantic flight from New York to Paris. On May 20, 1927, Lindbergh took off from Roosevelt Field for Paris in the *Spirit of St. Louis*. He landed at La Bourget, prompting headlines and mass enthusiasm. Some 1,800 tons of shredded paper flew from New York's office buildings. Reflecting on the acclaim accorded to the 1927 Lindbergh flight, Allen surmises that the American public was essentially disillusioned and there was "something that people needed" that was "missing from their lives . . . romance, chivalry, self-dedication."[18] Even with the fanfare, Allen suggests that a "sense of disillusionment . . . was the keynote of the 1920s."[19]

In *The Modern Temper* (1929), Joseph Wood Krutch argues that the scientific paradigm had drained the world of God and thus reduced humanity. He contends that if God is only a psychological need or an intellectual principle of order, there is no vitally transcendent resource for people. Eliot refers to this need of the times in *The Waste Land*. Jewish theologian Martin Buber referred to the "eclipse of God." Paul Tillich spoke of the ground of Being and urged courage and faith amid the "shaking of the foundations," while Karl Barth advocated neo-orthodoxy. Religion was popularly discussed in many books and popular magazines as a "debatable subject," Allen notes. In his survey of public attitudes, he observed that commentators of religion were asking if the war was at fault for a decline of "moral energy" or if prosperity had encouraged a "comfortable belief."[20]

In the interim, people turned to films, sports, and fads for recreation. Film attendance increased, with films drawing millions of moviegoers, while church attendance decreased. On January 1, 1924, Richard Simon and Max Lincoln Schuster started Simon and Schuster, originally known as the Plaza Publishing Company. Their crossword puzzle book became a national fad. Meanwhile, sports seized the public's attention. Arriving in New York in 1920, George Herman Ruth became the undisputed home run king of baseball. The Yankees began a streak of pennant victories. In 1921, Babe Ruth hit fifty-nine home runs, one shy of the record of sixty he would hit in 1927. Ruth's sixty-homerun year was followed by the famous 1927 World Series in which the Yankees played against the Pittsburgh Pirates. In 1921, boxer Jack Dempsey beat Georges Carpentier in three rounds at Boyle's Thirty Acres in Jersey City. Reporting on the fight, the *New York Times* recalls Aaron Burr's fateful trip to New Jersey for a duel. Bobby Jones was becoming a legendary golfer, and William Tilden was setting records in tennis. Tilden beat William Johnson at Forest Hills in 1920. In the football locker room in South Bend, Indiana, Knute Rockne was urging Notre Dame to "win one for the Gipper." In Illinois, Red Grange was running past defensive linemen. On October 19, 1924, the *New York Times* announced the football exploits of a "flashing, red-haired youngster."[21] Grange, who scored five of his team's six touchdowns against the University of Michigan, would become one of the greatest running backs in the history of the game.

MODERNISM AND POPULAR CULTURE

Literature had a unique place within this popular culture. It could provide entertainment, like the college football game, or it could be an engagement with characters and ideas that stirred thoughts and feelings. Likewise, literature could be an aesthetic experience, an encounter with the art and craft of how writers use language. It could enlist a reader's sympathy or create a sense of wonder—an "ah-ha" experience of recognition.

One way of reading this period in literary terms has been to point to the origins of modernism before World War I. Then there are the great postwar works of Eliot, Pound, Joyce, and Woolf. From this perspective, one considers the momentous works of 1922 in English literature—like *Ulysses* and *The Waste Land* and *Mrs. Dalloway*, and then begins to see a cohort that emerged and endured into the 1930s. In America, we prize the laconic minimalism of Hemingway and verbal flights of Faulkner. The former, who threw tight punches to the body as an amateur boxer, created clean prose that pummeled dialogue back and forth. The other, who once flew Royal Air Force training maneuvers, performed death defying aerial twists of language as if smoke-writing on air. He plumbed the depths of the psyche as he once flew the heights of the sky. These unique stylists, Hemingway and Faulkner, were modernists. Their modernism has been canonized as not only belonging to this period, but characterizing it. Oftentimes branded elitist or considered difficult, modernist literature fit into American culture, existing alongside popular novels and popular culture, interacting with American readers.

The late nineteenth century industrialized books. The expansion of literacy, growth of complex urban culture, and institution of compulsory education promoted the development of the book. By the 1920s, the movement of publishers toward commercialized mass-market production had increased. Some thirty literary agencies had merged in London by 1914, and many more had appeared in New York by the last year of World War I. The Book-of-the-Month Club started its mail-order distribution of selected titles in the 1920s and effectively became a literary manager of textual production. Modernist work, with little magazines and small press runs, painstaking craft, and linguistic difficulty, separated itself from the widely distributed works that became popular.

Meanwhile, popular novels and pulp fiction magazines of the 1920s, like today's television programs, provided their audiences with a release from the pressures of modernity. The popularity of mass-market titles may tell us something about the tastes and attitudes of people in the 1920s; however, the literary novel of the time, or the literary middle-brow novel, more deeply explored the human condition through the artistry and craft of powerful writers. It is to these novels that we turn here. Those who bought popular fiction were not necessarily the same people who bought and read well-wrought literary novels. Clearly, both types of novels sold well, although popular novel sales usually far outstripped sales of the literary novel. We can ask what these works might tell us about the national ethos and the relationship to their world that readers saw in these books.

The Roaring Twenties began with a variety of popular books. British writer H. G. Wells's *Outline of History* was the best-selling nonfiction book of 1921–1922. Subsequent nonfiction best sellers included *Story of Mankind* (1922) by Hendrik Van Loon, Emily Post's *Etiquette*

(1923), J. Arthur Thomson's *The Outline of Science* (1922), and *The Story of Philosophy* (1927) by Will Durant.[22] America's creative writers were also creating a new literature. The once-prestigious Boston literati—Longfellow, Whittier, and Lowell—fell out of public esteem, and other voices began to enter the canon: Melville, Twain, Dickinson, and Whitman. The biographical debunking of Victorian figures by Lytton Strachey in *Eminent Victorians* had its counterpart in American biographies, for instance, Rupert Hughes's critique of George Washington. At the same time, Lewis's *Main Street* (1920) and *Babbitt* (1922) revealed small-town pettiness, prejudice, and lack of culture. With acid satire that matched that of the cynical H. L. Mencken, Lewis portrayed the yearnings and limitations of the residents of Gopher Prairie and the ambitions of Zenith. While his novels humanized these individuals beyond caricature, they largely neglected what Allen refers to as the "friendly sentiment and easy generosity" of these people,[23] which, as we will see, caused sharp reactions amongst some Midwestern readers.

H. L. Mencken, whose social criticism was even more acerbic than that of Lewis, seemingly stood against everything. His "idol-smashing" wit was aimed at mass behavior, religion, conservative thinkers, notions of patriotism, and social inconsistencies. Democracy, he believed, led to mass-mindedness. He approached his rejection of the common man— "*homo boobarus Americanus*"—with the fervor of philosopher Friedrich Nietzsche, whom he translated and rewrote in a form idiosyncratically his own. When asked why he bothered living in the United States if he was so critical of it, Mencken flippantly replied, "Why do men go to zoos?"

Men and women went to work in factories, and humanists everywhere reacted to mechanization. Charlie Chaplin reflected on the problem of living in the machine age in *Modern Times*. In the theater, Elmer Rice critiqued it in *The Adding Machine*, and Eugene O'Neill responded to it in *Dynamo*. Lewis Mumford, in the *Freeman* (September 17, 1929), criticizes artificial values, "energetic, immature minds," dehumanization, and Ford Motors. Aldous Huxley would satirize Ford in his novel of the future, *Brave New World* (1932), set in the "year of our Ford." Sherwood Anderson lashed out against standardization in an essay in *Vanity Fair* in November 1926. For him this was not a new theme. He had treated the topic in his novel *Poor White* (1920), observing the machine-oriented abstraction of industrial progress and a Midwest society's development from a simple to a complex economy. Waldo Frank, in the *New Republic* (November 18, 1925), argues that American society needed "metaphysical consciousness." "Primitivism" also was considered a feasible response. Created by whites, this notion distorted racial realities. Some equated primitivism with instinct or something precivilized. A spontaneous and visceral way of living would oppose standardization and science in its social applications. Jazz became a musical signature of this for some; it held the promise of breaking out. It was a time when musical innovation sounded in dozens of nightclubs, and songs were captured on recording devices.

TIN PAN ALLEY AND POPULAR SONGS

An extraordinary phase of American song emerged from vaudeville and the blues and jazz. George M. Cohan, a star performer, wrote a string of hit songs, including "Yankee Doodle Boy," "You're a Grand Old Flag," "Give My Regards to Broadway," and "Over There," the most popular wartime song of the Great War era. By the 1920s, "Tin Pan Alley" had begun to emerge. At Union Square, music publishers developed the idea that songs could be created for special events and distributed by song pluggers. M. Witmark distributed free sheet music to performers from vaudeville. One technique was to plant singers in the crowd in theaters to extend the chorus of a song and get the house singing.

Irving Berlin developed into a giant of songwriting during this time—the king of Tin Pan Alley syncopation—with many of his songs drawing on ragtime. Born in Russia, his given name was Israel Baline. Berlin began as a lyric writer. He wrote lyrics to other people's melodies and became a staff writer for Seminary Music Company. The *New York Journal* paid him to write verses for the newspaper. After his lyrics came his melodies. His famous "Alexander's Ragtime Band" is a march. "Everybody's Doin' It" started a "turkey trot" dance craze. The musical *Watch Your Step* was filled with ragtime. Berlin provided material for the Ziegfeld Follies, and "A Pretty Girl Is Like a Melody" became its theme song. Later, for Kate Smith, he wrote "God Bless America," sung for the first time on the radio on Armistice Day, November 10, 1938. It was subsequently recorded on the Columbia Record label. Berlin's shows on Broadway included *This Is the Army* and *Annie Get Your*

Gun. He also wrote lyrics and music for film. He was one of America's central popular song composers. Oscar Hammerstein once famously commented on the sound of Berlin's line, saying, "all alone by the telephone."

Words and music form a symbiotic relationship in the songs sometimes described as the "Great American Songbook." The lyricists of the 1920s and 1930s frequently worked within a 32-bar format. The main part of the song was typically introduced by a verse in which the vocalist moved somewhere between speech and song. Lyrics to songs would appear in AABA structure. The chorus provided most songs with a popular and memorable center. Collaboration with a composer was at the center of the art of these lyricists. Ira Gershwin wrote clever lyrics to his brother George's pentatonic melodies, as in "I Got Rhythm." While George experimented with jazz harmony, Ira offered sparkling wit. Wittiness also appears in the lyrics of Lorenz Hart, for example, in "Mountain Greenery" and "To Keep My Love Alive," written with Richard Rodgers. Lorenz Hart was a master of surprising rhymes. In collaborating with Richard Rodgers, both Hart and Oscar Hammerstein needed to listen for Rodgers's tendency to hold long notes or provide surprising notes at the end of phrases.

Cole Porter, who wrote both lyrics and music, represents the truth that lyrics and music need to be inseparable in a song. As a composer, Porter often exchanged major and minor modes, and his lyrics observed the contrast, as in "Night and Day." Porter wrote clever lyrics to such snappy compositions as "Begin the Beguine" and "Let's Do It," and he provided many memorable hits, most notably "I've Got You Under My Skin," for future vocalists like Frank Sinatra. The lyrics were usually about romantic love. In songwriters' frequent creation of love songs, we begin to see a pattern that has continued to this day.

While Larry Hart, like a medieval troubadour, sobbed about unrequited love ("This Can't Be Love," "Glad to Be Unhappy"), Ira Gershwin wondered about falling in love. Cole Porter made wry observations about relationships and played with end rhymes. For the Gershwins, George's music usually preceded Ira's lyrics, and Ira worked off of his brother's rhythmic figures. Richard Rodgers's music and ideas for titles often started Lorenz Hart on his lyrics, as Hart listened for what was most unique in Rodgers's melody; however, when Oscar Hammerstein worked with Richard Rodgers, his lyrics often came first. To write this way, a lyricist has to be attentive to pauses, held notes, and rhythms, as well as the needs of the potential singer of the song and the style of the composer with whom he or she is working.

Operetta developed in the 1920s through the work and vision of Oscar Hammerstein and the composing of Sigmund Romberg, Jerome Kern, and others. Dorothy Donnelly wrote lyrics to Sigmund Romberg's *The Student Prince* (1924). Oscar Hammerstein and Otto Harbach set lyrics to Romberg's *The Desert Song* (1926). Dorothy Fields brought lyrics to Romberg's *Up in Central Park* (1945). *Show Boat* was the first fully American operetta, drawing on American scenes and themes. Hammerstein's lyrics supported a book in which he broke barriers by treating romance, miscegenation, and race relations. In *Show Boat*, Hammerstein and Kern's "Ol' Man River" moved audiences with its baritone echoes of African American tradition. "Can't Help Lovin' Dat Man" introduced the mood and attitude of the blues into the American musical. Hammerstein also wrote *Music in the Air* (1932) with Jerome Kern. A significant amount of America poetry and fiction developed in relation to a sense of music and within the musical and artistic context of the time.

AMERICAN LITERATURE COMES OF AGE

Van Wyck Brooks had announced *America's Coming of Age* in 1915. Nonetheless, at the end of the 1920s, Joseph Wood Krutch, in *The Modern Temper* (1929), observes a loss of belief in American society. People had no rational or unreasoning faith, he says. Science had divided the modern soul. One could no longer write tragedy with faith in the nobility of humanity or human heroism. Krutch wrote at a time when poets like Carl Sandburg (in *Smoke and Steel* [1920]) were reacting to the force and power of technology, industry, and the machine. He did not comment on recent advances in science, for instance, Einstein's theory of relativity or quantum physics and how they opened up areas of mystery and inquiry that were likely to change this equation.

The Stock Market Crash of 1929 was a blow to national faith in the economy. After the October economic collapse, thousands of businesses went into bankruptcy. The U.S. Bank followed suit in 1930, and more than 4,000 uninsured deposits were lost. Unemployment escalated during the next three years. Nearly one-quarter of the U.S. population faced unemployment in 1932, when Franklin Delano Roosevelt became president. People lost their apartments and houses. About 1.25 million New Yorkers were on relief. In Manhattan, makeshift attempts at housing, sometimes called "Hoovervilles," appeared along the borders of the Hudson and East rivers. F. Scott Fitzgerald's personal demise has sometimes been seen as mirroring the 1930s decline.[24]

* * *

Throughout this period, two of the most illuminating chroniclers of the literary 1920s were Malcolm Cowley and Edmund Wilson. Cowley takes the position that he can be a representative voice for his generation. Early in his recollections, he states that the forces that contributed to his generation were "already in motion."[25] In *Exile's Return* (1950), his account of the literary 1920s, Cowley immediately asserts that Fitzgerald or Hart Crane never spoke of a lost generation.[26] In his view, this was a useful tag through which an older generation could begin to describe a generation that was recognizably different from their own.[27] He does suggest that writers like Fitzgerald and Crane were "representatives of a new age"[28] and that his generation had developed a "common attitude" during this time of "rapid change," one that Fitzgerald called the "greatest, gaudiest spree in history."[29] Yet, perhaps the term *lost generation* had some credence. Before arriving at what Cowley calls "their achievements," members of the postwar generation were uprooted, and they attempted to break with the values of their elders and seek another way of life. Some of these writers chose "exile," a key word in Cowley's assessment of the age. In his view, they were not Dantean exiles, disillusioned in a wasteland. Their era was shaken, and they were looking for direction during a time of transition.

Cowley believes that in the early 1920s many members of his generation were too immature to be as depressed about the modern world as T. S. Eliot apparently was.[30] Still, Cowley soon gives us an image of a site in Weehawken where Alexander Hamilton and Aaron Burr faced one another on a fatal day early in our history. The image is one of a street veering off into limbo, where he and Kenneth Burke stood, sometime before 1920, watching barges bobbing in the Hudson River across from 42nd Street.[31] New York, he says, was a place where everyone came from another town.[32] He calls New York the "metropolis of curiosity and suspicion," a "city of anger." It is, he says, a place of impermanence, where "violent emotions" circulate "moment to moment . . . at the tips of the nerves."[33]

The Greenwich Village "bohemians" came from the same class as readers of the *Saturday Evening Post*, Cowley observes.[34] Nevertheless, he sees the village's bohemia as a form of self-expression and spontaneous living in the moment. The ideal was a sense of liberty, equality for women, and openness to change. The natural child, as in Jean Jacques Rousseau's sense, could live freely, sexually unrepressed, in a new paganism.[35] Cowley suggests that the war made it increasingly possible to write about love, adventure, and death.[36] He returned to the United States in August 1923. Recalling his return, he presents the image of exiles returning to the United States, with the Statue of Liberty in the background. The song "Yes, We Have No Bananas" is in the air. While there may be no bananas, there is liquor, despite Prohibition. Cowley's associative thinking moves from the stock market to the idea that American literature was also "entering a period of excitement and inflation."[37] Returning from Europe, young Americans wanted to remake their environment, he insists.[38] He also claims that people imitated fiction. College girls were modeling themselves after Brett Ashley in *A Sun Also Rises*. Men were posing as Hemingway heroes.[39]

Edmund Wilson, like Cowley, was one of the key literary critics of this decade and beyond. In *The Shores of Light*, Wilson gathered his essays on literature and culture in the 1920s and 1930s. Looking back from the 1930s, Wilson observes that the dynamics and trends of the 1920s would not help America in its new situation. He begins his essay "The Literary Consequences of the Crash" by noting that 1920s attitudes already seemed a "long way off."[40] He offers a brief retrospective of features of the 1920s before assessing the repercussions of the 1929 Stock Market Crash. He lists the superior attitude of the ironic Mencken-style, as well as the "smugness" of some of the old New England stock and those who dreamed that American prosperity and progress would reveal America's exceptionality; however, what Wilson calls the "mad hilarity and heartbreak of jazz" did not last, and he says that many people now recognize the superficiality of these attitudes and fads. The United States is now faced with a real crisis. Wilson asserts that the "dignity of the Parthenon" cannot be found in the stock exchange and that the world is run by salesmen and brokers. He begins to sound like someone waving an "Occupy Wall Street" sign.

Wilson was also an important voice for the 1920s because he embraced popular culture. Like his friend Gilbert Seldes, he saw the potential of popular culture in America. With *The Seven Lively Arts* (1924), Seldes expressed what Wilson calls this new orientation. Seldes loved the Krazy Kat cartoons, vaudeville, and Charlie Chaplin movies. Radio and movies, Wilson observed in 1950, were to Seldes the "great engines of democratic entertainment and culture," but if they moved toward uniformity they could mean a destruction of democracy.[41] Popular culture, Wilson insists, must remain varied and energetic.

In *The Shores of Light*, the first of his books on the 1920s, Wilson refers to many writers, Ring Lardner, Sherwood Anderson, Willa Cather, and Eugene O'Neill among them. The text brings together descriptive journal entries, published reviews, and a variety of essays. Wilson diverges into a discussion of George Gurdjieff, the theosophical mystic, whom he criticizes as a charlatan. Gurdjieff brought mystical reflection, movement, and dance with him to the United States. A. R. Orage, a writer and editor, was his strongest American disciple and proselytizer. He edited a publication called *The New Age*. Wilson mentions that during the 1920s, people sought faith or meaning within church settings, as well as outside them, but that he resisted all of it and "caught a wave" from Marxism. He had become more politically oriented with the onset of the 1930s. He points out that the writers and artists of his generation, those of the "Big Business era," were not put off by the economic slump. They had been critical of the age of Harding, Coolidge, and Hoover and were energized by the "unexpected collapse of that stupid gigantic fraud." The bankers were troubled, but the writers and artists were "exhilarated" and felt a new energy for their work.[42]

Wilson's ideas on literary criticism and social life evolved throughout the 1920s. He devotes sections of *Axel's Castle* (1931) to James Joyce, Gertrude Stein, Marcel Proust, T. S. Eliot, William Butler Yeats, and French poets Paul Valery and Arthur Rimbaud. His focus is on modernism in Western Europe, and hardly a word is spoken about either Fitzgerald or Hemingway. *Axel's Castle* contains an essay on Gertrude Stein in which Wilson discusses Stein's *Three Lives* and *The Making of Americans*.

To read Wilson is to encounter many critical judgments on the writers of the age. In *The Shores of Light*, he recognizes the literary quality in Lardner's short stories, when Lardner was still being categorized as a popular journalist. Wilson compares him with Anderson, in whom he sees a "poet's sensibility."[43] Anderson's *Many Marriages* is a disappointment after *The Triumph of the Egg*, Wilson concludes. "I found it tedious," he writes.[44] Do we really need another story about a man who gets tired of his wife and runs off with another woman? That wife is unreal, no more than a phantom, he says. When Anderson is on track, he writes with beauty and ease, and his insight is like a "diving bell" going to depths of human nature.[45] Nonetheless, *Many Marriages*, Wilson asserts, is far from his best.

Cather's fiction is well-crafted, in Wilson's view, but boring. "If only *One of Ours* had more vitality," he laments.[46] He believes that Cather is a writer of "real feeling" who brings "real distinction" to the Midwest, but he finds the cramping of Claude Wheeler's passions on a farm a weak premise for a story and Wheeler's experience of the war lacking vitality. We are given great "accuracy," but we are not given what the war did to the "soul" of this character. Of course, at this point, in 1922 and 1924, Wilson admits that he had yet to read Cather's *My Antonia*. Thus, he had a somewhat limited view of the scope of Cather's work, and so he reiterates, "Willa Cather is a good craftsman, but she is usually rather dull."[47]

In 1922, Wilson regarded much of Eugene O'Neill's stagecraft as naturalism, even though he experimented with expressionism.[48] When he writes more in the vernacular about "humble people" he is like Anderson, Wilson says.[49] In 1924, Wilson saw expressionism in theater as an effort to break from realism, comparable to the cubism of Braque and Picasso.[50] Meanwhile, poetry also received his attention. Wallace Stevens was a poet who Wilson saw great promise in. He reviews *Harmonium* in the same piece in which he considers e.e. cummings, whose work he found innovative but less convincing.[51]

The emergence of Hemingway is something for which Wilson appears to take some responsibility. He was one of the first critics to review Hemingway's *Three Stories and Ten Poems* and *In Our Time*, which was published in the October 1924 edition of the *Dial*. Wilson calls Hemingway's work "prose of the first distinction," saying that it is "strikingly original" and represents a "distinctively American development in prose."[52] Hemingway responded that he valued Wilson's opinion as the only U.S. critic he had any respect for.[53]

Hemingway appeared as one of Wilson's hopes for the future of American fiction. In a June 30, 1926 essay, Wilson recognizes the "cause of an American national literature in independence of English literature" and the importance of contemporary ideas positioned against those of preceding generations.[54] He acknowledges the literary quality of Jean Toomer's fiction. Zona Gale is "given to terrible lapses into feminine melodrama," he writes.[55] Cabell was too filled with southern sentimentality.[56] Then he sets forth his hope in the new generation of writers: "I feel more interest in F. Scott Fitzgerald and Dos Passos than any of the writers mentioned [earlier]: they are younger than the others, and one does not feel that one knows exactly what to expect of them."[57] Wilson adds that Carl Van Vechten and Ben Hecht "applied the formulas of naturalism." Along with Fitzgerald, they expressed a "certain interest" in the history of American culture. He found the characters in Sherwood Anderson's novels to be "vague" but applauds his short stories as having an "almost perfect instinct."[58] Hemingway, Anderson, Stein, and Lardner, despite the geographical distances between them, seemed to represent a new school of fiction writing, and Hemingway has read and been influenced by all of them.[59]

Literary critic Joseph Wood Krutch found in Hemingway's *In Our Time* a "weariness too great to be aware of anything but sensations."[60] But Wilson saw something different in the author. Reviewing *Men without Women*, Hemingway's second story collection, Wilson points to "A Simple Inquiry" as a "glimpse of one aspect of army life."[61] Hemingway was writing about the kind of individual who had come a long distance from the character who liked a three-day fishing trip in the "Big-Hearted River." Hemingway, Wilson writes, was a writer "preoccupied" with the "problems of natural cruelty" and "barbarity of the world since the war."[62] In contrast with Dos Passos, Hemingway looks at men broken by the war who were resigned to human agonies.[63] Wilson concludes that like his characters, Hemingway is himself oppressed.[64]

When, on April 17, 1929, Wilson wrote "Dos Passos and the Social Revolution," he concluded that Hemingway, Wilder, and Fitzgerald were writers who "confront their own little corners" and not the entire situation.[65] John Dos Passos, in contrast, had a big canvas and tried to capture everything. Yet, Wilson was concerned that Dos Passos, who he considered more intelligent than Upton Sinclair or communist Michael Gold, misapplied his resentments, affecting his politics.[66] Dos Passos often emphasizes the "importance of America," Wilson writes, but there is "something lacking."[67] He always looks at the social organism; however-er, in *Manhattan Transfer*, in trying to make his characters sympathetic, he also puts them down.[68]

With Dos Passos's novel *The 42nd Parallel*, Wilson saw a movement from *Manhattan Transfer* and New York to a consideration of the United States in relation to the world. Dos Passos was so capable of rendering colloquial American speech and so keenly aware of America's tendency to ascribe everything about life to the values of business and advertising, "out of which they make their salaries and in terms of which they conceive their ambitions."[69] Dos Passos capably moves from city to city in his story, showing the culture of each place: Chicago, Minneapolis, and Pittsburgh. He intersects newsreels or scraps of news items with the biographies of contemporary American figures and weaves them into his narrative. These characters were submerged in the culture, Wilson reckons. "Dos Passos seems the only one of the novelists of this generation concerned with the large questions of politics and society" (March 26, 1930).[70]

Concerned with international relations and metaphysical meaning was Thornton Wilder, who was among Wilson's favorite writers. Wilder, who is best known as a playwright, wrote two novels during the 1920s. *The Bridge of San Luis Rey* (1927) won the Pulitzer Prize and was made into a film in 1929. He followed it with *The Woman of Andros* (1930). This novel shows the return from the dead of a man who relives an ordinary day from when he was fifteen years old. While set in a Greek underworld, the novel develops on the same motif Wilder would use for his character Emily in *Our Town* (1928), the play for which he is best known. Wilder suggests that each of us is most fully alive when we recognize the blessings we have in our everyday lives. Wilder is the only American to have won Pulitzers for both fiction and drama. In the 1930s, in the theater, Wilder broke with traditional forms. *The Skin of Our Teeth* (1942) asserts that people can survive any odds. It won the Pulitzer Prize during World War II. Wilder, who had been at Fort Adams in Rhode Island during World War I, reenlisted and served in U.S. Air Force Intelligence in Italy and North Africa. He was awarded the Bronze Star and Legion of Merit, and Britain made him an honorary officer.

The subtle meditation on life and death that gave shape to Wilder's *The Bridge of San Luis Rey* seems to have emerged from his family context. It was one that was steeped in literature and Biblical understanding. Wilder's father, a man with solid New England Puritan values, was an American consul in Hong Kong, and several of the Wilder children, including Thornton Wilder, spent some of their childhoods in China. The elder Wilder was also a newspaper owner and editor in Madison, Wisconsin, as well as in California, and he seems to have adhered to a strict moral code. His wife was a teacher, a poet, and an enthusiastic reader of literature who passed her ambitions on to her children.

Their eldest son, Amos Wilder (1895–1993), was a collegiate tennis star in the 1920s and played mixed doubles at Wimbledon. He published two volumes of poetry in the 1920s through the Yale Younger Poets Series: *Battle Retrospect* (1923) and *Arachne* (1928). Amos became a prominent minister who concluded his career as an endowed professor of theology at Harvard University. Like Hemingway and Dos Passos, he served as an ambulance driver in World War I. In his books on New Testament theology, he sometimes reflects on the power of narrative and story.

Isabel Wilder (1900–1995) wrote three novels and was probably the closest to Thornton Wilder, living in nearby Hamden, Connecticut, and acting as his personal agent, hostess, and spokesperson. Their sister Charlotte (1898–1980) was also a poet and a professor of English. After receiving a master's degree from Radcliffe, she taught at Wheaton College and Smith College. She moved to New York in 1934 and, with Ben Bellit, received the Shelley Memorial Award in 1937. Her health deteriorated following a nervous breakdown in 1941. Janet Wilder studied zoology rather than poetry. She married attorney Toby Dakin, and her interest in horses and equestrianism led to a book on training a Morgan horse.

Wilder's one-act plays and sketches of the 1920s were preparation for his playwriting thereafter. His work presented a self-conscious theater that made use of symbolism. The actors in his plays are not working to be convincing characters, but they allow themselves to be viewed as participants in a theatrical experience. A Wilder play is a "deliberate artifice," says Travis Bogards; it is a play that knows itself as a play.[71]

In August 1928, Wilson wished that Wilder would turn his "feeling for national temperaments" on the people of the United States. In *The Cabala*, Wilder writes of other places and appears to be influenced by Proust. In *The Bridge of San Luis Rey*, he shifts his attention to South America. Wilder obviously knew something about China and the culture of the French and the Italians, but "now we need him at home," Wilson declares.[72] On to the ancient world went Wilder's imagination, and Wilson was soon reviewing *The Woman of Andros* and a time before the beginnings of Christianity. He echoes his earlier call: Because Wilder is such a first-rate writer, "one would like to see him more at home."[73]

Wilson had written on Wilder before in an unsigned editorial in the *New Republic* (November 26, 1930). He comments on Wilder's attention to social situations and the likeness of his prose to that of Proust. Finally, Wilson turns his criticism on American capitalism. He remarks that the beauty in Wilder's imagination may be a "sedative for sick Americans."[74] People are attempting to bring such idealism to their occupations, he observes. Yet, the present economic system requires that to be successful they must be "swindling" and "cutting one another's throats."[75] Still, on May 4, 1932, Wilson responded after Michael Gold attacked Wilder as bourgeois in the *New Republic*. He recognized this as an appearance of Marxist issues.[76]

Wilson calls Wilder's novel *Heaven's My Destination* (1934) "his best book."[77] George Brush, the religious textbook salesman, was his most complete, well-rounded character. Wilson notices that Wilder brings humor to his portrayal of the life and misfortunes of George Brush. The material is similar to that of Lewis and told gracefully. Wilson compliments the lack of sentimentality and Wilder's reflections on the collapse of the San Luis Rey Bridge, which he views as "implausible to the nonbeliever."[78] He appreciates Wilder's rendering of an "imperfect and suffering humanity."[79]

That is the gift of these American writers: their ability to bring joy, insight, and a vision of imperfect and suffering humanity. Wilson recognizes that Wilder was one of America's most important literary voices in both fiction and theater. Wilder was able to reach the American public because at the heart of his work was a storyteller's imagination. As we look back on Hemingway, Fitzgerald, and Faulkner, to read their works again is to discover imagination that brings light to our age, for the strength of their stories carries our imaginations along. Where we are now in time and society, of course, makes a difference in how we read and interpret any narrative. These stories and songs are tied to their time, but they transcend their historical moment and speak to our time as well in interesting ways.

I

BEYOND THE WASTELAND

T. S. Eliot and the Postwar World

The wasteland stands as that desolate no man's land between the trenches, where breath met mud and opposing armies shot at one another in the smoke-filled air across the craters left by artillery shells. Beyond the battlefield, the enemies to humanity were impersonal economics, standardization, and priorities that dehumanized people. For the young generation, their elders had made these mistakes of war because they remained stuck in their archaic mindset. Yet, it was the young who were sacrificed to the war. For Fitzgerald, the wasteland included those areas surrounding our great cities, where refuse and ashes, oil tanks and machinery, covered the pavement. In *The Great Gatsby*, these were the zones of Wilson's garage, the eyes of T. J. Eckleburg gazing out through the dull electric light that never reached all the shadows.

This was the world of T. S. Eliot, who, in his long poem *The Waste Land*, provides the image of a Dante figure making his pilgrimage through arid modernity. But all was not wasteland if one embraced the energy emerging in America. Popular culture enlivened the Roaring Twenties. The young were breaking free from enervated late Victorian categories and attitudes. Frederick Hoffmann has seen the wasteland motif as archetypal: loss of meaning, inability to believe, walking numbly in circles. Yet, Frederick Lewis Allen, writing in 1930, saw the decade as one of vivacity, as well as one of disillusionment. That contrast was a central feature of the 1920s, one that found its way into the literature of the era.

Eliot's *The Waste Land* (1922) offers a symbolic framework for this age. We hear in Eliot a voice inaugurating the modern era. Eliot himself called claims that his poem reflected the anxieties of an age an exaggeration. Still, the work serves as a useful figure for the postwar period. We see the image of the wasteland and the disillusionment it suggests repeated by other writers of this time period. It is vividly presented in the valley of ashes in Fitzgerald's *The Great Gatsby*, where the watchful eyes of T. J. Eckleberg gaze across the desolate terrain that includes the Wilson's garage. It is in the bleak conclusion of *A Farewell to Arms* (1929), in which Hemingway, resisting grand words like glory and honor, seeks concrete language. It echoes in the phrase "the lost generation," which Hemingway used as a caption to his first novel, *The Sun Also Rises* (1926).

But this image of a wasteland refers to the moral texture of life more so than the disillusionment brought on by the war, and some critics have rejected the wasteland idea altogether. In *Exile's Return*, Malcolm Cowley insists that his generation was not the disillusioned one characterized by Eliot's piece. He maintains that the wasteland image was a product of Eliot's own idiosyncratic reading of the times. Jonathan Ebel contends that rather than casting the American nation into disillusionment and doubt, World War I prompted the reattachment of Americans to religious forms and structures. In letters and diaries, people suggest that the war, despite its horrors, was deeply meaningful. Some believed that something profound was at work amid the suffering.

Eliot's *The Waste Land* is important to a contemporary perspective on the 1920s novel because Eliot, writing in vers libre, in fragments, connects a city and spiritual wasteland in a quest myth that has implications for an entire era. Any dreams of the city as a pinnacle of civilization are contested by the poem, which begins with a caption from Dante and suggests the moral inversions of Dante's *Inferno* and the City of Dis. The loss of faith, tradition, and classical culture is suggested by Eliot, and this theme of loss is treated in various ways in the novels of this time. John Dos Passos's *Manhattan Transfer* (1925) extends the wasteland image into a city of broken and anxious lives. Anderson, in *Winesberg, Ohio* (1919), and Lewis, in *Main Street* (1920) or in the Zenith of *Babbitt* (1922), each find the wasteland in the American Mid-

west. Those who would put an ecological spin on the notion of wasteland only need look at the opening pages of Hemingway's *A Farewell to
Arms*, where the landscape has been devastated by war.

These novels emerged from and reflect the age in which they were
written. Henry James once pointed out that people want to see in literature their own image and some description of the world as they know it.
Novels showed readers of the 1920s their world. With the Great War,
that image seemed to shift, displaced from conventional mimesis. This
created a shift in the critical atmosphere. Modernism had already begun this process, but the war heightened it.[1] Eliot's poem suggests the
fragmentary nature of modern life, a loss of fertility and sustaining
values, and a desperate need for cultural renewal. The age's literary
novelists were, in their own ways, each feeling this atmosphere of their
time.

Much of Eliot's concern was driven by his response to secularism.
He sensed a waning of religious belief in Europe similar to that characterized by such poems as Matthew Arnold's "Dover Beach," which was
written long before the alarums of the Great War in France and Bel-
gium could be heard from Dover's rocky cliffs. Eliot recognized that
prior to World War I, vitalism had become a watchword of intellectual
society amid increased secularization. In *Goodbye to All That* (1929),
Robert Graves speaks of priests in the war's trenches, a search for
belief, the difficulty of burying the war dead, superstitions, and stories
of miraculous or curious happenings. After the war, the problem arose
of how to restore and reconcile faith and reason. Some religious thinkers offered new perspectives. After serving in the trenches or in close
proximity to the field of battle, Teilhard de Chardin and Paul Tillich, for
example, both intensely reflect on religious meaning. In *The Future of
an Illusion* (1928), Sigmund Freud calls belief in God wish fulfillment.
By then, Eliot had begun his own movement from the Unitarianism of
his youth, through what was likely agnosticism, to his conversion to
orthodoxy. These concerns entered his poetry and later underpinned
his plays.

World War I ended nineteenth-century notions of progress and ra-
tionality. War destroyed a framework, the idea of history as steady
progress. This affected novelists like Hemingway, Fitzgerald, and Dos
Passos. It was questionable whether anyone could have confidence in a
world so shattered. During the years before the war, there had been, in

intellectual circles, much desire to connect the sacred and the secular. Edwardian synthetic philosophy "tried to make everything a part of everything else," observes Jonathan Rose. War strained secular religion and the Edwardian synthesis. For many, war destroyed faith, and churchgoing declined. Others sought information about life after death, turning to spiritualism. As Rose points out, "Spiritualism pointed toward a new religion far more easygoing than the old Christianity—a Christianity stripped of all its unpleasantness, moral strictures, and demands of faith."[2] Post–World War I Britain saw the diminishment of neo-Hegelian philosophy and the increasing influence of logical positivism (or logical atomism). In this milieu, orthodox Christianity also saw a resurgence, including the works of Karl Barth, C. S. Lewis, and G. K. Chesterton. Perhaps this was, in part, a reaction to the horrors of war.

As fragmented as a stained glass window, Eliot's 1922 poem refracts the light of its age and ages past as it engages in a search for form and renewal. As the poem begins its first of five sections, we begin to see the outlines of the themes that are to follow. It loosely follows the search for the Holy Grail and the story of the Fisher King and suggests not only decline and fall, but also ways to bring life back to Western culture. Eliot also sends his readers on something of a quest in search of an understanding of the poem. He challenges readers with his lack of transitions and draws attention to the process of reading. Moreover, he alienated some readers by the eclectic gathering of foreign-language phrases, literary allusions, and references to Buddhism and Hinduism. While abstruse, the poem calls for a revitalization of symbols, love, faith, and fertility. The modern condition itself seems to call for this. Eliot reiterates this concern with modern society in *The Hollow Men* (1925).

Given a poem that seems so obscure, it is easy for a reader to believe that Eliot was intentionally trying to alienate readers and distance his work from anything that could be popular. Yet, during the 1920s, he was a transatlantic poet and critic who wrote about the border of high culture and the popular arts. Eliot sensed the social presence of music, as T. Austin Graham observes.[3] Song emerges at several points in *The Waste Land*; one hears ragtime, Wagnerian music drama, Hindu chants, and drinking songs. Eliot's exposure to ragtime came when he was a child in St. Louis. There the St. Louis Blues were born amongst the Chestnut Street and Market Street bars and brothels. Ragtime filled late nineteenth-century St. Louis, and Eliot puts forth bits of street piano songs in his early poems. In the "Game of Chess" section of *The Waste Land*, the O sounds of vocalizing precede the oddly spelled Shakespeherian.[4] In the "Fire Sermon" section, we read of the typist who taps typewriter keys rather than a piano. Her life is as repetitive as the click of the typewriter: "She smoothes her hair with automatic hand/ And puts a record on the gramophone."

The Waste Land sometimes sounds a lament that classical culture has been shattered and had given way to the typist, ragtime jazz, and Madame Sosostris. On the other hand, Eliot's work and his letters show that he had a strong interest in jazz and black minstrelsy, as well as opera, radio, print, and film and Marx Brothers' comedy.[5] The poet was aware of the auditory impact of changes in contemporary music. Eliot's poem was written at a time when such composers as Arthur Schoenberg and Igor Stravinsky had pulled away from traditional harmony. He had recently attended a performance of Stravinsky's *The Rite of Spring*.

Eliot also knew that the modern listener carries many songs in his or her mind.[6] *The Waste Land* was published two years after radio broadcasting began, and songs were increasingly available on radio and gramophone. A tune might, unbidden, suddenly pop into one's mind. Graham points out that musical references create an intimacy between Eliot's poem and its readers. He inspired associations in their minds.[7] Ralph Ellison later commented on the work, writing, *"The Waste Land* seized my mind. I was intrigued by its power to move me while eluding my understanding."[8]

Those readers who listened to classical repertoire recognized a section of Eliot's poem that is modeled on the song of the Rhine daughters from Richard Wagner's *Das Rheingold*. The poem itself presents similarities to Wagner's musical technique of leitmotif. In *Tristan and Isolde* we find motivic development. "The Tristan Chorus" pulls away from traditional harmonies and moves toward some dissonance, in the direction that would later be taken up in atonal composition by Schoenberg. Wagner practices harmonic suspension: beginning a theme and interrupting it, and later returning to it in resolution. Wagner builds on cadences, drawing audience expectation. He introduces discordance. He takes a theme, breaks off, and resurrects it later. Eliot suggests something similar with his poem. From the rutty grooves of earth, or the grooves of a record, this age might modulate to a new key.

The wasteland idea took on a different shape in American fiction. In the 1920s, the United States was shaping its own voice, or, as Ann Douglas puts it, shedding its borrowed past.[9] In literature, as Van Wyck Brooks recognized, America was coming-of-age. The expatriate Eliot believed that English literature was of one piece, and he said little about "American" literature per se. In "Tradition and the Individual Talent," Eliot addresses the need for writers to recall and interact with the literary voices of the past. He insists that a new work of literature belongs insofar as it is connected with what has preceded it. For him, this meant an indissoluble link of American writers to their English forebears. The novels of the 1920s emerged from a preceding heritage, just as our contemporary works maintain a relationship to the novels of previous generations. Eliot's literary allusions in *The Waste Land* are an appeal to societal memory of a long literary tradition.

In his social thinking, Eliot was greatly influenced by T. E. Hulme, whose most important work was written before the commencement of World War I. Eliot describes it as the "antipodes of the eclectic, tolerant, and democratic mind of the last century."[10] Hulme experienced World War I as an "ash-heap of cinders," with no connection, no "order." One had to impose order like a "kind of manufactured chess board laid on a cinder-heap."[11] In *The Waste Land*, Eliot states, "I can connect/Nothing with Nothing." In "The Second Coming," William Butler Yeats delivers the following arresting lines: "Things fall apart; the center cannot hold/Mere anarchy is loosed upon the world."

Eliot recognized that Hulme's solution to such a crucial time was that one must create ethical values. Hulme asserts that a return to orthodoxy and transcendent religion could confront the division between sacred and secular, an "absolute division," and the "reestablishment of the temper or disposition of mind that can look at a gap or chasm without shuddering."[12] Hulme had a powerful impact on Eliot, as well as the Imagists. Both Eliot and Ezra Pound objected to the weak Romanticism of the late nineteenth century. The Imagists sought to express themselves concisely, with concrete imagery, and avoid abstraction. Hulme had anticipated that poets of a new century would avoid Romanticism and write "dry, hard, classical verse."[13] As Imagist poets did this, Eliot, in his literary criticism, developed ideas that would be valuable to the New Critics. He became one of the twentieth century's most important voices in the fields of poetry, drama, and literary criticism. The notion of the wasteland reverberated throughout American fiction.

OVER THERE: "THE WAR TO END ALL WARS"

The wasteland theme was concerned with modernity. The Great War, which dwelled in recent memory, was a stark expression of the collapse of values in the modern age. To American youth, it seemed like a disaster. America had arrived late to the war in Europe. While young men engaged in the conflict "over there," most Americans were spectators, imagining something afar in France. In April 1917, Germany began submarine warfare, putting American shipping at risk. The United States declared war on April 6, 1917. There was a quick mobilization and deployment of troops following the first nationwide draft in U.S. history.

American writers of war fiction had gone to Europe before the United States joined the fight in April 1917. Hemingway, Dos Passos, cummings, Faulkner, and others sought action. Some became ambulance drivers. Faulkner joined the British Royal Air Force. Dos Passos later said that he was "very anxious to see things at firsthand."[14] Experiencing the war brought these young men close to violence, to the encounter with death nearby. Hemingway was injured when a shell burst nearby while he was in camp on the front in Northern Italy. Faulkner was injured in a plane crash while in training. Cummings was falsely arrested in France, and he and his friend, Walter Slater Brown, were incarcerated at La Ferte Mace for more than four months (August 1917 to January 11, 1918) in a harrowing incident he recalls in *The Enormous Room*. He insisted that their arrest for suspected "treasonable correspondence" underscored the absurdity of France's wartime official bureaucracy. Affected by his experience of the enormous room, cummings became a decidedly unconventional poet.

Paul Fussell writes that war prompted the vision of "binary deadlock." People saw "simple antithesis everywhere"—us versus them. In this condition, the "mode of gross dichotomy came to dominate perception and expression everywhere, encouraging finally what we can call the modern versus habit," in which one thing is ever opposed to another.[15]

In the United States, the war advanced reforms for women. A sense of mission and series of temperance crusades promoted by women had led to Prohibition. With the war, a cry went out to boycott the German beer industry. Appeals for suffrage reform emerged, with a call for the vote. Many women entered the labor force while soldiers were away in Europe. The energy of their support for the United States during the war was obvious, and Woodrow Wilson addressed the U.S. Congress September 30, 1918, on behalf of women's suffrage. The United States concluded its part in the war on November 11, 1918, Armistice Day, a day we continue to recognize as Veterans Day. America lost 126,000 men in the war. European countries were devastated, with heavy losses. Treaty of Versailles negotiations were underway by late 1918. Most of Woodrow Wilson's "Fourteen Points" were defeated, and the United States did not support his goal of a League of Nations.

According to Gertrude Stein, World War I brought forth and accelerated the modern spirit. The war "forced . . . everyone" to be contemporary and self-conscious, she writes in "Composition as Explanation." [16] Meanwhile, Ann Douglas contended that the American imagination was working to keep up with a reality moving at "speeds hitherto unknown." [17] She calls this a "culture of momentum." [18] Into this changing environment came the novels of young writers, offering their recollections of the war. The American readership was primed for their stories by the events of the war. These writers were generally critical of the war. Hemingway distrusted inflated language. The poetry of cummings and his name were written in lower case. What words stood for was being scrutinized. The rhetoric of high ideals had been used in speeches, slogans, and battle plans to support an impossible war. It was now time to begin again, to make language new, forceful, and true.

Among the first war novels was *One Man's Initiation* (1920) by John Dos Passos. In it, Martin Howe and his friend Randolph see the destruction of not only physical structures, but also nobility. The devastation of art represents the callous destruction of the human spirit. Civilization itself is represented in an abbey torn to shreds by German artillery. In *Three Soldiers* (1921), John Andrews is in a hospital, thinking about the disintegration of everything that people value; what had been preserved in intellectual tradition has been shattered. Andrews muses, "There must be something more in the world than greed and hatred and cruelty." [19] The wisdom of "Democritus, Socrates, Epicurus, Christ" seems to have been devoured. The culture that Matthew Arnold once prized, that of the best that has been thought, has been turned into empty clichés. Andrews imagines that he might turn misery into music, recalling the rebellious John Brown in a composition he will entitle "The Body and Soul of John Brown." For how else, he wonders, can a man find meaning when he is trapped in a mechanism in which past values no longer seem to matter? Dos Passos's readers encountered his arguments against dehumanization. The individual, lying in a hospital bed, has been subjected to formation in "Making the Mould" and blasted by a cruel war of "Machines," "Rust," and "Under the Wheels." In his introduction to the 1969 reprinting of *One Man's Initiation*, originally printed in 1917, Dos Passos calls Woodrow Wilson's change from American neutrality to involvement in the war a "bitter disappointment" that turned him toward Socialism, for it soon became clear that "war was the greatest evil."[20]

American readers also consumed Ford Madox Ford's four-novel cycle dealing with the "world as it culminated in the war." It was a world that, in moral terms, had mismanaged the war. *The Good Soldier* is the most acclaimed and enduring of these novels. Tietjens, the protagonist, is a determined member of the ruling class. The soldiers might say that this class "caused the war to happen," and Tietjens feels a sense of responsibility for the outcome of the conflict. His participation is a matter of honor. He lives by a moral code that is pulling away from conventions. In his earlier collaborations with Joseph Conrad, Ford explores this theme of a moral code in a changing world. The postwar scene is revealed as one of irrationality in the final novel of the tetralogy, *The Last Post*. Erich Maria Remarque's *All Quiet on the Western Front* echoes this irrationality with its thesis that the Great War was unreasonable, bloody, and pointless. For Dos Passos's characters, this is summarized by one of Martin Howe's friends, who casts the war as unreal, "like Alice in Wonderland, Drury Lane pantomime, like all the dusty futility of Barnum and Bailey's circus."[21]

The postwar American reader included many soldiers and their families. More than 1 million Americans served overseas in World War I. About 350,000 of these men were African Americans who served in segregated troops. Among returning veterans, some 204,000 of them had been physically wounded. In addition, there were many undocumented cases of traumatized soldiers or shell-shocked veterans. In June

2012, in "Shell Shock," Dr. Edgar Jones of King's College in London described the symptoms of these World War I soldiers as "fatigue, tremors, confusion, nightmares," and impairment of sight or hearing.[22]

Hemingway had a sure sense of this struggle of the physically or psychologically wounded veteran. The implication in the short story "Soldier's Home" is that a soldier, like his character Howard Krebs, could not go back to his hometown and former life. He had experienced something momentous and life changing and could not adjust to the conventions of his home. After the war, some returning soldiers experienced disenchantment—a loss of faith in that world. In distancing themselves from the habits of their culture, they had become that "lost generation." Harry Crosby's war letters were published in 1932, following his suicide. He had witnessed "shell-gutted ravines, pock-marked hillsides, frightful roads, masses of debris."[23] As he stood by the ambulance he was about to drive, he saw a boy injured by an exploding shell. Sacredness itself seemed desecrated as artillery tore through a church, leaving only a statue of Christ, arms stretched in crucifixion over the debris.[24] He was chilled by a night attack by the Germans.[25] In his postwar letters, Crosby appears to cling to something religious to sustain him. He seeks normalcy in his home environment. Crosby's *Shadows of the Sun* (1928) chronicles his revisiting of the battlefields, of which he says, "It is still a wasteland."[26] The book is filled with suggestions that he was a shell-shocked veteran trying to adjust but unable to cope.

For Hemingway and Dos Passos, it was impossible to live conventionally after the war. Hemingway's Frederic Henry, in *A Farewell to Arms*, and Dos Passos's Martin Howe, in *One Man's Initiation*, were both scathed by the experience. Hemingway's Harold Krebs returns home psychologically shattered. Dos Passos's John Andrews searches for meaning amid the disintegration of values. The characters of these writers who experienced the war firsthand are quite different from those of Wharton and Cather, whose values were anchored in tradition. Wharton responded to the war with personal humanitarian aid, assisting the Red Cross in Paris. In her fifties when war broke out, she approached these times with a sense of mission. In her novel *Son at the Front*, George Campton is principled and eager, but the psychological complexity of Hemingway's Harold Krebs and Frederic Henry is missing. In contrast with Wharton's fiction, there is a vivid intensity to the works of Hemingway and Dos Passos.

Dos Passos was particularly incited about the effects of systems on the individual. His emphasis on visual and structural techniques may suggest that he became increasingly distrustful of words.[27] Against the mechanistic forces that would crush him, the fragmented world of the individual must be given voice or be newly formulated. The novel itself would be a new construction, an architecture that would involve the reader in a visual aesthetic and the new rhythms and patterns of a changing world. The fragmented individual would find integrity within the diverse features of this world. In Dos Passos's view, mechanistic ideologies or empty rhetoric should not manipulate the person or deny an individual's hope.

Both Dos Passos and Hemingway point out the destruction of the landscape by the machinery of war. In *Three Soldiers*, the military machine tears through the Loire Valley, betraying the artistic beauty of the place. The world can no longer express an "ideal state of wholeness" or provide a "basis for . . . a faith in man."[28] As John Andrews is arrested, a windmill positioned against the sky is "turning, turning," like a circular machine, a wheel of fortune gone wrong. In the first pages of *A Farewell to Arms*, the impact of the war on the land is equally clear. We see a shattered landscape, the machines of war camouflaged within it.

Dos Passos became a member of the Norton Harjes Ambulance Corps in 1917. He was a multitalented artist who had attended Harvard and could work in several media, including painting, theatrical scene design, and poetry. His poems in *Pushcart at the Curb* (1922) appeared first, before his fiction and experimental drama. In his first novel, *Streets of the Night*, his character Wenny commits suicide. Fanshawe, an intellectual, resigns himself to prosaic repetition. Nan cannot give herself to either of them, and she vanishes into Boston and tries to contact Wenny's spirit with a Ouija board. *One Man's Initiation* sold only sixty-three copies in the first year after its publication. Martin Howe seeks experience on the Western Front and recognizes his need for initiation. With *Three Soldiers*, Dos Passos faces the war, crafts an original style, and appeals to some members of the war generation. The novel is long—more than four hundred pages—and critiques Western civilization. Like Jean-Jacques Rousseau, who begins *Emile* with the thought that man is free but is everywhere in chains, Dos Passos sees modern men and women in a similar dilemma. Fuselli comes from San Francisco and Chrisfield from the Midwest, and John Andrews is a musician from Virginia, who, like Dos Passos himself, has attended Harvard. Their war is one of mechanism and devastating irony, much like we see in Stanley Kubrick's film *Paths of Glory*. H. L. Mencken applauded Dos Passos's *Three Soldiers* as the best of the war novels to appear soon after the war. About 3,000 to 4,000 copies were distributed, and they sold well.

Dos Passos's art seems to have developed in him a uniquely spatial sense, as well as a curiosity about time. The war confined space into a broken field: that muddy, blasted zone of territorial combat. Fussell has written of the "gross dichotomies" of safety in the trenches and "no man's land."[29] Officers attempted to control time in coordinated movements of troops; however, an individual's personal experience of time, or *duree*, was something else, as Proust or Bergson would show. Time was indeed out of joint. Postwar writers like Joyce, Faulkner, Dos Passos, and Virginia Woolf would explore the simultaneity of events within a stream of consciousness. In *To the Lighthouse* (1925), for example, Woolf devotes many pages to the Ramsey family's long day in the Hebrides and less than a dozen to the many years of war in a section called "Time Passes." Dos Passos marks sections of his work as "Time Before" and "Time After."

Space and time were reconstituted in visual art by the cubists. The impressionists had challenged nineteenth-century realism many decades before. Paul Cezanne worked to redefine ways of seeing and imagining landscapes and space. Cubism emerged from his innovations. These painters would present multiple angles of vision simultaneously on a series of planes. Cubists, considering how the eye sees, across a series of microseconds, fragmented the object. The changing view emphasized subjectivity. Such writers as Hemingway and Dos Passos were drawn to cubism in developing their styles. *The Sun Also Rises* shows suggestions of cubist influence in his descriptions of landscapes. In *Three Soldiers*, Dos Passos attempts to reflect a convergence of simultaneous happenings, and in this respect, it is a precursor to his more developed cubist style in *Manhattan Transfer* and the *U.S.A.* trilogy.

The "impressionistic" technique used by Stephen Crane in *The Red Badge of Courage* may be seen as a precursor to Dos Passos's *Three Soldiers*. Crane records the impressions or sensory moments of Henry

Fleming's experience of battle as they occur. Dos Passos uses a similar method, moving into the consciousness of each soldier and placing the men in juxtaposition to suggest simultaneous experiences. Their sensory experiences intersect with one another. As Gertrude Stein claims, the war advanced cubism and reflected fragmentation.[30] The works of Picasso and Gris were a visual complement to the experimental tendencies in Hemingway and Dos Passos.

Such experimentalism was a feature of the poetry that Dos Passos's friend cummings was writing. In *The Enormous Room*, the poet's single lengthy prose work, he offers an account of the kind of delays in law that one sees in Dickens's *Bleak House*. His story suggests deprivations of imprisonment that one would later find in the prison camps of World War II or the caricature of incompetent war leadership that one sees in Stanley Kubrick's films *Paths of Glory* or *Full Metal Jacket*.

Edith Wharton, who carried out extraordinary relief efforts for the French and Belgians through the Red Cross, experienced a different kind of contact with the war. In Frederick J. Hoffmann's view, the Great War was a "mission for her."[31] In Wharton's *A Son at the Front* (1923), John Campton recognizes that his son George must perform his duty to fight in the war against Germany. He goes off to Europe, even as Wharton realized that some "meaning had evaporated" out of words like "honor."[32] Wharton returned to her novel *Son at the Front*, begun in 1917, after she had written *The Age of Innocence*, her story of New York elites in a "long vanished America." As Hoffmann points out, Wharton provides a hero whose "splendid death" speaks of a somewhat Victorian notion of heroism rather than the experience of bitter alienation. Her concern was with French culture and tradition, and an America that might best develop through its contact with the high culture of the old world of Britain and France.[33]

Further off from the war was Cather, whose *One of Ours* (1922) garnered a Pulitzer Prize for Fiction. In her novel, Claude Wheeler discovers culture in France that he did not know in Nebraska. Wheeler represents values, a sacrifice for what is loved, and nobility that may be likened to the Homeric sense of arête in Hector in *The Iliad*. Wheeler is not disillusioned like the characters of Dos Passos and Hemingway. Cather's experience was not anything like that of Hemingway, who wrote to Edmund Wilson that Cather had to get her war experience secondhand.[34] Her ideals were strong, but, like Wharton, she was a noncombatant. Both women were also two decades older than younger writers like Hemingway and Dos Passos, who appear to have directly experienced the psychological trauma of war and a search for meaning.

Faulkner, in his training with the Royal Air Force, remained concerned throughout the 1920s about the impact of the war. When his character Donald Mahon returns to Georgia in *Soldiers' Pay* (1926), his face is disfigured. Bayard Sartoris appears to have returned home undamaged, but he is wounded mentally. He is clearly struggling with posttraumatic stress disorder, as he misses the heightened energy of war and has to substitute drunkenness, hunting, and racing cars for being active in the war. The problems we see in *Sartoris* are contemporary ones for some soldiers who have returned from conflict in Iraq or Afghanistan. In Faulkner's fiction, Horace Benbow comes back home from Y.M.C.A. service and runs off with Belle Mitchell, another man's wife. In "All the Dead Pilots," the narrator says that the survivors all died on November 11, 1918, Armistice Day. Their days of daring were over. They had to go home to suburban lives and forever sit behind desks, getting fat.[35] None of them was quite prepared for ordinary life. In the meantime, those who were too young to go, like Julian Lowe, lament that they could not participate in the adventure.[36]

The war brought to Europe writers like Hemingway, Dos Passos, and Faulkner, who began their work in small magazines on the continent. A strikingly imaginative novelist, Fitzgerald, would soon join them there. The publication of his first blockbuster novel, *This Side of Paradise*, had been accompanied by his marriage to southern belle Zelda Sayre, and the wild acclaim the novel received brought a reputation that followed them as they moved to Paris.

2

ERNEST HEMINGWAY AND F. SCOTT FITZGERALD

Friendship and Rivalry

America's most influential writers of the first part of the twentieth century found their testing ground and launched their careers during the 1920s. Ernest Hemingway and F. Scott Fitzgerald were uniquely different literary stylists of the same generation who began writing from within the context of this extraordinary milieu of the Roaring Twenties. The contact between Hemingway and Fitzgerald, who first met in Paris, has sometimes been described as a literary friendship; however, the relationship grew agonistic, especially in later days. A thread of competition existed between the two men.

Alongside this competitiveness, these writers had quite different visions and markedly individual writing styles. Hemingway wrote sparse dialogue in his short fiction. He searched for the right word, the concrete detail. He omitted things. Fitzgerald filled his short stories to overflowing with social gestures, fabulous characters, firecracker dialogue, and lyricism. These writers profoundly shaped the American imagination in their own unique ways.

HEMINGWAY IN PARIS

America in 1922 was a memory for Ernest Hemingway, one closely held, like winter air in the lungs, Paris in bad weather, or the pencil and blue notebook and the café au lait in the cup before him. From the Place St.-Michel, a good café, he could think of the United States and imagine a cold, windy day in Michigan, one of those brisk days with clear skies, far from the smoke of war, and put pencil to paper and, in short, clean lines, describe it. Not far away, at 27 Rue de Flueres, was Gertrude Stein, who took his stories seriously. She read them as she sat under paintings by Picasso, Cezanne, Gris, and Matisse, and she knew of such young writers as John Dos Passos and e.e. cummings and Hemingway, the boys who had been to war and become disillusioned, determined men. One day she said to Hemingway, "You are all a lost generation." The garage keeper had said that and Stein repeated it, and Hemingway would one day inscribe it as a caption on the flyleaf of his first novel.

In those days, Hemingway often wrote in an upstairs room that looked out on the rooftops of Paris. After writing steadily each morning from Rue Cardinal Lemoine, he might walk the steep road to the river, follow the Seine to the bookstalls for cheap American books, or go to Sylvia Beach's book shop, Shakespeare and Company, on the Rue d'Olean, where books lined the shelves. There he could see the author photos that filled the walls, and he might catch a passing glimpse of James Joyce, in conservative suit and rimless eyeglasses, or the bearded Ezra Pound in his sinister cape and Spanish hat. Hemingway knew that American reading audiences liked popular fiction. It was his intention to write something different—to make words count, to pin the world down in concrete images and spare, sure language.

The 1920s world of Paris that Hemingway recalled in *A Moveable Feast* (1964) years later was a place in which writers like Fitzgerald, Dos Passos, Faulkner, and others rediscovered their sense of America. There they began to shape the new American novel. So began a generation of American writers and a succession of their readers: men who talked like Hemingway characters, new women animated by the frenetic jazz age images of Fitzgerald, readers who wondered at the beautiful and damned, and the few who pondered the human terror under the magnolia and cypress shadows of Faulkner's southern world. Those readers were caught up in a world of change—that new era of advertising, radio, motor cars, and popular culture, and these novelists, in their fiction, captured this and made an impact on readers' lives. "Their sense of being different," Malcolm Cowley says, can be seen in their stories, as when Fitzgerald writes in "The Scandal Detectives" that some generations follow one another closely, but for others there is a "gulf . . . infinite and unbridgeable" between them.[1]

Hemingway, Fitzgerald, and Faulkner were of a new generation. The innovations that had begun to reshape the American novel came to them through older writers: Anderson, Wharton, Dreiser, and Cather among them. Hemingway was selective in his reading and sharp in his comments about the older writers. In 1920, Lewis's *Main Street* became a best seller, critiquing the American small town; however, for Hemingway this was already yesterday's fiction. He was after a new style, a new contemporary voice. He had begun to craft his own style, while observing the innovations of Stein and the textures of Anderson's fiction. He had become aware of new voices, like that of James Joyce, and had heard of F. Scott Fitzgerald and his novel of college life.

Hemingway knew that Fitzgerald's *This Side of Paradise* was wildly popular and that it signaled the appearance of a younger generation, his own generation. He also realized that Fitzgerald's novel made a good deal of money, although he was willing to subordinate the quest for income to a search for craft and sureness in his own work. In 1919, Fitzgerald earned $800 from his writing, but *This Side of Paradise* changed his fortunes. The publication of the novel and short stories for the *Saturday Evening Post* ballooned his income to $18,000 in 1920. Readers were becoming increasingly aware of a youth culture, the new woman, flappers, and the pulse of jazz—an indigenous African American art now transposed by white orchestras. They were, as of yet, unaware of Hemingway and Faulkner, both of whom had traveled overseas to Paris in the early 1920s. John Dos Passos had given readers his accounts of the war in *One Man's Initiation* and *Three Soldiers*. Fitzgerald's novel entertained readers with his account of college life at Princeton. A new generation of writers and their stories was beginning to break into American consciousness.

American fiction was changing with these new writers. Modernist writers, like Hemingway in *The Sun Also Rises*, let go of plot in favor of a wandering story. Before 1925, Hemingway published in journals with small circulations, while Fitzgerald was writing for such mass-market magazines as the *Saturday Evening Post*. Hemingway worked painstakingly on his fiction, producing his story cycle *In Our Time*, published by Three Mountains Press. Scribner's editor, Maxwell Perkins, learned about the book from Fitzgerald, who insisted that Hemingway (whose name he misspelled with two m's) had a "brilliant future." In October 1924, Edmund Wilson reviewed Hemingway's story collection, then entitled *in our time*, in lowercase. Fitzgerald began reading Hemingway and, upon his move to Paris, met with Hemingway at the Dingo bar in April 1925. The trade edition of *In Our Time* appeared half a year later. In March 1926, Fitzgerald's enthusiastic review of the book appeared in the *Bookman*. Thus began the long and often frequently conflicted relationship of these two writers, often discussed by literary historians and critics.

Fitzgerald played an instrumental role in bringing Hemingway's work to a wider audience through his contact with Perkins at Scribner's. Boni and Liveright had offered Hemingway a three-book contract. To fulfill this contract, Hemingway rapidly wrote *Torrents of Spring* (1925), critiquing Sherwood Anderson's *Dark Laughter*. Boni and Liveright, the firm that published Anderson, declined to publish the book. His next book was now free to be published by another firm. Fitzgerald recommended Hemingway to Scribner's, and *The Sun Also Rises* appeared in 1926. Hemingway's audience and sales would grow throughout time. His style, perhaps more than that of Fitzgerald or Faulkner, would influence a future generation of writers.

VISITING WITH GERTRUDE STEIN

Behind Hemingway's work at his craft at this time towered Gertrude Stein, who was in Paris beginning in 1903, and Anderson. They recognized in Hemingway a style that embraced conciseness, focus, simplicity of expression, and sensitivity to the weight of words. Hemingway thought about perspective and point of view in a narrative. The rugged naturalism of Stephen Crane, Frank Norris, and Theodore Dreiser held some appeal for him. In contrast, Wharton's *The Writing of Fiction* (1925) was remote from his style and purposes. He preferred the short stories of Anderson, who wrote of how word played against word, relating sound to sound.[2]

Hemingway frequently visited Stein's rooms at Rue de Fleures, and he encouraged Ford Madox Ford to serialize Stein's *The Making of Americans* in his *the transatlantic review*. Stein was proud of *The Making of Americans*—a long work and one that must be read with patience. Stein's work on the book dates from 1903 to 1911, but it was not published as a book until Robert McAlmon did so in 1925, through his Contact Press. The novel is subtitled *The Story of a Family's Progress*. Yet, it is hard to know if the family featured in the story progresses much at all. Stein's consciousness circles around, and the rhythmic pattern of phrase and nonlogical language appears to draw most of our attention. The Dehnings and the Herslands appear in the first of seven sections. Julia Dehning marries Alfred Hersland. In the next sections readers meet the Hissings and their daughter Fanny, as well as three women named Shilling, who are seamstresses. Fanny and her husband David's children are introduced in the next sections. If anything about America is suggested by this family, it may be a sort of dislocation. There are divorces as marriages, family, and community fail. Style takes precedence, and repetition becomes an important feature.

Stein appreciated Hemingway and mentions him in her memoirs, which are narrated as if they were from her companion, Alice Toklas. She titled the book *The Autobiography of Alice B. Toklas*, and Wilson thought that was a neat trick. Through Toklas's point of view, Stein looks at herself and her literary and artistic circle. In Wilson's review (October 1933), he points out that Stein truly creates a distinct individual character in Toklas, as if this account were a novel. For Wilson, the most interesting part of Stein's book is her recollection of World War I and her discovery of the works of Matisse and Picasso. He describes this section as one of "artistic adventure," as Toklas enters the Stein context. Jean Cocteau referred to this period as the "heroic age," and it was a time of nostalgia for independent magazines and art shows. Stein notes that sadness followed the death of Guillaume Apollinaire in the war. It seemed as if history had intruded upon their artistic circle.

Wilson calls the remainder of the book "less exciting."[3] Still, it gives expression to Stein's attitudes toward such familiar figures as Pound (a "village explainer") and Hemingway. The latter comes in for criticism as a pupil who "does it without understanding." Stein and Anderson were "funny" about him, says the narrator, Toklas, since "Hemingway had been formed by them."[4] Wilson believes that Stein's view was partly biased because she was the "ruler of a salon," and once her protégés left she believed less in them.[5]

Hemingway began to draw away from Stein by 1926. At the time, she was writing in *Composition as Explanation* (1926) that a writer ought to maintain a continuous present, "using everything," beginning again and again. Time and repetition and the movement from sentence to paragraph were the concern of the writer of fiction, she asserted. Her method argued for attention to the present immediacy of the thing seen. Hemingway was then writing with attention to the concrete image. The rhythm of repetition of the word *and* occurs in his novel *The Sun Also Rises*. The perspective he observed by looking at Cezanne's paintings is also in evidence here. For example, the location and movement of a truck is given spatially, in planes, as if on a canvas. The reader is given the foreground, and one's eye follows a truck up the road, riding toward the background. Commenting on this technique, Hemingway mentions that he learned something from Cezanne.[6]

Hemingway sought concrete facts, sure words, and action. His work sought dreams of order, writing as an alternative to the disorder of society. The individual deprived of ultimate purpose has to create. Performance was a way to create a goal. Jake Barnes only wanted to know how to live life. In *The Sun Also Rises*, his physical wound is also part of the psychic wound of expatriates adrift from their American past. In Hemingway's *The Sun Also Rises*, Frederick Hoffmann sees the "postwar landscape of unreason."[7] The novel portrays a cast of isolated individuals who are cut off from tradition and on a wandering journey. There is aimless sequence and a lack of order or meaningful happening.[8] The war wound of Jake makes him impotent. The character Brett drifts with a lost quality and has no normal or lasting relationships. The characters move from Paris to Spain and the Pyrenees, to Pamplos and the bullfights. In *The Sun Also Rises*, Wilson saw "heartlessness" and "atrocious behavior" in Hemingway's characters. The novel, he suggests, was about the attempt to either escape this world or find a code whereby to live in it.[9]

The first British edition of *The Sun Also Rises* was entitled *Fiesta*. As the novel circulated more widely, it became an important part of the Hemingway mystique. He was viewed as a man who liked women, sports, and violence. Hemingway repeated the bullfighting interest with *Death in the Afternoon* (1932). The Twentieth Century Fox film version of *The Sun Also Rises*, made in 1957, brought the story to a later audience. It was directed by Daryl Zannuck, with a cast of Tyrone Power, Ava Gardner, Errol Flynn, Eddie Albert, Mel Ferrer, and Julie Greco. The films of Hemingway's novels tend to focus on romance and sensationalism for a middle-class viewing audience. By 1954, when he won the Nobel Prize, Hemingway had become an iconic figure, and his style was frequently imitated by other writers.

A *Farewell to Arms* (1929) appeared during the same year as *All Quiet on the Western Front*. Both stirred recollections of World War I. Hemingway's tragic love story moved readers in Europe, as well as the United States. Erich Maria Remarque's novel embodied his plea that the Great War be the war to end all wars. Whereas Remarque underlines his argument with a call for pacifism, Hemingway is understated, working by pointing to concrete things. His words denote objects, things that can be pinned down. In the United States, the Book-of-the-Month Club distributed about 67,000 copies of *All Quiet on the Western Front* to subscribers.[10] *A Farewell to Arms* sold approximately 70,000 copies.

In Hemingway's novel, the romance of Frederic Henry and Catherine Barkley is driven by an attempt to escape the war. In their search for meaning, Frederic and Catherine find one another. The five books of the novel comprise a drama that includes the war, a romance, the retreat at Caporetto, Frederic's decision to escape with Catherine into Switzerland, and the fateful conclusion. Frederic recounts his story. He is an ambulance driver from the United States who is on the Italian front, at war with Austria. He has joined the war for adventure rather than any sense of purpose; he was able to speak Italian and there was a war in Italy, so he joined. Injured and convalescing in a hospital in Milan, he begins a relationship with his nurse, Catherine, who is English.

The war in Italy has become costly and difficult, and Frederic is going to be sent back to the front; however, Catherine informs him that she is pregnant. When Frederic leaves for the front, with this on his mind, he learns that the Italians have lost a significant battle at Caporetto. We receive a vivid description of their retreat in the rain. Frederic has decided to desert the army and bring Catherine with him. They make a dramatic escape to Switzerland. Perhaps because of their arduous journey, Catherine's pregnancy is disastrous. Hemingway offers a stoical approach to biological necessity, whose consequence is a kind of doom. It appears that Frederic could not help but fall into Catherine's arms any more than he fell into the arms of war. They bid good-bye to the military conflict but soon struggle with a serious conflict awaiting them. Catherine's very life must be saved, and tragedy strikes just when they seem to have escaped. In the end, there is the rain as they descend from the mountains—and with the rain comes loss.

Readers opened the pages of *A Farewell to Arms* a little more than a decade after the war had ended. Some critics saw surface realism in Hemingway. Yet, others recognized that he was a writer who made use of implication. When Cowley introduced *The Portable Hemingway* in 1940, he suggested that Hemingway was no realist but, rather, that he belonged with Poe, Hawthorne, and Melville as one of the "haunted and nocturnal writers."[11] In Hemingway, Cowley saw an "instinct for legends, for sacraments, for rituals, for symbols appealing to hopes and fears."[12] In Hemingway, the inner battle within his characters is often more important than the outer one. He writes laconically, with scenes stripped down, focusing on the action of his ordinary heroes.

A Farewell to Arms was launched to considerable public acclaim. Hemingway had completed revisions while in Key West, where he was visited by Maxwell Perkins. Scribner's offered $16,000 to run the story as a serial in their magazine. On June 24, 1929, Hemingway completed his work in Paris. He later told a reporter that he had revised his last page often, so he could "get the words right."[13] It appears that most readers responded enthusiastically to his novel, but Boston censors had moved to ban Scribner's magazine's run of the story, objecting to the unmarried love affair between Frederic and Catherine. Hemingway called this move an unhealthy one for a significant book.

The book was then published by Scribner's in the United States and Jonathan Cape in England. When Scribner's first printing of 31,050 copies was issued, each copy sold for $2.50. A second printing of 10,000 copies soon followed. The first edition of *The Sun Also Rises*, in comparison, had seen a print run of 6,000, followed by two more printings of 2,000. *A Farewell to Arms* was something different indeed: By January 1930, sales had surpassed 70,000 copies.

Letters from readers who are critical of Hemingway's novel appear in the Scribner's archives at the Firestone Library at Princeton University. These readers take issue with the stories on moral grounds, objecting to the affair between Frederic and Catherine and the pregnancy outside of marriage. A man from Maine wrote, "What modernists call realism reminds me of an artist picking out for a still life picture a half-empty milk bottle with milk souring and flies crawling over it, some stale and rotting vegetables and molding bread."[14] Nevertheless, there are also notes from fans of Hemingway and stories of those fans that later made efforts to locate him. In August 1944, after U.S. troops had entered Paris, twenty-five-year-old J. D. Salinger sought out Hemingway at the Ritz Hotel. The man who would write *The Catcher in the Rye* was then with the Counter-Intelligence Corps, and he drove his jeep to the hotel in search of one of his favorite authors.

A Farewell to Arms was Hemingway's first novel to be adapted into a film, and he was not entirely pleased with the result. Yet, the film catapulted the novel to greater sales. Director Frank Borzage and screenwriters Benjamin Glazer and Oliver H. P. Garrett took some liberties with Hemingway's story. Paramount advertised the film as a romance and considered two different endings. The writers wondered whether the story should end happily ever after or miserably, as Hemingway had written it. One of their endings shows Frederic (Gary Cooper) carrying Catherine (Helen Hayes) to a window, saying the word *peace* as the bells toll outside. It is a sad but poignant conclusion. In the other version, Catherine is healed and comes to life as the war ends on Armistice Day, and everyone outside cheers. Hemingway, needless to say, did not like that ending at all. Borzage highlights the romance between the couple rather than the war, which so greatly impacts their lives.

In his novel, Hemingway implies much about the stress of war. Frederic's desertion is likely a response to his malaise and anxiety, and Catherine's death mirrors war's bleak devastation of life. For Borzage, the war is a setting for the plot to unfold within: It is the context in which the couple's romance blossoms. Paramount had no difficulty filming the retreat from Caporetto: It won an award for cinematography. They censored the premarital sex between Frederic and Catherine, however. The couple had to be married and her pregnancy to be lengthened. Meanwhile, the Italians were embarrassed by the defeat at

Caporetto, and Benito Mussolini banned Hemingway's book. Paramount heard that the Italian dictator had insisted that all American films be banned in Italy if they contained any signs of Italian soldiers giving up or deserting the army. As a result, the film provides no verbal mention of Caporetto and only the mention of another battle that resulted in an Italian victory.

Ben Hecht's later screenplay for the remake of A Farewell to Arms is a bit different. He wrote more closely to Hemingway's novel. David O. Selznick had purchased the film rights from Warner Brothers and chosen Hecht, with whom he had worked on Gone with the Wind. As director, Charles Vidor replaced John Huston, who had begun work on the film but had a difference of opinion with the producer. Hecht builds the chaplain (Albert Sordi) into a hero, as Hemingway does in his novel. He gives us the retreat from Caporetto with no careful omissions and has Catherine die, as in the novel, without glossing over the tragedy of this. Vidor and Hecht attempted to include Frederic's interior monologues as Frederic (Rock Hudson) dwells upon Catherine (Jennifer Jones) and death and dying in the war. Hemingway did not like this film either, nor did the Catholic League of Decency, which called the film morally objectionable.

All Quiet on the Western Front by Erich Maria Remarque (Im Westen Nicht Neues) (1929) also became a popular film. The novel, written a decade after the war, reveals the war's harsh destruction and human cost. Remarque's story, partly autobiographical, is a pacifist response that underlines dehumanization and alienation. Paul Baumer and his fellow soldiers, many of whom were his comrades from school, are behind the lines on the Western Front. Baumer begins to see that ideas of heroism are empty and that they are caught in a hostile place. By the time Baumer meets a French soldier, he is no longer the nationalistic individual bent on heroism that he once had been. He becomes the last survivor within his military squad. Tormented by this loss, he is finally killed by enemy gunfire.

Lewis Milestone's film won the Academy Award in 1930 for best film. In his novel, Remarque makes use of fragmentation and impressions; however, the film moves along chronologically, following the scenes in Remarque's novel. There are scenes of warfare, and Baumer's experience provides the film's center. Milestone is faithful to the novel's theme: its pacifism and reflection on the effects of war. Baumer, who is played by Lew Ayres, is portrayed as a victim. Milestone creates several visual images that are not in Remarque's novel. In one, Baumer reaches his hand toward a butterfly that is fluttering above the trenches. A series of crosses are superimposed.

F. SCOTT FITZGERALD ON *THIS SIDE OF PARADISE*

When F. Scott Fitzgerald entered basic training in Montgomery, Alabama, he began writing hurriedly, certain that the war would claim him; however, what claimed him was the fascination of Zelda Sayre, whom he met at a dance in July. Inspired, he took *The Romantic Egoist*, a 120,000-word novel he had submitted to Scribner's, and recast it as *This Side of Paradise*. It was a story that Scribner's editor Maxwell Perkins became enthusiastic about, and he accepted it for publication on September 16, 1919. Fitzgerald's agent, Harold Ober, also sold "Head and Shoulders" to the *Saturday Evening Post*, which circulated to as many as 2 million readers. About twenty stories were sold to *Scribner's Magazine* and other publications that year.

Scott and Zelda Fitzgerald married at St. Patrick's Cathedral in New York on April 3, 1920, two weeks before *This Side of Paradise* appeared. Fitzgerald was suddenly the young writer of adolescent college exuberance—one who described a young generation's drinking, petting and kissing, and materialistic quest for success. Scribner's advertised the novel widely, calling it a "Novel for Flappers Written for Philosophers." Fitzgerald took this as a title for his short story collection *Flappers and Philosophers*. He cast himself as the dandy philosopher and his southern belle Zelda, with bobbed hair, as a flapper, and they were ready for prime time: The party was on. The public got its first taste of indulgence and alcohol-fueled antics. Scott and Zelda became the popular image of what he called the jazz age. Writing, however, requires discipline, method, and conscious planning. Fitzgerald was a professional writer, and he needed to curb the Dionysian frenzy and bacchanalia of partying to focus on writing.

There is a patchwork variety to *This Side of Paradise*, which is a composite of other works. Fitzgerald assembled a series of incidents and combined *The Romantic Egoist* with "Babes in the Woods," his "Debutante" play of 1919, and his undergraduate verse. *This Side of*

Paradise is the story of Amory Blaine's drift through his Princeton education and his efforts to live in a dreamlike world. He passes through World War I and becomes increasingly disenchanted. Filled with desire for life, a "sphere of epicurean delight," Amory imagines himself onstage or in love: "Oh to fall in love like that—to the languorous magic melody of such a tune."[15] He imagines an idealized existence and that the real world can be masked by theatricality. After all, Amory and Isabelle are "described in theatrical terms," as T. Austin Graham observes.[16] They also fall into a romance. Amory writes a love letter to Isabelle from his dorm room at Princeton: "O Isabelle dear—it's a wonderful night. Somebody is playing 'Love Moon' on a mandolin far across the campus, and the music seems to bring you to the window. Now he's playing 'Good-bye Boys, I'm Through' and how well it suits me. For I am through with everything."[17] As Graham points out, this song appeals to the memory of the reader, who then has to match it with the text.[18]

Drawn toward their first kiss, they hear in the background Jerome Kern's melody from the musical *Very Good Eddie* (1915), "Babes in the Wood." Alternating male and female voices join together. Yet, Schylur Greene's lyrics suggest that the ballad "Babes in the Wood" is not about passion. They are simply in the "same canoe," and the narrator says the moonlight is bright and tells the person he is speaking to that she ought to kiss him like a sister. As Graham notes, it is a "remarkably chaste selection for a novel that was considered quite racy in its time."[19] Perhaps, for Amory, it is more about the dream and less about the reality of a relationship. "It was always the becoming he dreamed of, never the being."[20]

When *This Side of Paradise* was published by Collins in London in May 1921, it was met with negative critical reviews from the *Times Literary Supplement* and slow sales of less than 1,000 copies. Some considered the first novel bereft of structure. Still, it can be said that modernist works were intended to be innovative and diffuse. Hemingway's *The Sun Also Rises* wanders like its characters. Hemingway consciously avoided plotting his novel like a popular thriller. Fitzgerald's patchwork quilt of a novel was within the spirit of the time. With *The Beautiful and Damned*, he sought form but ended up giving "care to the detail."[21] *Metropolitan Magazine* serialized the story in September 1921. It appeared in book form with a slightly different ending.[22]

This Side of Paradise sold 49,000 copies in its first year. It's popularity has prompted speculation from critics about the novel's audience. Were they drawn to his images of youth culture, college life, or romantic scenes? Was the novel popular because it captured social attitudes that were in the air and the spirit of the times? Was there a response to an underlying tone of disenchantment or the spirit of independence evoked by the novel?[23] The novel describes a generation, one that Fitzgerald would be associated with throughout his life. To be young in the 1920s, Kirk Curnutt suggests, is to be able to use entertainment in the construction of identity.[24] This is what Amory Blaine attempts to do. Fitzgerald's characters Amory Blaine, Nick Carraway, and Judy Jones in "Winter Dreams" encounter an intense life of passionate vitality. Fitzgerald wonders at a world of wealth and sense of privilege, which he critiques for its ostentation, lack of taste, sophistication, and pretense. Yet, he marvels at glitter and sparkle, social mobility, and freedom. He presents the youth culture of the flapper, bright and beautiful, and the choreographed movements of individuals of vanity and egotism. This is a culture at play, jazzed, seeking the ecstatic.

American youth were excited to see Amory's world in *This Side of Paradise*. Others were puzzled by it. The novel became talked about and was widely distributed on a wave of rumor and newfound popularity. *This Side of Paradise* was considered by some to be an insightful sociological study of youth culture. Fitzgerald seems to have caught on to the nation's changing attitudes toward youth. The *Bookman* called the novel a "Chronicle of Youth by Youth," and the *Philadelphia Evening Public Ledger* announced that in it, "Youth Writes about Youth."[25] Young people had become increasingly segregated amongst their own peers and, by the 1920s, had developed values, language, dress, and behavior specific to their own generational cohort. Fitzgerald himself announced that an author should write for his own generation.[26]

Edmund Wilson was harsh. In his March 1922 review, he describes Fitzgerald as a "rather childish fellow."[27] His novel is quite alive, but he is too occupied with himself and too little with the world, says Wilson. In contrast, Thomas Woodward (1898–1935) and Peggy Woodward (1898–1965) of Minneapolis assert that Fitzgerald was far more than a "flapper novelist." In 1922, Thomas replied sharply in the *St. Paul Daily News* to Wilson's review of *The Beautiful and Damned* in the *Bookman*.[28] Wilson then called Fitzgerald's *Tales of the Jazz Age* "spontaneous nonsense" and sarcastically criticized "The Lees of Happiness," a story of which Peggy Woodward said, "I read it . . . and wept over it."[29] The Woodwards' comments in a Minnesota newspaper did not carry the same weight as those of Wilson, who was writing for such national publications as the *Bookman* and the *New Republic*. Peggy had published a novel *The Love Legend* in 1922, and Thomas published his novel *Through the Wheat* in 1923. It was thought that Fitzgerald had been instrumental in getting these works printed. Hence, their critical opinions were not highly valued.[30]

CELEBRITY AND CULTURAL CRITICISM

In H. L. Mencken's review of *Flappers and Philosophers* (1920), he observes Fitzgerald's pursuit of both commercial success and critical success as causing a kind of dichotomy in his personality. Mencken refers to Fitzgerald as "ambidextrous."[31] Meanwhile, newspapers began to include gossip about Fitzgerald's own audacious behavior. The flappers he wrote about were theatrical, performing, making a show with dance, affectation, mannerism. Fitzgerald recorded in his fiction a cultural grasp of the sights and sounds of the 1920s, the onstage behavior of his peers, much as sociologist Erving Goffmann would later offer in more staid language in *The Presentation of Self in Everyday Life*, in which he thoughtfully examines a society of gestures, poses, and roles. The 1920s initiated a time when commodities were heralded as marks of distinction for the middle class. Cars, clothes, and other material products became signs of belonging. Amory Blaine is attentive to clothing, fabric, color, and other sartorial surfaces that would give Thomas Carlyle's *Sartor Resartus* heartburn, and he proceeds to dress like a dandy. His life becomes a semiotic social landscape of signs and appearances.

Fitzgerald was an astute observer of social change, a professional writer who seemed to search for some moral grounding in a shifting world. His own odyssey brought the temptations of Circe. With notoriety came excess, a quest for drama, and a theatrical self that reflects today's Hollywood obsession with facelifts and image. Today our popular media can project Fitzgerald's world of spectacle with special effects. As in the 1920s, entertainment, fads, and reality television have promoted a culture of pleasure and fun rather than one of self-development and civic responsibility in building community, nation, and world.

Fitzgerald's fiction was mostly autobiographical. He could dash off some short fiction, relying on his imagination and lyrical gifts, but for other stories he became a conscious planner.[32] *The Beautiful and Damned*, his second novel, required some planning. It sold more than 50,000 copies, and he followed with a short story collection, *The Jazz Age*, which sold 24,000 copies. In the fall of 1922, Fitzgerald moved to Great Neck, Long Island. In 1923, he sent scripts and scenarios to film studios and earned about $13,500 for film rights from his stories; however, Edmund Wilson and John Peale Bishop, both of whom were familiar with Fitzgerald from their days at Princeton, criticized the uneven quality of his work. Many of his stories, they concluded, were ephemeral, like noisy New Year's Eve party horns—squealing, sensational, and dispensable. This affected Fitzgerald's critical reputation, even while such stories as "Diamonds as Big as the Ritz" and the well-crafted "Winter Dreams" were clearly works of quality. Stories like "Winter Dreams" (1922), "Absolution" (1924), and "The Sensible Thing" (1924) deal with the theme of a poor boy in love with a rich, inaccessible girl, and they associate romantic love with money. These stories would lead to *The Great Gatsby* (1925), which has become one of the touchstones of twentieth-century American writing.

The Beautiful and Damned is principally about the decline and fall of Anthony Patch, a privileged hedonist in New York who aspires to be a writer but loses his family inheritance, joins the army, fears he has an unfaithful wife, cannot keep a job, and never writes the work he says he is going to write. In his bathroom, Anthony sings "My Beautiful Lady" from the musical *The Pink Lady* (1911), imagining that he is the seductive violinist described in the lyrics. Anthony listens to "Ring Ting-a-Ling," a song sung by Ada Jones, accompanied by a brass band, which has a melody punctuated by the ringing of a phone. Listeners can hear the comic, conversational delivery. Muriel arrives with songs: "You ought to have a phonograph out here in the country," she says, "just a little Vic—they don't cost much. Then whenever you're lonesome you can have Caruso or Al Jolson right at your door."[33]

The *Saturday Evening Post* printed many of Fitzgerald's stories between 1923 and 1924, earning him $16,450. Scott and Zelda went to the French Riviera, where they met Gerald and Sara Murphy, a cultivated couple who were trendsetters and supportive friends. While in France, Zelda's affair with French aviator Edouard Jozan created difficulties in the marriage from which the couple would never quite recover. Nonetheless, they stayed together, in spite of financial difficulties and Zelda's breakdowns.

CREATING GATSBY

In the spring of 1924, Fitzgerald was determined to write an "intricately patterned" novel with a focused plot and sense of mystery. *The Great Gatsby* was revised several times, including following Maxwell Perkins's suggestions late in 1924. The extensive revisions that Fitzgerald applied to his novel show him as a craftsman of literature. Attracted, dazzled, and enticed by glitter and laughter like the sound of money, we are suspended, caught in Nick's anticipations, ever wondering with him just who this Gatsby fellow is. Even as the darkness settles on West Egg, even as the waves of the Sound lap upon the shore fifty yards from Nick Carraway's home, we watch with him the lights going on, distantly flickering across the seemingly vast reach of night between those who, like the ambitious Gatsby, have much and those—the affluent and charming—who have ever more. There is Gatsby, who Nick says "turned out all right," yet who, with calculated ambition, fell into a mistaken path with his fabricated chivalry and is caught in Nick's troubadour lament of courtly love.

The Great Gatsby is filled with imagined jazz, vaguely described "yellow cocktail music," and several identifiable pop songs.[34] When Nick is with Jordan Baker in Manhattan, they hear girls singing in the West Fifties "The Love Nest," a song from George M. Cohan's musical *Mary*, with lyrics by Otto Harbach and music by Louis A. Hirsch. Still familiar to contemporary audiences is the frequently covered "Ain't We Got Fun" (1921). "Beale Street Blues" can be found on YouTube, with *Louis Armstrong Plays King Oliver* (1954). The song "Sheik of Araby" (1921) was written by Ted Snyder, with lyrics by Harry B. Smith and Francis Wheeler, following a novel of that title that became a film.

When "Three O'Clock in the Morning" appears in *The Great Gatsby*, Nick wonders about the song's effect on Daisy. He wonders what in the song "seemed to be calling her back inside."[35] It is a three-quarter time waltz by Julian Robledo (music) and Dorothy Terriss (lyrics) dated 1922—that watershed year for modernism during which *The Waste Land* first appeared. On YouTube, one can find Irish tenor John McCormack singing the song. Also on YouTube, the Paul Whiteman Orchestra plays the song as an instrumental. Inserted into the song is a tinny, ringing sequence of notes that have since been used for doorbells. Nonetheless, "Three O'Clock in the Morning" suggests the passage of time, the waning of the night, song, and romance. Music is characterized by change in time, repetition, a passing that may only be retrieved by replaying the record. Gatsby might believe he can repeat the past. Yet, at best he can replay the phonograph record. At the end of the Redford film, it repeats it over and over, as life dissolves.

On March 12, 1925, Fitzgerald wrote to Perkins that he wanted his book's title changed to "Gold-hatted Gatsby" and that he still liked "Trimalchio" as a title. In his correspondence, he spells Hemingway with two m's and said he would "look him up" in Paris. On April 10, 1924, he wrote to the editor that he hoped to finish his novel in June.[36] By June, he was telling August Fowler that he felt "old too, this summer" and remarked to Perkins that he was thinking of the poet Percy Bysshe Shelley: "Shelley was a God to me once."[37] The novel, he suggests in his letters, was about the "loss of those illusions that give such color to the world."[38] Fitzgerald wrote *The Great Gatsby* during that summer into the autumn of 1924 and revised during the winter. On October 10, 1924, he urged Perkins to keep an eye on that young writer named Hemingway, who, he said, "has a brilliant future."[39] Days later, on October 27, 1924, Perkins received a manuscript of a little more than 50,000 words. On November 18, Perkins wrote to Fitzgerald, saying, "I think the novel is a wonder."[40] He then called *The Great Gatsby* an "extraordinary book" and offered some suggestions for chapters six and seven. From Rome, Fitzgerald corresponded with Perkins on December 20 and again in January, typing a letter about revisions.

The novel was published on April 10, 1925. Fitzgerald told Perkins that he was sick of rewriting it five times. Zelda liked the book's dust cover jacket. Fitzgerald, who had devoted a great deal of time to refining his work, returned to the magazine story writing that brought about $2,000 per story. In the interest of maintaining his lifestyle, he also began to think about writing for motion pictures. In the spring of 1925, Scott and Zelda Fitzgerald moved to Paris.

The Great Gatsby initially sold about 25,000 copies. Two weeks after the novel was published, Fitzgerald met Ernest Hemingway at a café, the Dingo Bar. Fitzgerald deeply admired Hemingway's writing and encouraged his publication at Scribner's. Hemingway would later become one of Fitzgerald's critics—puzzled by his inability to hold his liquor, recalling Fitzgerald's insecurity about his anatomy and sexuality, and calling Zelda "phony as a rubber check."[41] While living at 14 Rue de Tilsitt on the Right Bank, Fitzgerald wrote to Edmund Wilson that Hemingway was taking him to meet Gertrude Stein.[42]

Fitzgerald's work was much appreciated by Jewish avant-garde writer Gertrude Stein, a rich woman who weighed some two hundred pounds and was sharply in contrast with her dark-eyed, wiry companion, Alice Toklas. Stein had studied psychology at Radcliffe and medicine at Johns Hopkins. On her walls were paintings by Pablo Picasso, Henri Matisse, and Juan Gris. She was writing experimentally, creating *The Making of Americans*, and thinking about generations, culture, and history.

Fitzgerald was also in contact with other authors. In April, Fitzgerald wrote from Capritto to Willa Cather, mentioning *My Antonia* and *A Lost Lady* and her short stories "Paul's Case" and "Scandal." He recognized that he had been reading *A Lost Lady* while writing *The Great Gatsby*.[43] To Sinclair Lewis he sent a copy of the novel, noting that he had sent for *Arrowsmith*. He told Lewis that he hoped that his own book would be the "second best book of the spring."[44]

With Marya Mannes, Fitzgerald shared the idea that female readers "haven't generally cared for it."[45] This was, he thought, possibly because of the novel's emotionally passive characters. Hazel "Patsy" McCormack, an aspiring writer from St. Louis, was one of the readers who had been critical of several of Fitzgerald's stories in 1924, and Fitzgerald began a lengthy correspondence with her. "The stories you objected to were necessary," he wrote, asserting the worth of "Absolution" and "The Baby Party." He calls his novel in progress, *The Great Gatsby*, "wonderful" and conveys his hope that it would be "out by the spring."[46] McCormack wrote again in May 1925 that she had read and liked *The Great Gatsby*. Fitzgerald wrote back that her letter had done much to "lift [him] up from the fact that it isn't going to sell. Not like the others."[47]

Before long, Fitzgerald was wondering if *The Great Gatsby* would be published in England.[48] Perkins confirmed that it would be, and Fitzgerald responded on October 20, 1925, noting that 19,640 copies had been sold in the United States. There would not be strong sales in England, however. One reviewer insisted that the subject matter was too American. T. S. Eliot, in a letter, brightened Fitzgerald's spirits by telling him that *The Great Gatsby* was the "first step" in American fiction since Henry James.[49] Fitzgerald inscribed a copy to him in Paris in October 1925.

Fitzgerald's reading public in Britain always remained relatively small compared with that in the United States. His short story collections *Flappers and Philosophers* and *Tales of the Jazz Age* were published by Collins in London; however, the publisher rejected *The Great Gatsby*. Perkins told Fitzgerald that they had called the novel's "atmosphere . . . extraordinarily foreign to the English reader."[50] Chatto and Windus published the novel in England in 1926. The reviewer for the *Times Literary Supplement* recognized *The Great Gatsby* as "undoubtedly a work of art and of great promise" but disliked the characters.

❋ ❋ ❋

Clearly, Fitzgerald's themes in *The Great Gatsby* resonated far beyond the 1920s. Bob Batchelor, in the first book in this series, refers to *The Great Gatsby* as a particularly culturally significant work, pointing to a "meta-Gatsby" that resonates throughout American culture. It is the book by Fitzgerald that is most often read, taught, and adapted. Some contemporaries saw the merits of the novel. Gilbert Seldes reviewed *The Great Gatsby* twice, in the *Dial* and *New Criticism*. William Rose Benet relates that Fitzgerald had unearthed the "depth of philosophy."[51] The reviewer for the *New York World* disparaged it, with a headline that asserts, "F. Scott Fitzgerald's Latest a Dud."[52] One may look back on the curious irony of such a criticism. Whereas the *New York World* was discontinued long ago, *The Great Gatsby* is still very much alive in our culture.

The popular image of 1920s as being filled with fun and good times that appears in Fitzgerald's novel might be described as a kind of breaking away from the Victorian emphasis on self-improvement and austerity. In Freudian terms, it was the bursting free of the superego. Sensual

dance and syncopated rhythms suggested a kind of sexual liberation—
intimate, throbbing, twisting, and breaking free of corsets and garters.
Fitzgerald implies this in the parties in *The Great Gatsby*, where flappers dance "quite individualistically," as well as quite clearly in *Tender
Is the Night*, where Dick and Rosemary dance closely, "clinging together," and later entwine in the coatroom.[53] The dancing at the Gatsby
party is fueled by alcohol, and the Eighteenth Amendment and the
Volstead Act are futile, unable to stop the buzz. And so Fitzgerald
propagates a myth of the libidinous pulse and stereoscopic swirl of
1920s abandon. These Roaring Twenties were only heard by some.
Most Americans were not invited to Gatsby's parties. Still, these images
stay in our minds, almost one hundred years later, as one of the chief
features of this lively era.

"You've got to sell your heart," Fitzgerald once told Frances Turn-
bull, a young correspondent, in November 1928. "This is especially true
when you begin to write," he said. Before a writer has developed the
tricks of the trade that make characters interesting, what makes fiction
convincing to readers is a writer's emotions. "This is the experience of
all writers," Fitzgerald added, pointing to Dickens's *Oliver Twist*, Hemingway's *In Our Time*, and his own *This Side of Paradise*, of which he
said, "I wrote about a love affair that was still bleeding."[54] A love affair
still bleeding was also at the center of Jay Gatsby's dream.

The Great Gatsby captures many of the trends and concerns of the
1920s: romance, crime, and consumer spending. As Curnutt and others
have pointed out, Fitzgerald presents the automobile as a way of seeing
human life becoming increasingly mechanical.[55] Thus, Daisy Buchanan,
distracted by something other than texting with her friends, drives Jay
Gatsby's car into a fatal crossroads, where it strikes her husband Tom's
mistress, Myrtle Wilson. People have succumbed to mechanism, and
Myrtle, a pathetic aspirant to glamour, has died in the impersonality of
it all. Yet, in the midst of the tragic dream of Jay Gatsby, the man who
believed he could repeat the past, there is the archetypal quest of the
American dream. Jay Gatsby can be read in multiple ways, and so can
the horizons of that dream.

A POPULAR STORY WRITER

Fitzgerald's third short story collection, *All the Sad Young Men* (1926), appeared less than a year after *The Great Gatsby*. It sold about 16,000 copies in the first year. The collection contains the stories "Winter Dreams" (1922), "Absolution" (1924), and "The Rich Boy" (1926). In the *Chicago Daily News*, Harry Hansen enthusiastically writes that Fitzgerald's stories are ones that "scintillate." Yet, in comparing the collection with Hemingway's *In Our Time*, he preferred Hemingway's artfulness. Reviewing the collection for the *Saturday Review*, Benet comments that Fitzgerald was caught in a conflict between money and art. Fitzgerald, he says, had an "astonishing facility" for writing marketable stories; however, it seemed to Benet that Fitzgerald was denying "his true nature."[56]

It was more doubtful whether Fitzgerald's "true nature" could be found in Hollywood. He received an offer from United Artists in 1926 to write for film. He headed to California by train in January 1927. Attempts had already been made by Hollywood studios to turn *The Beautiful and Damned* and *The Great Gatsby* into movies. In Hollywood, Fitzgerald's effort on a script, "Lipstick," was rejected. He would return to Hollywood in 1931 and spend his last years struggling to write screenplays.

In April 1928, Scott and Zelda were back in Paris, at 58 Rue Vaugirard, which was near Gertrude Stein's place on Rue de Fleures. Fitzgerald met James Joyce during this time through Sylvia Beach, owner of the Shakespeare and Company bookstore on l'Odean. Zelda wrote and took ballet lessons from the Daighilev ballet school, presumably trying to dance away her inner demons. Living in an increasing alcoholic haze, the Fitzgeralds returned to the United States in September 1928. In response to some criticism from Hemingway, Scott suggested that his great creative output between 1919 and 1924, while "living at top speed," was something that "may have taken all I had to say too early."[57]

It seems that life got in the way of the innovative follow-up to *The Great Gatsby* that Fitzgerald hoped for. He wrote fifty to sixty stories during the decade between *The Great Gatsby* and *Tender Is the Night*. Still, the hoped-for novel about Francis Melarky, an American expatriate, did not take shape. The work had to be reconceived and reworked into the story of Dick and Nicole Diver, which became *Tender Is the*

Night. The reception of *Tender Is the Night* in the 1934 depression-era United States might have been called lukewarm. The difficulties of Zelda's breakdowns and issues of finances delayed work on the novel that many critics call *The Last Tycoon.* Fitzgerald planned the work with many notes, but the difficulties of life likely contributed to the fragmentary qualities of his final narrative.

THE JAZZ AGE

F. Scott Fitzgerald coined the term the *Jazz Age* as a title for his second collection of short stories in 1922. "Jazz age" was a name for manners and culture, a designation given to a society in the grip of change. "Jazz" was, for Fitzgerald, not only music, it was a lifestyle. "The word jazz in its progress toward respectability first meant sex, then dancing, then music," Fitzgerald writes.[58] Jazz was a "state of nervous stimulation, not unlike that of big cities behind the lines of a war." The word *jazz* reflects the social mood of a generation, which came of age in the 1920s. The word *jazz* meant flappers, petting, and glitz. It meant recklessness, immediacy, the tinkling sound of money, and the jitterbug of a new nervousness. For a largely white culture, it intersected with the rhythms of African American life, where jazz and blues were the song of daily life. For American culture, World War I was an "emotional stimulant from which it was not easy to taper off," writes Frederick Lewis Allen in his close-up retrospective of the 1920s, *Only Yesterday.*[59] Fitzgerald concurred, saying that something had to be done with all that nervous energy.

The Great War, as World War I was then called, brought about a state of mind that encouraged a carpe diem attitude, Allen believed that one should eat, drink, and be merry, for tomorrow they could die. This was a time of ferment in which the growing independence of women promoted the suffrage movement, Freudian analysis revealed the unconscious mind, and the automobile changed the landscape of the United States and Americans' sense of mobility. It was an era of Prohibition, films, confessional magazines, and sensational news stories, an age in which advertising and popular culture increasingly influenced society, and the United States came into its own as an international power. "I am restless. My whole generation is restless," says Amory Blaine, Fitzgerald's prototype of the disaffected 1920s youth.[60] Indeed, this was a restless generation, experiencing the push and pull of a new world in the making.

The old order was breaking apart. Beneath the transition was uncertainty. In Britain, young writers like Lytton Strachey sharply critiqued the conventions of his Victorian predecessors. "You are all a lost generation," Stein told Hemingway, even as she pointed out that World War I had emphasized changes and trends that were already in motion. "The circumstances of American life have been transformed," Allen tells readers on the first page of his book.[61] As the 1920s came to a close, Allen saw American culture spinning like a ride at Coney Island. Jack Dempsey was taking punches. Babe Ruth was hitting home runs. Women had lifted their skirts above their ankles. Allen acknowledges that some smoked cigarettes, danced, and "got blotto." A presumably sophisticated and smart set were contesting conventions, tossing off modesty, embracing trifles, and finding new enthusiasms. Perhaps they were running from the darkness of a postwar wasteland, seeking the city lights beyond the ash pits and the gaze of T. J. Eckleberg, the oculist billboard ad of Fitzgerald's *The Great Gatsby*. "It was an age of miracles," Fitzgerald noted: one of art, excess, and satire. In this vibrant, transitional time, as Allen recognizes, an "upheaval of values was taking place."[62]

Fitzgerald documents this new world in his fiction. In Amory Blaine, in his first novel, *This Side of Paradise*, we see a rather brash, self-centered young man working hard at being sophisticated and smart, testing out roles, and figuring out the rules of life. By the end of the novel, Amory is questioning the values by which American society has been traditionally structured. Amory, the flawed and sometimes irritating protagonist, is perhaps now open to change and the idea that a new world is in the making. By 1925, this image of a boy-like dreamer had grown into the figure of Jay Gatsby, a man lost in his illusions and for whom money is the key to persona and self-creation. Gatsby and his outrageous parties glittered, but in many ways he was merely "jazz": a tinkling surface that masked the ambitious yearnings of a lonely man.

In his review of *The Great Gatsby* for the *Baltimore Sun*, Mencken suggests that we might cast Fitzgerald as a social historian. Fitzgerald, he says, was a witness to the "florid show of American life," to a "high carnival" of people of wealth who indulged in their "idiotic pursuit of sensation." Mencken, a sharp wit who criticized almost everything, complains that Fitzgerald's books were like the "improvisations of a pianist playing furiously by ear but unable to read notes." The analogy with jazz musicians of his time is clear. Mencken's perspective on the fierce and fluent production of Fitzgerald's commercial fiction takes us back to jazz: a highly improvisational form.[63]

Perhaps the nervous energy that Fitzgerald spoke of in "Echoes of the Jazz Age" and "The Crack Up" found its complement in the brisk vigor of jazz music. Ragtime, with its ragged, syncopated rhythms, emerged in popular music during the first decades of the century. Dixieland bands from New Orleans and Chicago—King Oliver, Louis Armstrong, Bix Beiderbecke, and Fletcher Henderson among them— brought the novelty of new sounds to white audiences. They were sounds that were, at first, perhaps better understood by the black culture that initially created them. Jazz was often misunderstood, called a "slew of fancy noise," a sound that "concealed all the tune and melody," by one Cornell University student. Jazz had replaced the romantic violin with the "barbaric saxophone."[64] Such impressions of jazz are, of course, shallow. Nonetheless, there appears to be a similar notion operating in Fitzgerald's treatment of jazz music as something not quite as substantial and serious as the European classics, as he associates jazz music and dance with the popular culture of "jazz."

For example, in the opening pages of "A Freeze Out" (1931), culture and personal taste appear to be at stake as Forrest Winslow of Minnesota steps into a music store. High culture and low culture appear to clash as Forrest reads, "with horror," such song titles as "When Voo-do-odo Boop-boopa doop, There'll Soon Be a Hot Cha-Cha." A girl standing nearby asks for Prokofiev's "Fils Prodique," and Forrest is resigned to purchase "Huggable, Kissable You." Another customer asks for a copy of Stravinsky's *Firebird* and Chopin waltzes: a mix of atonal innovation and nineteenth-century chromaticism. The next titles on Forrest's list of potential purchases are "Digga Diggity," "Ever So Goosy," and "Bunky Doodle I Do." Reflecting uneasily on this, Forrest thinks to himself, "Anybody would take me for a moron." He crumples up his list and asks for Beethoven's "Moonlight Sonata."

Prokofiev and Stravinsky works were, at this time, stretching the boundaries of concert music. Stravinsky's *Firebird* (1909–1910), with its almost mechanistic rhythmic pulse, was a precursor to *The Rite of*

Spring (1911–1913), which shocked and dismayed its audience with its syncopation, dissonance, and rapid changes. Prokofiev's piano pieces, with their experimental harmony and dissonant percussive effects, including *Suggestion Diabolique* (1908), *Sarcasms* (1912–1914), *Visions Fugitives* (1915–1917), had their premieres before 1921. These are modernist musical innovators who, like the best jazz musicians, were creating musical gestures that became physical in dance or pieces that were often strikingly rhythmic and propulsive. Forrest's selection is of a standard tune, Beethoven's "Moonlight Sonata," which had been domesticated.

Aesthetic taste and moral taste are likewise in question in *The Great Gatsby* (1925). Jazz plays a role in Fitzgerald's novel, suggesting the superficial life of a party that is fundamentally empty beneath its dazzling surface. The story's narrator, Nick Carraway, tells us of the music that came from his neighbor's house on summer nights. With the motion of the earth into darkness came lights, "yellow cocktail music," and voices, excitedly rising to a "key higher." This modulation suggests increased giddiness and drunken excitement: a wide lawn and rooms filled with voices and a patio humming with music and laughter. We can imagine a flapper dancing her frenetic dance of nervous sensation, an energetic romp of physical contortions. The party has begun. Old men dance with young girls in "eternal graceless circles." People grab banjos from the orchestra and begin to strum them. They perform "stunts." The moon rises like a silver coin reflecting the water of the Long Island Sound. The air is full of sparkle and champagne, and the moon trembles to the "tinny drip of banjos on the lawn."[65]

Jay Gatsby stands apart. He has called upon the sound of unfamiliar guests—their tinkling voices, music, and laughter—to fill his rooms. During his party, it is announced that Gatsby has requested a jazz piece by Vladimir Tostoff, whose name, like that of Prokofiev and Stravinsky, is clearly Russian, perhaps suggesting something revolutionary. This imaginary piece by an imaginary composer bears the pretentious title "The Jazz History of the World." The presumptuously entitled jazz piece is indicative of Gatsby's lack of taste. It is notable that neither Nick nor Gatsby actually listen to the music. As the piece begins, Nick's eyes fall on Gatsby, who is "alone on the marble steps." Gatsby is conspicuously alone.

Gatsby is the hollow man: a man who, without roots in culture and history, is the ephemeral romantic song of the times. He is a symbol of jazz age dreams, its illusion, and its disillusion. Gatsby invents himself, like a solo jazz player improvising; however, he invents only embellishments. He jazzes his life up, creating a hollow world of appearances, a play of sound and lights lacking substance. While daydreaming of Daisy Buchanan, Gatsby has made moral compromises to purchase his gaudy palace at West Egg. He has brought to it an illusion of Camelot filled with wine, glitter, and excitement: Jazz for everyone. Gatsby's jazz party gives way to disillusionment. While Gatsby holds on to his dream to the tragic end, with Nick we begin to see the emptiness of his life. Jazzby's chaotic jazz-jam has disappeared, and all that remains is the lone, solemn blues trumpet of Nick's narrative thoughtfully bidding him farewell.

The blues are the downside of jazz. In many respects, the blues are at the roots of jazz, offering a state of mind that is given to self-expression. The blues provides the emotional, poetic soul of jazz, and from the blues jazz derives its phrasing. What distinguished the younger generation, writes Walter Lippmann, was their "disillusionment with their own rebellion." Allen calls this disillusionment the "keynote of the 1920s."[66] In music, the key is the tonal center of a musical composition. If we were to compare the 1920s with a piece of music, the jazz age would be music with some flats in the key signature. It might be suggested that the apparent frivolity of the jazz age had a darker side, one rooted in the blues.

America's new experiences of jazz music and new experiments with atonal music and "primitivism" were reflective of the times, for the jazz age was a time of great experimentation. The old harmony had changed and now came a dissonance and new rhythm. Jazz music is syncopated, that is, its accents or beats are varied; its stresses are set in unexpected places. Likewise, the stresses and accents of the jazz age fell in unexpected places. Jazz is a genre of music that may happen spontaneously as players solo and improvise. It expresses itself as inventive musical language. The 1920s marked the emergence of one of the most innovative periods of literature and art in America and Europe in recent times. Writers and artists offered new ways of looking at the world. In Harlem and Paris, there was a strong interplay of collaboration within creative communities. When William Wiser wrote his ragged montage of those days in Paris, he called his book *The Crazy Years*. The title may be suggestive of the times. The irrational arose from the depths or became more obvious at a time when Sigmund Freud was mapping the strange territory of the human unconscious. Society's unconscious seemed to break forth. One might claim that the strong superego structures of the enlightened Age of Reason and the Victorian age were cracking open. A wild, adolescent Id sprung forth, imbibing prohibited alcohol and dancing the Charleston.

Yet, there was something serious going on amid this so-called "craziness." A deep and lasting change in how people looked at themselves and their world was taking place. Artists led the way in their search for a new language, a new sense of meaning and purpose to live by. Ernest Hemingway insisted on a code by which a person would create his or her life. At the center of this code was an emphasis on truth, discipline, awareness, and an honesty and purity or style in one's action. From this would come a sense of meaning—a purpose to live by. In a world disrupted by the war, Hemingway sought to pin down reality in clear, concrete terms, as he points out in *A Farewell to Arms*. T. S. Eliot responded to a perceived loss of meaning in the modern world by seeking fundamental truths of the human condition as expressed in myth. Eliot worked to carve out a core of meaning that seemed to some to be lost or hidden during this time of transition.

Fitzgerald, in contrast, appears to have been fascinated with the emerging popular culture, writing for the movies and popular market stories for the magazines. In one of his early stories, "Dice, Brassknuckles, and Guitar" (1922), the meaning of Fitzgerald's term "jazz age" is suggested. A man from Georgia introduces himself to a woman named Amanthis. His car has broken down on the road. He tells Amanthis that he was planning on making use of the car as a taxi in New York City. The man presents his business card: James M. Powell, J. M. The J. M. stands for jazz master. Powell has operated a jazz academy. We soon learn that this "jazz" school teaches not jazz instruments and musicianship, but the jazz that "first meant sex, then dance." Of course, the students' parents assume it is a music academy and dancing school. The jazz academy is popular amongst the younger generation, but it is not approved of by the fashionable and flurried Mrs. Poindexter Katzby (one may note the name) and Mrs. Clifton Garneau. They are in search of their daughters. Their "old music" is played by the orchestra, while

James Powell insists to Amanthis that "our music" is the new music of jazz, the music that is claimed by the younger generation as its own. In this story, the horns are "fashionable" and people "shuffle" to the beat.[67]

In "Offshore Pirate" (1920), a group of black singers gather on the deck of a luxury cruise ship, which is the central setting for the story. Ardita, a narcissist, is on deck reading a book one day when she sees men in a rowboat and hears them singing. In the playful lyric they sing, Fitzgerald rhymes carrots and peas with knees and breeze, and fellows and bellows with Goldbergs, Greens, and Costellos. The group's leader, Curtis Carlyle, is standing on the bow of the boat waving a baton. Ardita asks if she is seeing the varsity crew or escapees from the country nut farm. The voices of the Negroes on deck with Carlyle rise in a haunting melody. Adapting a blues-folk form, the singers recall a dialogue between Mamma and Pappy. Meeting Ardita, Curtis calls her a "flapper," which she resists. Meanwhile, Trombone Mose, the biggest of the singers, changes the name of the cruise ship from the *Narcissus* to the *Hula-Hula*. We learn that Curtis Carlyle's musical experience began in Tennessee, where he played the kazoo and at piano parties. He later played a battered violin in little cafes in Nashville. With the "ragtime craze," he brought six Negro singers with him on the Orpheum circuit and went on to Broadway, exploiting both the blacks and his sense of rhythm.

A sense of rhythm: According to a character in Fitzgerald's sketch "The Lost Decade" (1939), that is what composer Cole Porter came back to the United States from Paris for. Porter returned because "he felt that there were new rhythms around."[68] New rhythms: That was part of it all. This was the new age of the automobile, the radio, advertising, and a pace of commercial urban life that brought new rhythms to American society. It brought *jazz*—a term resonant with a variety of connotations. Jazz was the lifestyle of Fitzgerald's flappers and philosophers. Jazz was, at times, a kind of superficiality and pretentiousness devoid of good taste. Yet, even so, jazz was fun. Whatever its "lack of taste" the jazz age brought significant changes to the landscape of American life and culture. As girls "dramatized themselves as flappers" and youth "corrupted its elders and eventually overreached itself," as F. Scott Fitzgerald observes, the novelist captured the images, voices, and movements of change in fiction.[69] The novelist and short story writer F.

Scott Fitzgerald was, as Mencken notes, a social historian of this period of change. Yet, so were they all, these novelists, in their various ways, critics of culture, observers of a bright and unique era.

REVIVING FITZGERALD THE ROMANTIC

F. Scott Fitzgerald was a Romantic at a time when T. S. Eliot and others were eschewing the weak Romanticism of the late nineteenth century and asserting that it did not fit with the spirit of modernism. He was lyrical, ornate, and formal, focusing on dreamy possibilities and tragic relationships. Eliot and Pound implicated the vital Romanticism of the late eighteenth and early nineteenth centuries, although they both, in their teens, read a steady diet of the work of British Romantic poets. The young Eliot was given the works of Keats and Shelley for his birthday. Ezra Pound was deeply attracted to the troubadour poets of Provencal, and the favorite poet of his friend William Carlos Williams was John Keats. Now Eliot and Pound and the New Critics who followed them attacked romanticism as escapist and too emotional. Modernity called for experimental styles, technique, and detachment. One had to "make it new" and put away Victorian and the Romantic predecessors.

Fitzgerald, however, was not about to give up on the fantastic, the moody, or the ups and downs of human emotion. He believed that writers like Joyce were breaking with the past and that his generation was formulating something new; however, a new cynicism in the wake of the war included romance and that sense of loss so well captured in Wordsworth's *Prelude*, "Ode: Intimations of Immortality," or "Lines Composed a Few Miles above Tintern Abbey." Romantic disillusionment, as portrayed by Keats in "La Belle Dame sans Merci" or Coleridge in "Dejection" would be important to *The Great Gatsby* and *Tender Is the Night*. Amory Blaine's quest in *This Side of Paradise* is likewise a romantic, heroic journey for some ideal self. Imagination and what Amory refers to as "consuming introspection" would transform the world. Likewise, the disenchantment of the world of Dick Diver is romantic. *Tender Is the Night* takes its title from John Keats's poem "Ode to a Nightingale," a poem of longing in which the speaker unhappily regards the nightingale's brightness and the changing season.

Fitzgerald was a self-making seeker of grandeur, a romantic who was no stranger to modernist techniques like the stream of consciousness interiority of a character, shifting point of view, or the symbolism of a stark modern wasteland that arises so forcefully in the bleak terrain surrounding Wilson's garage in *The Great Gatsby*. He combined theatricality, marketplace savvy, and a romantic sensibility with modernist awareness and a keen eye for the culture of his age.

The revival of Fitzgerald began after World War II. In 1950, Lionel Trilling viewed Fitzgerald as a moralist.[70] Stephen Vincent Benet, who appears to have anticipated the future potential for nuclear radiation in "By the Waters of Babylon," saw the future in Fitzgerald, the writer of "Babylon Revisited," when he forecasted that Fitzgerald's *The Great Gatsby* and his strongest stories would bring about his acclaim as an important American writer.[71] Curnutt points out the progress of this rediscovery of Fitzgerald at a time when critics sought to dissociate Fitzgerald from the 1920s. Early in the 1950s, Mizener's biography of Fitzgerald, *The Far Side of Paradise* (1951), was a best seller. Several critics argued that Fitzgerald's primary theme in *The Great Gatsby* is the "American dream." With this in mind, Marcus Bewley wrote "Scott Fitzgerald's Criticism of America" (1954).

The 1960s and thereafter brought what Curnutt sees as an attempt to historicize Fitzgerald: To see him very much within the context of the 1920s.[72] This historical contextualizing appears in Curnutt's *A Historical Guide to F. Scott Fitzgerald* (2004) and Ruth Prigozy's *The Cambridge Companion to F. Scott Fitzgerald* (2001). In 1981, *Some Sort of Epic Grandeur*, by Fitzgerald scholar Matthew Bruccoli, appeared, leading the way for many other biographies of the lives of Scott and Zelda Fitzgerald. The ongoing competitiveness between Hemingway and Fitzgerald is illustrated in Scott Donaldson's *Hemingway vs. Fitzgerald: The Rise and Fall of a Literary Friendship* (1999). Whatever one's definition of "friendship" may be, it is clear that their interaction spurred each of them onward. It is also clear that their drive to create resulted in some of the most significant and lasting fiction of this era.

3

WILLIAM FAULKNER

A Southern Voice in the Age of Modernism

William Faulkner is unquestionably one of the most important American novelists of the twentieth century. He became a critically acclaimed author following many years of obscurity. The closest that Faulkner came to touching mass popularity was as a screenwriter behind the scenes, a silent partner in Howard Hawks's films in the 1930s and 1940s. His fiction, bursting from conventional form, is often a fascinating and difficult read. Although it deals with sensational, psychological disturbances, as well as sex, violence, and mystery, a Faulkner novel is seldom what we might call a page-turner. Rather, it is more often an exploration of the abyss.

The social and cultural context of Faulkner's writing is significant. He shows us a different picture of the 1920s than the one we have been looking at to this point. The historical ground of Faulkner's fiction predates this decade; however, it reflects issues that still burned in his conscience during the time that he was writing.

Faulkner was a haunted writer, one who dealt with such troubling subjects as racial tension, miscegenation, incest, the fracturing of families, and distortions of southern culture. He was also a modernist writer of searing vision. As Richard Brodhead points out, the first generation of Faulkner's readers "failed to recognize his greatness."[1] He has most often been the subject of literary criticism that remarks on his experimentalism with form. Recent works, however, have corrected the "deficiency" that Brodhead saw in 1983, in Faulkner criticism that primarily focused on the writer's stylistic and formal innovations. Today Faulkner is recognized as a great American writer whose imaginary world of Jefferson and Yoknapatawpha County intersected with historic regional and national issues. Even so, he is seldom read outside of classrooms. Even there, students encounter his work with some difficulty.

A social world surrounded Faulkner's fiction. Unique in his vision and often private in his life, he was embedded in this social world. To approach him from the vantage point of southern intellectual history has some limitations, observes Eric J. Sundquist.[2] We might consider the myth of a South gone with the wind, a "fallen aristocratic dream," or a romantic continuity as in Wilbur Cash's idea of the "mind of the South." Yet, Faulkner and Cash are critics of that romantic consciousness, adds Sundquist, who points out that Faulkner perhaps tells us most about one major issue: race and the problems that arise from it.[3] The resurgence of Jim Crow laws and the Ku Klux Klan in the 1920s is a historical fact. On movie screens, the white-hooded figures of the Klan appear in D. W. Griffith's *The Birth of a Nation.* In the 1920s, the estrangement of the races was a situation that Faulkner inevitably had to deal with in what Irving Howe calls a "journey of self-education."[4] Faulkner faced the social problems of his age and region as a man troubled, observing, inquiring.

Faulkner's first novel, *Soldiers' Pay* (1926), is a postwar narrative that might be read alongside Dos Passos or Hemingway. For his next novel, *Mosquitoes* (1927), Faulkner meditated on aesthetics, which did not intrigue as many readers as his first. With *Flags in the Dust*, later retitled *Sartoris* (1929), Faulkner began to find characters of his southern locale that he would develop in future novels. *Sartoris* was a rambling gathering of many strands that would be improved by later editors. Faulkner's friend Ben Wasson had insisted that it was six novels rolled into one. *The Sound and the Fury* (1929), which soon followed, is widely regarded as Faulkner's pivotal work, a stunning experiment of modernist thought that many have considered the launching point of Faulkner's greatness as a novelist. In this story, he explores the interior stream of consciousness of three brothers—Benjy, Quentin, and Jason Compson—as they think of their sister Caddy and unfold the troubled life of their dysfunctional family.

Faulkner was a student at the University of Mississippi during the same years Fitzgerald attended Princeton. It was probably not easy to teach a student as recalcitrant and independent-minded as Faulkner. When he was asked by his English professor, D. H. Bishop, what Shakespeare had in mind in giving lines to *Othello*, Faulkner responded, "How should I know . . . I wasn't there."[5] Despite this obstinacy, he published poems, stories, and drawings in the *Mississippian*, including "Landing in Luck," about a military pilot's first solo flight. Some of his ink drawings are reminiscent of the art of Aubrey Beardsley. Faulkner told his war stories to Wasson, who would later become a lawyer and Faulkner's agent. Professor Calvin S. Brown, who wrote about the relations of music and literature, encouraged Faulkner with an annual prize. Later, in response to Faulkner's racy novel *Sanctuary*, he wondered why anyone would ever write a novel like that.

CONVERSATIONS WITH SHERWOOD ANDERSON

In 1922, Faulkner met with Sherwood Anderson when he was in New Orleans. Faulkner had briefly worked at a bookstore in New York City with Elizabeth Prall, who would later be Anderson's wife. Anderson stayed in an apartment in the Pontalba Buildings on the south side of Jackson Square. Faulkner would meet the writer with the deep-set eyes and sit with him on a bench in Jackson Square, near the cathedral. He would make use of Anderson's library and read James Frazier's *The Golden Bough*.[6] He was soon living in an apartment with artist William Spratling in a place called Orleans Alley, which overlooked St. Anthony's Garden.[7] He spent many afternoons listening to Anderson's tales.

Faulkner was working on the novel *Mayday*, which later became *Soldiers' Pay*. He wrote longhand and later typed what he had written so that he could revise it as he was doing so. Among his best stories was one he told to people he met. He said that his plane had been shot down in the war and he had a plate in his head and that he drank to numb the pain. Of course, Faulkner had never seen active combat, but it was a good excuse for drinking. Recalling his time as a Royal Air Force pilot, he wrote the essay "Literature and War," a piece consisting of only five paragraphs in which he reviews the World War I writings of poet Siegfried Sassoon, novelist Henri Barbusse, and novelist R. H.

Mottram, who had written about British soldiers in France in *Spanish Farm*.[8]

Faulkner's story "Mirrors of Chartres Street," featuring a beggar who uses the narrator's money to go to a movie instead of getting food, was printed in the *Times-Picayune* on February 8, 1925. "Damon and Pythias Unlimited" followed on February 15, with the story's narrator being brought to the horseracing track by someone named Morovitz, who is met by his accomplice, a former jockey named McNamara, who has "certain death in his eyes."[9] For this story, Faulkner played with the detective mystery genre. He bought yellow copy paper at Canal Street, bothered the other tenants of the building with his typing, and carried his work over to the *Times-Picayune*. Three more stories came in April 1925.[10] There was Jack Potter in "Cheest"; a "wanderer" in "And Now What's To Do"; and a seventeen-year-old vagabond in "Out of Nazareth," which appeared in the *Times-Picayune* on April 12, 1925.[11] Joseph Blotner, one of Faulkner's principal biographers, also charts other stories, including "Nympholepsy," "Chance," "Sunset," and "The Kid Learns" (May 31, 1925), a story about bootleggers in which "little Sister Death" appears to at last claim Johnny.

Many of Faulkner's stories take place in the area around the fictional town of Jefferson. This creation of a locality recalls the model of Anderson's *Winesberg, Ohio*, or the single day in Dublin of Joyce's *Ulysses*. The people of one small town might be made to speak, and they would appear as a microcosm of the larger society.[12] Faulkner read Anderson's *Winesberg, Ohio*, as well as his short story collection *Horses and Men*, and recognized that Joyce was, in part, behind the rhythms of Anderson's novel *Dark Laughter*. He appreciated the older writer's work and identified him as a "giant of [his] generation" but he later suggested that Anderson was really only a one- or two-book man.[13] Anderson was, Faulkner thought, most effective as a short story writer. The falling out between the two men was characterized by Elizabeth Anderson as a case of two sensitive men who were "too much alike."[14]

Anderson introduced Faulkner's work to publisher Horace Liveright at Boni and Liveright. Those close to Liveright said that the publisher seldom read books but that he had a shrewd and intuitive sense of what would sell. Faulkner later said that Liveright should have been a stockbroker. When Liveright first entered the business, he had married the daughter of a paper company owner, who made him president of a toilet paper company. When the prospects for toilet rolls spun out of control, he headed for New York and teamed up with Albert Boni, a newspaperman. An investment of $25,000 from Liveright's father-in-law got the Modern Library going, and the Boni and Liveright Publishing Company was born.

Boni and Liveright became one of the most successful New York publishing forms of the 1920s. From under its roof emerged Theodore Dreiser's *An American Tragedy* (1925); Hemingway's first short story collection, *In Our Time* (1925); and Faulkner's first novel, *Soldiers' Pay*. Anita Loos was successful with *Gentlemen Prefer Blondes: The Illuminating Diary of a Professional Lady* (1925).

THE EARLY STORIES

In Oxford, Mississippi, where spring brought magnolias and roses, Faulkner brought his stories to his friend Phil Stone, while Sallie Simpson typed them. Out the stories would go to magazines, and they would often come back again, rejected. During the summer, he wrote at the home of the Bairds on wooden benches constructed in the shade of a powerful oak on the front lawn. *Soldiers' Pay* received positive reviews. Blotner writes that E. C. Beckwith applauded the novel in the *New Republic* as unique among the fiction of veterans. Larry Barrette of the *Herald Tribune* calls it "almost a great book," but one lacking restraint and discipline. L. S. Morris of the *New Republic* recognizes a "nervous, swift talent." In the *International Book Review*, Louis Kronenberger echoes this sentiment but acknowledges that the story "achieves a vividness." Writing for the *Nashville Tennessean*, Donald Davidson saw Joyce's techniques at work and placed Faulkner with Dreiser, Lewis, and Dos Passos.[15] Perhaps more interesting was the noncritical reception of the veterans who identified with the book.

In New Orleans, Faulkner lived in the French Quarter with William Spratling, in an apartment that looked out on St. Peter's Square. They made gin with alcohol in gallon cans. Faulkner went for coffee in the mornings, walking down toward the river and the French Market.[16] In the meantime, he was waiting for word on his second novel, *Mosquitoes*. In New York, it was being read by a young publishing assistant, Lillian Hellman, who would become one of America's significant playwrights. She recommended the novel—a story of Mississippi hill people and the tenant farmers who came in to take their land. The story is set in the town of Jefferson, the town that would become a center of Faulkner's fictional world of Yoknapatawpha County. He began writing the story of Flem Snopes, a man with a hard stare in his eyes and a tight mouth who chews tobacco as he stands in the twilight. His working title was *Father Abraham*, and he scrawled it on legal paper in small black print. With some sense of his own mortality, he wrote fiercely, turning to the history of what he then called Yocoma County, creating the legends of a local family, old Bayard Sartoris leaning over the memorabilia in his attic: a Bible, swords, and two pipes. It is a family inclined to embrace lost causes. [17]

In Paris, in late summer of 1925, Faulkner wrote a novel he called *Elmer*. Drawing on Joseph Conrad's experiments with point of view and shifts in chronology, he developed techniques—unconventional ways of telling his stories. Joyce and Flaubert were also behind his early work, claims Blotner, who adds that Faulkner's style increasingly became more like that of Honoré de Balzac, who was more concerned about people and what he called the human comedy to worry much about style. [18] He walked along the Seine, watching children, feeding bread to sparrows, seeing wagons loaded with vegetables or flowers passing by. [19] Faulkner talked with William Hoffmann, appreciatively read Margaret Kennedy's *The Constant Nymph*, and lived the life of a bohemian artist in the French Quarter. Blotner surmises that a "brief angry involvement" with Lewis Lewisohn's "Literature and Life" prompted Faulkner's own aesthetic reflections. [20]

In December 1925, Faulkner returned to the United States aboard the *Republic* and arrived at the docks in Hoboken, New Jersey, on December 19. Blotner speculates that he immediately caught the ferry across the Hudson River to Manhattan and visited the offices of Boni and Liveright on 48th Street. The brownstone on 48th Street, between 5th and 6th avenues, stood next door to a speakeasy called Toni's. Neither is still there.

From New York, Faulkner took a train back to Mississippi. Once home, he turned his attention to writing short stories: "Divorce in Naples," "Mistral," and "The Devil Beats His Wife." [21] Then came the idea for *Sanctuary*, one of his most notable and best-selling novels. In Memphis, he heard from a woman in a nightclub the story of a gangster who was impotent and used objects to compensate for his sexual inadequacies. The woman described how a gangster raped a woman. Faulkner mulled over the horrible story and embellished the gangster figure, one that critics have identified as one Neal Kerens Pumphrey, known locally as Popeye. With his short story "The Big Shot," Faulkner began creating a character. A frame narrator introduces him, much like Joseph Conrad had a frame narrator introduce his sailor-narrator Marlow. In this story the gangster is protected by a political boss from charges for traffic offenses. He shields the gangster from prosecution again, only to find out that the victim of the gangster's hit-and-run accident was his own daughter. This story of corruption was the seed for Faulkner's controversial novel *Sanctuary*.

Meanwhile, *Soldiers' Pay* appeared in February 1926, with a first printing of 2,500 copies. Faulkner, while living in New Orleans, read Anita Loos's *Gentlemen Prefer Blondes*, which was on its way to becoming a best seller. During the summer, he spent time with Helen Baird at Pascagoula, writing his novel *Mosquitoes* on a bench under a group of oak trees. He dated his conclusion of the story "Pascagoula, Miss/1 Sept 1926."[22] He returned to his rooms in the French Quarter with Spratling and began to think about the South and its history, and a cold man he named Flem Snopes. In small black print on white pages, he began a story he called *Father Abraham* and another story he would call *Flags in the Dust*.

As 1927 began, Phil Stone was pitching an announcement of Faulkner's *Mosquitoes* to the *Oxford Eagle*. He mentioned the novels his friend was working on. One was the historical saga of the Sartoris family: high-minded but sadly destined to dissolution. In the meantime, Faulkner made some extra money by painting houses. In the summer of 1926, he created a forty-seven-page book for the Baird girl, Victoria, called Cho-Cho, offering her a fairy tale he called *The Wishing Tree*. A girl named Dulcie awakens to wonder at a red-haired boy named Maurice, who is standing next to her bed. They go in search of the wishing tree and discover a castle, where Maurice works his magic. There is an old man with a beard of silver whom the narrator calls the "good Saint Francis." Dulcie receives a bluebird for a present, and the reader learns that St. Francis has given her some words of wisdom: "If you are kind to helpless things, you don't need a Wishing Tree to make things come true."

The vulnerability of a little girl and a wishing tree may lie behind Faulkner's masterpiece, *The Sound and the Fury*. The name Maurice may have become transmuted to "Maury," who becomes the retarded Benjy Compson, in whose jumbled thoughts we begin the story. Benjy is indeed a "helpless thing," and the tree that Caddy climbs to see into her grandmother Damuddy's funeral is a central figure in that novel. Other connections with Faulkner's later work have been made by Blotner. The figure of Saint Francis makes a curious appearance in *Mayday*, in which "little Sister Death" appears. In his canticle, Saint Francis speaks gently of "brother sun, sister moon" and "sister bodily death." Blotner sees the golden flecks in Maurice's eyes in those of Pete in *Mosquitoes*, and a phrase concerning "gentle ponies" is repeated in *Father Abraham*.

In writing *Flags in the Dust*, Faulkner was examining generations, how times had changed, and how a way of life had disappeared. The town of Jefferson, his story's central location, was about twenty-five miles from Oxford, Mississippi. It was a "mythical town," Blotner notes, one that shared characteristics with New Albany, Ripley, and other places in the area.[23] With *Flags in the Dust*, Faulkner was creating a milieu, the groundwork for many novels. This was a world of the South peopled with the burdened, faded aristocracy of the Sartoris family and yeoman farmers, white sharecroppers, Negro workers. From it rose characters like Horace Benbow—the "poet"—a man trapped in futility. This is the novel that Wasson said included six novels rolled together. In a sense, he was right. In it are the roots of the Faulknerian world of Yoknapatawpha County and novels yet to come.

Mississippi was troubled that year, beset by flooding. In 1927, the Mississippi River rose and broke through the levees, pouring tons of water into the Mississippi Valley—the most destructive and far-reaching flood in U.S. history. The scene was similar to the destruction caused by Hurricane Katrina, which damaged New Orleans, only the calamity in 1927 was geographically more widespread. River waters flooded areas from southern Illinois and Missouri to Arkansas, and thousands of workers tried to reinforce the levees of New Orleans. By April 20, some 25,000 people were homeless, and the waters showed no signs of receding. The flood covered 9,000 square miles, raising fears of typhoid and the need for a remedy to prevent an epidemic. The Red Cross came. On April 30, dynamite was used to blow up a dam at

Poydras. Faulkner's *Mosquitoes* was published in New York on a day when the threat of mosquitoes carrying germs had become quite real in Mississippi. Tornados came in May, adding further injury and threat to the Atchafalaya Basin. People were evacuated. Others ran into the wilderness. Towns were submerged. Muddy water and earth left silt, waste, and destruction. Damage was estimated at $236 million. The human distress was incalculable.[24]

Faulkner had published two well-received, although not so popular, novels by the summer of 1927. That autumn, he waited on word about *Flags in the Dust*. The message arrived in November. Liveright had rejected the novel, remarking to Faulkner, "you don't seem to have any story to tell."[25] Faulkner, unhappy, asked for the novel back and decided to dissolve his relationship with the publisher. Of course, he still had to fulfill a contract that called for a book for Liveright. He sent Wasson to act as his agent in search of a publisher. Meanwhile, he worked on short stories. He taped a list of magazines to the back of his closet door. He wrote the name of a story and the date he sent it out next to each one. He might have marked the date each story came back rejected. Not a single one was published, but at least he had decorated his closet.

During this time, while painting houses and doing odd jobs, Faulkner crafted additional short stories. One in particular intrigued him – the story of the Compson children. According to Blotner, "That Evening Sun" took shape from earlier sketches like "Never Done Weeping When You Wanted to Laugh." In this eight-page piece, Nancy, a Negro cook and laundress, appears in a story told by Quentin Compson, who is recalling his childhood. Quentin, Candace, and their younger brother Jason see that Nancy is going through a difficult time. Her lover Jesus is creeping around outside near her cabin, jealous and angry that she is pregnant with the child of a white man. In the darkness, Jesus holds a razor. The shadow of Faulkner's troubled tales of miscegenation had begun to lengthen. In "That Evening Sun Go Down," Faulkner contrasts the adult world with that of children.

He followed this with "A Justice," in which Quentin listens to the story of Sam Feathers, a Negro-Indian blacksmith. With the onset of winter, he began a story he called "Twilight," and it began to expand. One moment, the children were splashing one another in a brook. Then Caddy was climbing out on a branch to see the corpse of Damuddy.

Faulkner was soon absorbed in the wandering thoughts of a retarded boy, behind his iron fence on the edge of the golf course, where men were "hitting." He was one who lived forever in the moment, amid the smell of trees and the sight of Caddy's muddy pants disappearing. He was unable to interpret anything. The reader, feeling perhaps disoriented in Benjy's world of sensation, has a lot of interpreting to do.

With the rejection of *Flags in the Dust* by Boni and Liveright, Faulkner seemed to have hit his own personal wasteland, a desolation in which he decided to simply write for himself, with no care for any market. From this marginality, came the voice of Benjy—innocent, tortured, searching for the missing sensitivity of his sister, who he could no longer find in this world. From these sensations, inarticulate moans, and confusing sighs for a lost love came a new kind of story: one of voices, images of timepieces, a tree shading a stream, water and mud and funerals and clocks, children growing to adulthood trapped in obsessions.[26] This would begin Faulkner's series of formal experiments— *As I Lay Dying*, *Light in August*, and *Absalom, Absalom!* In these novels there is a tension of the regressive and the innovative, as David Minter points out.[27] They seem to ask if any sense of purposeful chronological time or a moral, meaningful world can be found in modernity. The town of Jefferson begins to take shape on this uncertain nexus of family, home, and childhood.

In the interim, a contract for *Flags in the Dust* came from Harcourt Brace and Company, dated September 28, 1928. Wasson had pitched the manuscript to his friend Hal Smith, one of the company's editors. Smith had previously read *Soldiers' Pay* and liked it. He was less certain about the new book, which was now being called *Sartoris*. He wondered if the novel could be trimmed a bit. Faulkner was adamant that he did not want to cut anything. Smith asked Wasson to talk to him. "The trouble is," Ben told Faulkner, "you had about six books in here."[28]

THE SOUND AND THE FURY

In the fall of 1928, Ben Wasson was living in a brownstone at 146 MacDougal Street in Greenwich Village. Faulkner went to New York City to visit him and again joined his friend William Spratling in a nearby apartment. There he worked on his revision of *The Sound and the Fury*. An ink marking on the carbon typescript for the novel indicates that Faulkner finished typing in New York in October 1928. Wasson recalls that Faulkner walked into his room, tossed the manuscript on the bed, and said, "Read this, Bud. It's a real son of a bitch."[29] He met Hal Smith for lunch on Christopher Street, where Smith urged him to bring *The Sound and the Fury*, to Harcourt Brace. The editors rejected it on February 15, 1929. Perhaps they found it inscrutable or unmarketable. Smith would not give up on Faulkner, however. When he left that firm for Jonathan Cape, he brought Faulkner's novel with him. Three days after Harcourt Brace had turned down the narrative, Jonathan Cape agreed to publish Faulkner's fiction—one of the most important novels of the twentieth century.

The Jonathan Cape contract for *The Sound and the Fury* indicated that Faulkner would receive a $200 advance and 10 percent of royalties on the first 5,000 copies. This would increase to 15 percent once sales reached that mark. This was not a mass-market publisher, but *The Sound and the Fury* would eventually sell well beyond the firm's expectations. Reviewed with some acclaim, the novel's sales fell off with the Depression that followed the October 29 Stock Market Crash. There were 1,789 copies printed. These sold gradually and several copies remained a year and a half later. Nevertheless, subsequent publication and critical attention during the Faulkner revival in later decades would make the novel one of the author's most lasting and important works.

Faulkner recognized that the first section of his story—the Benjy section—was hard to follow. Wasson suggested page breaks, but Faulkner disagreed; he wanted the story to flow without interruption. He preferred the use of italics and shift in typography. In a Village speakeasy, Faulkner suggested to Wasson the use of different color inks to indicate time sequences in the Benjy section.[30] For publishing in 1928–1929, such a procedure would have been expensive and difficult. In 1932, Bennett Cerf of Random House considered the color scheme when he brought out a limited edition of the novel on an imprint, Grabhorn Press; however, only recently has a limited Folio edition (London, 2012) been produced, featuring those different colors and a bookmark card that indicates the time sequence. A two-volume set in a sturdy slipcover, the novel is bound in red alongside a gray-covered glossary and commentary by Stephen M. Ross and Noel Polk. The editors' *Reading Faulkner: The Sound and the Fury* was published in 1996, to assist readers of the novel.

Writing of the novel appears to have been both exhilarating and taxing for Faulkner. His friend Jim Devine recalled that he and Leon Scales went to visit Faulkner in October 1928 and peered in on him sprawled out on the floor, surrounded by empty liquor bottles. They took him uptown to 111th Street, near Columbia University, where Scales attended classes and Devine sometimes sat in on the lectures of philosopher John Dewey. Faulkner soon moved in to a fourth-floor apartment at MacDougal and 6th with artist Owen Crump, who had come from Shreveport to study with the Art Students' League in New York. He wrote in notebooks he bought at Woolworth's, tucking them into a valise, and the two shared gin and dinners in the Italian neighborhood near their apartment. Their favorite spot was the Black Rabbit, a front for liquor bootleggers. When it wasn't acting as an illegal distribution center, its cooks made some great ravioli and spaghetti. When Faulkner returned to the New York area in 1931, he and Devine would hang out in Hoboken, New Jersey, where bars and eating establishments still line Washington Avenue.

* * *

The Sound and the Fury contains little plot. The story is centered on four children and their pitiable broken family. Faulkner sets forth a central image of a little girl climbing out on a tree limb to witness her grandmother Damuddy's funeral; the funeral-goers can see the seat of her pants as they look up at her. Caddy is moving away from her brothers—out on a limb toward the complications of her own life—and she is recalled through the needs of her brothers and their inner psychological conflicts; however, in a move that might prompt a casual reader to scrap the novel, Faulkner tosses linear progression. But for a patient reader, one willing to read recursively, an extraordinary work of fiction awaits. Faulkner's novel gains its vitality from rhetorical innovation, startling shifts, and juxtapositions. The patience of readers is challenged by this technical virtuosity. One looks for markers, indications of when things are occurring in time.

To the extent that Faulkner's contemporary readers could follow Benjy's ramblings, his effusive sentiments led them to sympathy with his dependent, voiceless, repetitive life. They were then further disrupted as Faulkner portrays a tragic world in Quentin's memories and his peculiar idealism and sense of chivalry. Quentin's jumbled thoughts reveal a world of failure in his father and himself. He circles through self-focused obsessing about Caddy's promiscuity and expresses grief in aesthetic musing, pushing away pain and insight. Jason follows with his claim to negative attention with selfish schemes. Dilsey's section, in omniscient point of view, comes as quite a relief for most readers.

The Sound and the Fury, Sundquist observes, may be read as an allegory of the South, a reflection on time, a probing of the Oedipal complex, or an ironic symbolism of Christ's agony.[31] It is a story of brokenness, a family splintered, scattered into separate consciousnesses, as is the very form of the novel. One might say that the novel is drawn and quartered, a rack of punishment, brutally pulling in four different directions. It begins in the mind of an idiot—Benjy, a retarded individual who has no sense of time and to whom all moments are present. For the lost Caddy, his sister, he is ever seeking, as is his psychotic, introspective brother Quentin and his mean, vicious, self-serving brother Jason, who acts out his loss and psychological wounds and steals Caddy's daughter's money. The novel, presented through the first-person views of these three characters, concludes on Easter Sunday in the perspective of Dilsey, the black housekeeper who patiently endures, keeping the Compsons' fractured world together as best she can. Dilsey is not only a source of strength amid the family's alienation. Her section, presented in third-person point of view, can help readers overcome the alienation of a challenging text.

These separate narrations of experience make up a novel that is quite different from Faulkner's earlier works. The roots of *The Sound and the Fury* lie in two short stories: "That Evening Sun Go Down" and "A Justice." In a third tale, called "Twilight," the story of the Compson children begins to take shape. Howe recognizes that scenes in which black and white children play together are the only happy ones in *The Sound and the Fury*.[32] Dilsey serves as a moral critic, he contends. She is a window to a historical world that is disappearing.[33] In sharp contrast with Quentin's narcissism or Jason's self-centeredness, Dilsey respects everyone around her. She is a home-center in contrast with the homelessness experienced by the Compson children as adults or the homelessness of Faulkner's later character, Joe Christmas, in *Light in August*.

Dilsey is a coming home for a novel that veers off in directions that some readers have found obscure. It is Dilsey who brings Benjy to the Negro church and affirms that "the good Lord don't care" whether he is smart.

The South, observes Howe, is in Faulkner a "muted shadow, a point of reference."[34] In *The Sound and the Fury*, the broader suggestion of a doomed South lies latent in this story of a doomed family. Like the Compson family, it is broken and divided. With the loss of Caddy has come the loss of childhood innocence, the loss of the virgin land, the myth of an idyllic time. Following Quentin's emphasis on honor and purity, his sister's lost virginity represents what Wilbur Cash has seen as the South's "cult of womanhood."[35] From the standpoint of cultural history, the lost time of an antebellum world has vanished into the less hospitable terrain of post–Civil War rapacity. Quentin's stream of consciousness narrative ticks away in questions about time. "I was in time again," he writes as his grandfather's watch ticks on relentlessly. He insists on virginal purity for Caddy and seems trapped within the fate of his fathers, damaged by an alcoholic father without hope in the world, weakened by a weak, self-focused mother, and cursed by heredity and heritage. With suicide Quentin attempts to free himself from time.

SANCTUARY, AS I LAY DYING, LIGHT IN AUGUST

In the 1930s, Faulkner wrote a string of powerful novels set in the South, in the same "postage stamp" locale, as he called it: *Sanctuary*, *As I Lay Dying*, *Light in August*, and *Absalom, Absalom!* They underscore the South's troubled history, turbulent family histories, and the persistent issue of race. His work would gather strength as the fictional cultural history of a region, mapping ambivalent feelings. These were novels of social and historical significance that Robert Penn Warren recognizes as stories of southern lives expressing what had been "lying speechless in their experience."[36] The intense critical attention that would follow in later years largely explored the formalistic aspects of Faulkner's fictional structures and innovations.

In *The Sound and the Fury*, Faulkner contests and dissolves the linear structure of family and history, but Faulkner's theme becomes more historically rooted and apparent in later works, probing and pushing the credibility of legends of Confederate times that remained in the air of his own. *Light in August* casts into relief the shadow of the "Negro" and shows the breaking forth of the unconscious repression of the secrets of miscegenation of white masters and black slaves. We see a "black" character, Joe Christmas, who is also "white."

A certain doom follows Joe, a man whose very identity is in question because of his origins. He is mulatto, white and yet black, and he is caught in the opposition of black and white. As Faulkner wrote, this character emerged in a novel that initially focused on a country girl, Lena, and a troubled minister, Gail Hightower. Race, as Brodhead points out, became a "structure of consciousness" rather than a given: It was a construction, a label given to Joe within a world of racial tension.[37] He has been cast as a "reminder of the ancestral phobia," notes Howe.[38] Indeed, Joe has no sense of community, as Cleanth Brooks points out.[39] He is pursued by a mob that would lynch him. Joanna Burden is ambivalent about Joe's blackness. She needs to escape the genetic determinism of the Burden family history. Perhaps miscegenation might also suggest a world beyond black and white: something that may be a hope for some and a threat for others.

Meanwhile, Reverend Gail Hightower is a "disillusioned man," caught in a cold Protestantism that focuses on a "God of justice rather than of mercy."[40] Lena can redeem him as a "female principle," a woman who carries an unborn child: the promise of a possible future world that can bring these people back to community. Brooks notes that evil for Faulkner stemmed from a "violation of nature."[41] Faulkner's characters have to face a world that has become unnatural; however, the instinctual is not necessarily good either. One must find courage, face evil, and make moral choices and efforts to "achieve goodness."[42]

As I Lay Dying, which emerged from *Father Abraham,* was finished on October 25, during the time when Wall Street panic broke out. The novel was written to the hum of a powerhouse machine. Faulkner wrote during the night shift at a place where coal was shoveled out into wheelbarrows and fed into a boiler. The title of his novel came from the words of Agamemnon, which are spoken to Odysseus in the Underworld in Book Eleven of *The Odyssey*: "She even lacked the heart to seal my eyes with her hand."[43] Fifteen different points of view make up the novel. The new novel was about the Bundrens, again a troubled family in the Deep South.

Faulkner knew that his novels were difficult. He also knew that his experience in writing *The Sound and the Fury* had been extraordinary and the writing of *As I Lay Dying* had been less so. He began another novel—the one he would call *Sanctuary*. For it he would develop the story he had heard in a Memphis nightclub years before—and a harrowing story it was. Gangsters were clearly part of the 1920s. Chicago and nearby Cicero, Illinois, had witnessed the bloody rampages of Al Capone and rival gangs. Memphis was only slightly less notorious. With its Tenderloin district nightspots and backstreets, the city had been named the "Murder Capital of the U.S.A."[44] The story of Horace Benbow, a failed lawyer fighting the evil Popeye, a gangster, and Temple Drake, the sympathetic heroine, would be a thriller that was sure to be shocking.

Sanctuary was read at Cape and Smith. The readers were appalled.[45] Faulkner, however, sensed that the novel would be a sensation. His dark imagination was spinning new stories. In late 1929, likely seated at a fragile writing table, he wrote the strange and disturbing story of Emily Grierson in "A Rose for Emily." From the blue ink on legal pad sheets came the story of a deeply troubled woman who had hidden away in her rooms, unwilling to yield to change or society, holding on to the corpse of her father and then sleeping beside the skeletal remains of her beau, Homer Barron. Often anthologized, it is for some college students their first look at the probing stories of William Faulkner.

FICTION, ART, AND FILM

Faulkner's prose has been described as lyrical, a verbal art of incantation. From the dialogue of *Soldiers' Pay* to the experimentation of *The Sound and the Fury*, he required his readers to listen and then work at reading his fiction. A reader of Faulkner is compelled toward close reading, or even recursive reading—that is, reading twice. It is a common experience for a reader who is first picking up a Faulkner novel to struggle a bit with the story. This is especially true when time, in one of Faulkner's stories, is not linear or when a character's stream of consciousness moves in unexpected ways. Thus, Faulkner's novels were never popular fare. It took years for the first printing of *The Sound and the Fury* to sell out. It was only when Faulkner wrote the sensational and violent story *Sanctuary* that anything like a popular audience responded to his work. Yet, Faulkner is unquestionably one of the most important American writers of the twentieth century.

Faulkner was also a fairly private man. Unlike Hemingway and Fitzgerald, he appears to have had little contact with other writers during his brief time in Paris. Still, with his verbal and narrative techniques, he was very much part of modernism as it developed during that time. He never met Hemingway, Pound, Eliot, or Stein. His contact with Anderson was in New Orleans. He spent some time with his artist friends in New York. Most of Faulkner's time was spent in Mississippi, except for his stint as a screenwriter in Hollywood in the 1930s. There was also a private quality to his work and craft. He did not talk about what he read. His storytelling was fundamentally in an oral tradition. In him we see modernism's thrust toward the well-made story, one emerging from what Hugh Kenner relates stemmed from "tireless revisions" and requires the "skilled reader."[46]

Faulkner drew upon many sources for his unique experimentation. In 1924, he got a copy of the fourth printing of *Ulysses* from his friend Phil Stone. It has been suggested that he made use of Joyce's techniques.[47] Faulkner, nonetheless, had his own unique sensibility, and his movement toward stream of consciousness writing and experimentation with fictional form extended beyond Joyce's innovations. One might say that modernist creativity was in the air of the times. Behind Faulkner's attention to a locale was Sherwood Anderson's *Winesberg, Ohio*, as much as Leopold Bloom's day in Dublin in Joyce's *Ulysses*.

Faulkner's keen eye for imagery was partly developed through his sketching, drawing, and painting. He drew cartoons, line drawings, and ink illustrations. He painted less as he became a novelist, but his attention to French Postimpressionism and modernism is evident in his fiction. For his stories, he drew on his sense of art. Paul Cezanne's art suggested to him the direct use of color and pigments and strong brush strokes. The work of visual artists may have led Faulkner toward what one critic has referred to as his "spiral form."[48] Observing the loneliness of Joe Christmas in *Light in August*, Ilse Dusoir Lind compares his experience to a spiritual condition of isolation in de Chirico's empty spaces and barren buildings on canvas.[49] The racial themes of *Light in August* are underscored through the play of white and black in the text.

There is Joe's white shirt and black pants. Joe has been described as a crucified Christ-figure who suffers at the hands of others. Lena, in her blue dress, will give birth to a son—a new hope. Gail Hightower, a minister, faces a spiritual crisis. Faulkner may be said to have, in a sense, painted them, as well as described them. [50]

Faulkner's work in Hollywood film lay ahead in the later 1930s and 1940s. Many of his screenplays and treatments were for director How-ard Hawks's films. Hawks had read Faulkner's *Soldiers' Pay* and mentioned him to his friends, including writer Ben Hecht. *Sanctuary* (1931) led to a MGM contract, although Hawks passed on this, expecting censorship. Paramount Pictures then produced *The Story of Temple Drake* (1933). Faulkner began writing screenplay treatments, none of which were produced. In 1932, his work on *Turn Around* showed Faulkner apparently agreeable to making the changes that Hawks suggested. Hawks liked linear structure, finding that it was easier for audiences to grasp than the time shifts in Faulkner's fiction. Faulkner liked montage. Hollywood films, while they have the stamp of a director's vision, are collaborative works. None of Faulkner's scripts have been used in their original form and in their entirety to produce a film. His work was usually rewritten or reworked. Among his most memorable scripts are those for *The Big Sleep* and Hemingway's *To Have and Have Not*. Faulkner participated in writing *Drums along the Mohawk*, *Gunga Din*, *Mildred Pierce*, *Submarine Patrol*, *Escape in the Desert*, *Land of the Pharaoh*, *Adventures of Don Juan* with Errol Flynn, *Today We Live*, and *The Road to Glory*. Several scripts were never produced. These include *Dreadful Hollow*, a vampire thriller; *War Birds*; *Country Lawyer*; *Stallion Road*; and his own *Flags in the Dust* and *The Unvanquished*.

To read Faulkner is to think with him about the racial problems that troubled him and have troubled the United States. His setting is the rural South, a land of ancestry and memory. Yet, one might also think of the Gulf Coast wracked by Hurricane Katrina and the lives of displaced people. Most of Faulkner's stories do not take us to New Orleans, but the Mississippi Delta and all that surrounds it is of a piece. Sometimes in Faulkner's stories we hear of Memphis—in "The Vendee," "The Unvanquished," or "Two Soldiers," in which a rural boy is in search of his big brother, who has enlisted in the army. Faulkner's attention is oftentimes on characters in Jefferson, in rural settings like those that appear in "Barn Burning," "The Tall Men," "Dry September," or "Delta Autumn." Faulkner is a storyteller who gives us characters' voices and invites us into the places where his characters live, places where many of us have never been.

But thinking of Faulkner, one might also imagine an era of jazz bands, bright sounds from New Orleans rooftops, and the music of the city's gaiety slipping into a history long ago. Back then, one might have seen a funeral parade rounding the corner: men with instruments in their hands and teary eyes betraying the celebration. In 1920, one might have spotted Louis Armstrong leaning out from a terrace or heard Lil Harden humming a tune they had been practicing. Or we might find ourselves in the French Quarter during the peak of summer at Jackson Square, where Faulkner is sitting on a bench with Sherwood Anderson, talking to him across from the cathedral in the shade of trees. By the black iron fence one might see artists painting; there is a man eating crawfish gumbo, and the air is sweet with the scent of fresh beignets and the smoke from the pipe Faulkner is holding in his fingers. He then walks slowly home, toward Pirates Alley, sunstruck, with the outlines of a story coming to his mind.

4

MODERNISM AND POPULAR CULTURE IN THE AGE OF EZRA POUND AND JAMES JOYCE

They were modernists—Hemingway, Fitzgerald, and Faulkner—and they had been born into a new world. They sought to create a new fiction in this new world. The details of the first decades of the century were highlighted under electric lights and documented in photographs. There were cars, planes, and an array of modern ways to wage war. Technologies had increased the pace of life. News of the *Titanic* disaster in 1912 was reported six hours after the incident. Yet, that incident also pointed to a somewhat naïve faith in technological power. The war would further break down that hope in the machine. Faulkner, with *Soldiers' Pay*, Fitzgerald, with *The Great Gatsby*, Dos Passos, with *Manhattan Transfer*, and Hemingway, with *The Sun Also Rises* and *A Farewell to Arms*, would turn the hard edge of their work into crafted, searing fictional interrogations of relationships and society.

The work of modernist writers was not immediately popular. Focused as they were on the art and craft of fiction, their painstaking efforts were at times obscure and difficult. Fiction that is unconventional and not easily accessible aims at a highly literate, aesthetic audience rather than the broader audience that is entertained by popular fiction. Modernism broke away from the realist novel by looking to the interior life of consciousness. Writers began to imitate the stream of human awareness, casting in words the fragmentary, impressionistic glimpses of experience. Virginia Woolf claimed that the world had changed in

December 1910 or thereabouts. Mrs. Brown, the new woman, would no longer be satisfied with the realism of Arnold Bennett and John Galsworthy when she considered the interior life. The Victorian world's language, its moral structures and sense of God and humanity, had long since begun to break down or transform into a new modern era. Marching off to war, jubilantly, Britain's soldiers might go to Flanders fields or to the Somme with slogans on their lips; however, such chivalry was a vestige of a bygone era. Their patriotic fervor and the sport of kicking balls across the trenches soon dissolved into a nightmare. Civilians at home could no longer rest secure in relative safety, for now attack could come by air, as well as sea or land. Likewise, literature set out to meet the new challenges of Post-Impressionist art, psychoanalysis, and a changing culture. America's young writers met a perilous new age.

In the years before 1920, the modernist artist faced a dilemma. Amid an expanding publishing industry, the writer inherited contradictory models of authorship. On the one hand, the author needed to make a living, and if the author was a professional, he or she ought to be obtaining money, but the writer also needed to maintain aesthetic quality. To sell out in the interest of gaining a wide audience was anathema to the modernist writer. Such authors as Ernest Hemingway, William Faulkner, and F. Scott Fitzgerald had to negotiate this divide, as did their European counterparts, for instance, James Joyce and D. H. Lawrence. Fitzgerald's remedy was to write short stories for the lucrative magazine market while crafting his novel *The Great Gatsby*. Fitzgerald and Faulkner would later turn to Hollywood for income, exploring the new medium of film. Faulkner wrote numerous screen treatments and portions of scripts through the 1930s; however, as he had begun to do in the 1920s, he reserved his novels for experimentation with form.

However intent those writers' aesthetics of distance and attention to their craft may have been, the sale and distribution of the novels of Hemingway, Faulkner, and Fitzgerald depended on promotion and publicity. The modernist author preserved a reputation amongst a small coterie of readers. Nonetheless, money and art could not remain antithetical for long. Artistically, these three writers, in their different ways, subscribed to the view that narrative control of point of view was extremely important in their fiction. Meanwhile, the economic success of their work during their lifetimes was also important to them. In Hemingway's case, this material success came with the growing Hemingway myth of the masculine sportsman who liked to box, fish, and attend bullfights. He became an influential model of gutsy masculinity in the 1940s and 1950s. With Fitzgerald, the myth of the man and the jazz age he virtually invented seemed to grow larger than the obvious merits of his best fiction. Faulkner wrote dozens of film treatments in Hollywood but preferred the relative quiet of his home in Oxford, Mississippi.

These eventual literary giants became familiar to thousands of readers. By the 1920s, the literacy rate in the United States was at about 95 percent. This meant the presence of millions of potential readers. A modernist writer might only write for a select few readers. Yet, mass distribution, film, advertising, and the professionalization of authorship and commercialization of the publishing industry had changed the equation. The avant-garde audience was interested in distinguishing itself from the mass popular audience. The modernist writer's goals were rhetorical and aesthetic: Integrity meant a willingness to challenge the reader, to write without compromising one's uniqueness. Even as these writers resisted popular demands, genre fiction, romances, and conventional formulaic stories sold briskly. Fitzgerald negotiated both the popular magazine audience with his short stories and the demands of the well-crafted novel with *The Great Gatsby*. Hemingway, whose first story collection, *In Our Time* (1925), was published in the United States by Boni and Liveright, increasingly reached a broader audience once his novels *The Sun Also Rises* (1926) and *A Farewell to Arms* (1929) were published widely by Charles Scribner's Sons.

In the first decades of the twentieth century, a writer might wonder who his or her audience was. In the nineteenth century, Charles Dickens encountered a small segment of his readership as he brought his public readings to the public. Mark Twain later met some of his audience face-to-face on the lecture circuit; however, by the 1890s, that sense of author–reader connection had changed. Oscar Wilde, during his trial, commented, "I have no knowledge of the views of ordinary individuals."[1] Literary works operated in a cultural field that involved publishers, distributors, sales people, and reviewers. The common reader was less visible. He or she was obviously an important participant in the literary communications circuit. Still, as critics glibly addressed the critical reception of a novel, it was other critics' comments in major periodicals to which they generally referred. It was assumed that most readers shared those opinions or might be influenced by them. Few

critics took the time to find the letters, journals, library records, autobiographies, or newspaper comments of common readers that might
tell us otherwise.

Yet, writers like Hemingway and Faulkner aspired to contact with an
audience of fine, literate readers, and they both exercised careful control of their writing. They knew that they could not control what became of their work once it was published. Likewise, Willa Cather, although not often considered a fellow traveler with high modernism,
practiced a modernist attention to craft and point of view, as well as
what she referred to as "fine readers." These authors tended to be
uninfluenced by the broader public's expectations. Serious modernist
fiction controlled point of view. It offered a character's way of thinking,
as in Frederic Henry's reflections in *A Farewell to Arms*. Sometimes
this articulation of a point of view could be baffling for readers, as with
Faulkner's Benjy in *The Sound and the Fury* (1929): a retarded character who has no sense of time—past or present—whose disconnected
narrative forces readers to become patient interpreters who reread the
text.

With the further emergence of mass production and commercial
publishing, the reader had become more difficult to identify. Publishers
produced a variety of books, some of them designed for a limited and
influential audience. From this they could obtain both sales and a kind
of prestige—what Pierre Bourdieu has referred to as "cultural capital."[2]
Their image of their readers influenced sales and distribution decisions.
Commercial publishers thus produced manuscripts in the hope of
creating a best seller, as well as manuscripts designed for minority audiences. The writer expected the work to have a social dimension, and the
publisher was the intermediary.

The notion that popular art and well-crafted literary art were antithetical was another reaction by some writers and critics to the expansion of the reading public. The potential audience for fiction had grown
by the turn of the twentieth century, and changes in the reading audience had resulted in a high–low dichotomy. Literary practice entered a
time of transformation. Indeed, with Postimpressionist visual art and
interiority in fiction, a new spirit of the times was afoot. American
literary critic Irving Howe, in "The Culture of Modernism," proposes
that modernist fiction is always difficult, self-consciously so.[3] A goal of
the writer was to remain aloof from popular demand, industrial output,

and sales projections. In *Fiction and the Reading Public*, Q. D. Leavis asserts that a highbrow novel in the 1920s could be a best seller by selling about 3,000 copies.[4] A sales index was no sure measure of the impact of a novel or its literary worth. The modernist novel was a success if it reached a significant audience.

As the literate audience for novels expanded, writers sought ways to connect their work with readers. Authors like Joseph Conrad, Willa Cather, and F. Scott Fitzgerald developed point of view as one means of doing this. The voice of Marlow in *Heart of Darkness* (1900) or Nick Carraway in *The Great Gatsby* becomes a confidante, a lens through which the action and events of each novel may be encountered. The modern novel had to find some interpersonal connection with its audience, even as publishers recognized the diversification of readers. If a book was to achieve strong sales, it would need to appeal to a variety of readers, and it would not appeal to all of them for exactly the same reasons. There were economic advantages to editing and producing books of quality.

A great deal has been written about modernism and the artistic trends that appeared in the first decades of the twentieth century. Modernism showed the many ways in which the different arts can be brought together. Literary writing met with music, film, theater, photography, and visual art. This was a time of intermediality, one in which such new technologies as the gramophone, radio, and telephone stimulated modernist art. Marshall McLuhan has argued that our information technologies provide extensions of the human senses. The electronic media of the 1920s turned the attention of artists to perception.

During the past two decades, critics have closed the binary of high–low culture associated with modernism by showing how modernist writers became involved with popular culture. Films, songs played on phonographs, newspapers, music halls, Broadway theater, music revues, and Nickelodeon all intersected with modernist writing. Mass-market publishing, advertising, and periodicals were connected with popular culture, as Lawrence Rainey has shown. Avant-garde experimental works shared an "ironic interdependence" with popular culture, observes Michael North.[5] Edmund Wilson embraced the vitality of a "literary vaudeville" of many cultures—high and low—interacting during this time period. He enjoyed popular entertainment, for example, the Ziegfeld Follies, and held that to place popular culture alongside literature would help us to better understand the entirety of American culture.

The myth of the modernist writer's aesthetic detachment, his legendary lack of concern about money or audience, has been studied by critics. They have concluded that most modernist writers thought about their audience, evaluated popular culture, and had a relationship with popular entertainment. Some disliked popular culture and inscribed their rejection of it in their work. Discourses about popular culture promoting standardization and commercialism came from several quarters in the century's first decades. These critiques of mass culture parallel the work of Theodor Adorno, who, in "On Popular Music," considers popular music an empty reflection of the "culture industry" that turned listeners into passive consumers.[6] But modernist writers wanted to reach an audience, and some, like F. Scott Fitzgerald and T. S. Eliot, were conversant with some of popular culture's forms, for instance, the music of Tin Pan Alley. Eliot writes, "The most useful poetry, socially, would be one which could cut across all the present stratifications of public taste—stratifications which are perhaps a sign of social disintegration."[7]

One of the most striking features of literary modernism is the innovative and experimental nature of the fiction, drama, and poetry. The challenging design of Eliot's *The Waste Land* passed under the watchful editorship of Ezra Pound, who, in his critical writings, self-consciously recognizes the experimentalism and aesthetic attention that lay behind artistic explorations of the time. The poet advanced Imagism and Vorticism; fostered the development of small magazines; called for newness and clarity; and reclaimed troubadour poetry, Dante, the sound of language, and French poetry. Ten years before Eliot's poem appeared, Pound had set forth principles of Imagism with H. D. (Hilda Doolittle). The object would meet with imaginative perception, and the poet would seek pure imagery and the precise word to reflect the object. There would be an economy of expression. With "The Serious Artist" (1913), Pound sought morally responsible art. *Des Imagistes* (1914) was followed by Richard Aldington's *Some Imagist Poets* (1915). Eliot was familiar with these approaches and drew on such French symbolist poets as Jules Lafourge, as well as the entire tradition of English poetry.

Eliot, like other writers of his time, was also aware of the importance of Sigmund Freud's psychoanalytic explorations of the subconscious. Along with the revelations of Freud came literary works increasingly inclined toward introspection, mental reflection and soul-searching. The period included criticism of conventions and a shunning of Victorian constraints, which were associated with repression. In his writings, Freud referred to the drama of Sophocles, Shakespeare's *Hamlet*, the poetry of Heinrich Heine, and Goethe's *Faust*. He beckoned writers to explore the world of dreams, as did surrealism, which tapped into the creative potential of the subconscious. On the stage, Eugene O'Neill's plays made considerable use of Freud and Strindberg's *Dream Play* in experimental works of the 1920s. O'Neill's *The Emperor Jones* (1920) and *The Hairy Ape* (1921), *The Great God Brown* (1926), *Lazarus Laughed* (1928), and *Strange Interlude* (1928) make use of Freudian concepts, as do *Desire under the Elms*, which explores the psychology of motive, and the later *Mourning Becomes Elektra* (1931). Novels like Conrad Aiken's *Blue Voyage* (1922) were also heavily indebted to Freud's theories. The stream of consciousness writing of James Joyce, Dorothy Richardson, and Virginia Woolf likewise expresses a pattern of associative thought that reflects the methods of Freud and the insights into time as *duree* of Henri Bergson.

Consciousness and the prosaic lives of modern men are explored in Joyce's *Ulysses*, which appeared in book form in 1922, the same year as Eliot's *The Waste Land*. Those who closely followed Joyce were already acquainted with characters Leopold Bloom and Stephen Dedalus from serial installments in the *Little Review* in 1918. Modernist works like Joyce's novel usually appeared in small magazines during this time, where they found an undersized but sometimes influential audience. The novel attracted the interest of New York publisher B. W. Huebsch, who arranged to print it; however, the deal was withdrawn when the *Little Review* was censored. In Paris, Sylvia Beach printed her own run of 2,000 copies.[8] Samuel Roth produced an unauthorized printing of the book. Beach followed with a 1922 publication that sold fairly well.[9] The ban on *Ulysses* in the United States was rescinded in 1933, enabling Random House to put forth an edition. In 1934, the novel was accompanied by *How to Enjoy James Joyce's Ulysses*.

With *Ulysses*, James Joyce clearly placed a fierce demand on his readers. It is paradoxical, observes Alisdair McCleery, that this novel, featuring a common man, Leopold Bloom, was not easily read by common readers.[10] McCleery, who charts the movement of *Ulysses* from avant-garde text to classic, observes that publishers sought what Pierre Bourdieu has called "cultural capital" in Joyce's works. In McCleery's view, it was the 1969 Penguin edition of *Ulysses* that made Joyce's novel a "safe" classic in the canon for academic study.[11]

Joyce biographer Richard Ellmann has said that the author set as his goal the moral improvement of his readers. In a letter, he frames this as a determination to provoke and transform Irish character. He was engaged in "creating at last a conscience in the soil of this wretched race."[12] This is eloquently phrased in the narration of Stephen Dedalus in *A Portrait of the Artist as a Young Man*: "I go to encounter for the millionth time the reality of experience and to forge in the smithy of my soul the uncreated conscience of my race."[13] Joyce's goal required offending those readers, and he stubbornly asserted the need to keep in his book what Grant Richards and his readers found to be objectionable passages and phrases. Among these was the adjective "bloody," which Joyce insists was the "exact expression" he intended to create an effect on his readers.[14]

Joyce argued for a "looking glass" in which his Irish readers could see themselves.[15] In 1909, Maunsel and Company in Dublin agreed to publish *Dubliners*. This did not work out well. Discouraged, Joyce claimed that "present circumstances worked against his will to write."[16] "I am not a literary Jesus Christ," he insisted.[17] He struggled with *A Portrait of the Artist as a Young Man* and was in need of material support. Richards relented in 1914 and published *Dubliners*, which did not sell well. In 1915, the book sold 499 copies, missing royalties by a single copy. Joyce had by now completed *A Portrait of the Artist* and had begun *Ulysses*.[18] In *Ulysses*, Joyce shuns conventions in experiments with style and form. There is no particular character's point of view, although we enter the stream of consciousness of Stephen and Leopold. Hugh Kenner sees a clear stylistic departure in the "Sirens" episode and notes that Joyce created "screens of language."[19]

Commercial publishing interest in Joyce followed the publication of *Ulysses*, with Boni and Liveright in the United States making an offer for *Finnegan's Wake* at $2,000 and 15 percent royalties. That offer then increased considerably. Nevertheless, Joyce held out for another offer, which came from Random House and Bennett Cerf in 1932. He further pushed his experimentation with *Finnegan's Wake*, departing from language conventions and challenging intelligibility. Meanwhile, his writing had a strong impact on such American writers as Conrad Aiken and William Faulkner. Aiken's *Blue Voyage* (1927) was modeled on Joyce's *Ulysses*. Demarest is much like Stephen Dedalus, and Aiken has him journey on a ship bound for England, thinking of his fiancé. He soon discovers that she is onboard the same ship, and she greets him coldly. Demarest spins out an unconscious reverie, quarrels with his censoring analyst, and explores states of consciousness.

Faulkner likewise explores states of consciousness throughout *The Sound and the Fury* (1929) and several works in the 1930s. It might be said that when his character Candace Compson left home, she set in motion the responses of her retarded brother Benjy, her brothers Quentin and Jason, and housekeeper Dilsey. Faulkner's novel appears to ask to be read more than once and discursively. He takes his readers into the consciousness of each character. In Benjy there is no distinction between past and present, and change is not realized. Benjy is innocence, believing that Caddy cannot be gone. He bellows and cries, perhaps sensing disorder. Quentin is rational, introspective, and troubled, and he tries to overcome time. His father's watch represents time, memory, and wounds that will not heal. For Quentin, time cannot progress. Caddy must remain virginal and society chivalrous and honorable. His ideal has been destroyed. The style of writing in this section reflects the difficulty that Quentin is having. Quentin covers his emotional life with intellectualizing and abstracts reality. Jason is a materialist, one who lives on the level of sensation. This common sense rationalist appears to lack any moral scope. He takes Caddy's money, which was intended for her daughter. His rational world is defeated by the irrational. It is only when we come to the third-person point of view narrative in which Dilsey is a viewpoint character that we find any potentially harmonizing influence on this fractured family and the divided subjectivities of this text. Faulkner leaves the text open-ended, and the complex world of the Compsons beckons to us for another reading.

MIDDLEBROW AUDIENCES AND THE POPULAR NOVEL

The realist novel was markedly affected by the emergence of modernism. The experimental novels of William Faulkner make no attempt to capture the interest of a wide popular audience; however, broader audiences were also being catered to by periodical publishers. Popular fiction aimed at entertainment for the middle-class reader. While Faulkner's novels displayed innovative craft and Eliot's *The Waste Land* presented readers with a confrontation with the modern age, popular fiction was readily accessible. Some critics, like Lewis Mumford in the *Freeman* (April 18, 1923), portrayed these novels as escapist best sellers: diversions for sensation seekers that were the fiction equivalent of tabloid newspapers and movies.[20] The perspectives of New Critics contributed to the split between high culture and popular culture.

A new reading public had emerged with the expanding middle class, which now had more leisure time and income. Advertising and the cinema further encouraged this growing readership. While modernism appealed to a well-read, educated audience that had the ability to be patient with textual difficulty, popular fiction appealed to middlebrow audiences, which were increasingly important to publishers and writers in the 1920s. Writers of middlebrow women's fiction included marginal figures the likes of Rosamond Lehmann, Rose Macaulay, and Elizabeth Bowen. There were also less literary writers like Stella Gibbons and Dodie Smith, whose novels made the Book-of-the Month-Club-lists. Their novels emphasize romance and domestic matters. With *Dusty Answer* (1927), Lehmann ventured a story with lesbian contact. Margaret Kennedy's *The Constant Nymph* tells of sexually active adolescent girls. Romance had long been associated by male critics with lowbrow tastes and a world of shop girls attracted to ephemeral women's magazines, but now women's writing was attracting a broader audience. Such writers as Dorothy Canfield and Jessie Fauset, who appealed to the black middle class, wrote well, in a manner that could be considered both literary and popular. Mystery genre writers like Daphne du Maurier, Mary Robert Rinehart, and Agatha Christie were clearly fine writers who wrote suspenseful stories.

New fiction was created that appealed to a changing sense of identity and class, and the binary of high/low, or literary and popular, was challenged. According to Nicola Humble, book review columns in English periodicals suggested the need for a category of middlebrow.[21] A reviewer for the *Observer* acknowledges that a book he was reviewing was not highbrow, nor was it lowbrow.[22] For example, Kennedy's *The Constant Nymph* (1924), Michael Arlen's *The Green Hat* (1924), and Anita Loos's *Gentlemen Prefer Blondes* (1925) were middlebrow best sellers, all daring for that time in their content. The middle class read books like these and a variety of periodicals. To classify a book as middlebrow may have suggested that that book was relatively easy to read. A book became a best seller not because of its inherent literary quality, but because it was categorized and marketed well to its largely middle-class audience. George Orwell pointed out that in this emerging market for the popular novel, detective fiction was among men's preferred leisure reading.[23] The fiction of S. S. Van Dyne and Dashiell Hammett was directed toward this audience.

Publishers played a role in this network of reading, as did libraries, which advocated reading purposefully or reading the best. Some librarians held notions about reading for self-improvement, rather than as escape or a tranquilizer. These approaches have different ways of expressing the power of the text and role of the reader. When we consider readers, we might ask to what extent that reader extracted meanings and to what degree he or she produced an idiosyncratic sense of the text while reading.

For example, some readers of Sinclair Lewis's *Main Street* who lived in Minnesota and others in South Dakota rejected the author's image of Gopher Prairie. Their comments show us a different reception of the novel from that of professional critics in New York who appreciated the writer's satire. Readers are unique, and the same novel can be read in different ways. Class, gender, and geographical location have shaped the orientations of readers. Many different acts of reading were taking place in that same historical period of the 1920s. Book historian Roger Chartier points out that readers "obey rules, follow logical systems, imitate models."[24] Sociologist Anthony Grafton refers to the "obstinate, irreducible individualism" of the reader.[25] Individuals, situated in history and society amid these institutions, may practice unique reading styles or "cultural acts of defiance." Readers may be "self-fashioned," as Stephen Greenblatt states, or engaged in "self-authorization," as Barbara Sicherman points out.[26]

READING CIRCLES

Reading is not only a solitary activity; there are also networks in which readers may be involved. For many years, people have shared books in clubs and reading groups. In the nineteenth century, reading aloud during family gatherings was a common practice. To look at the reading practices of reading circles gives us a way to consider the associational life of Americans. The study of this may go back at least as far as Alexis de Tocqueville's observation in *Democracy in America* that Americans often joined groups and affiliated themselves with organizations.[27] More recently, however, some sociologists have lamented what they view as a breakdown in community life. In the 1980s, Robert Bellah and associates asserted that many Americans were individualistic to the point that those "habits of the heart" that translated to civic spirit and community participation were being lost. Robert Putnam writes that people were "bowling alone." He asserts that what bound Americans together was loosening, and "social capital" was decreasing. Elizabeth Long points out that Putnam's focus was on formal groups. Women's groups, including their reading groups, have been more informal.[28] Women's reading groups have again expanded in number in recent decades.

Many of the readers who gathered in reading circles in the 1920s were women. Books by Edna Ferber, Mary Robert Rinehart, Kathleen Norris, and Temple Bailey graced the best seller lists and were read by them. The "new woman" appeared in Diana Mayo in *The Shiek* (1921) and Lorelei Lee in *Gentleman Prefer Blondes* (1925). A search for these readers and what they were reading usually requires an examination of the minutes of these reading circles. Newspaper reports appear to have been more attentive to the atmosphere of women's reading clubs than what they were reading and discussing. For example, on June 1, 1922, *Women's Enterprise* of Baton Rouge reported that "Mrs. Washburn, the charming hostess for the Twentieth Century Book Club yesterday . . . placed Marie Antoinette baskets filled with fragrant lilies in the reception rooms of her home."[29] Nonetheless, amid the refreshments and décor, books were sometimes discussed. It appears that American history was a popular subject.

In June 1920, Mrs. Warren Ward was the new president of the Round Dozen Book Club. On October 27, 1922, the Winsboro, South

Carolina, newspaper reported that Mrs. J. F. McMaster was the hostess for a discussion on Martha Washington.[30] The Tallulah Madison Parish book club in Louisiana held a "pageant" known as "America" on Tuesday night, May 8, 1922, at the Lyric Theatre. The sixty-five members, who met regularly in private homes, offered a public presentation on American history in three parts: "The Spirit of Indian Days," "The Spirit of Wilderness," and "The Spirit of Patriotism."[31] The club met on Thursday evenings throughout that spring and summer, including a meeting at Mrs. Holt's home June 4, 1921, during which her daughter entertained with music and reading.

Janice Radway has recognized that readers of romance novels found personal value in their reading. Radway observed that a mass cultural form does "not necessarily dictate that it be used in ways completely in keeping with the ideology embedded in its narrative structure." Readers can "remake" what they read into something useful.[32] Reading romances has often been categorized as low-culture reading, but Radway's work shows that these novels play a valuable role in the lives of their female readers. Both Radway and Laura Struve have noticed that what is quite important is how romance readers talk about what they read with one another, developing a kind of community among them. In *Loving with a Vengeance,* Tania Modleski holds that female readers of romances are allowing themselves to accept their limitations and dependency and read these books as tranquillizers.[33] Kay Mussell argues that these readers are well-adjusted, but the passivity of the heroines in this fiction can mirror their own passivity in life, as they wait for a man to define their desirability. Laura Struve provides counterarguments, indicating that romance readers are not isolated women waiting for Prince Charming.[34] Rather, they seek other women in groups with whom they can share their reading. She points out that some 273 romance writers have interactive websites. There is a Regency Novel Database, and there are numerous websites devoted to romance reading.

In the 1920s, communities of readers were developed by people who created reading circles. Others were enticed to read by activists like Katherine Johnson, who distributed books to African American readers. Johnson had been working with the Y.M.C.A. overseas during World War I. In 1922, she was an itinerant bookseller, working out of her Ford coupe. She thought about how to get books into the hands of Negro readers. She packed books into the back seat of her car and drove up and down the East coast, meeting with people in black communities at churches and social groups. By 1925, she had covered ten states, says Elizabeth McHenry. In two years, she sold more than 5,000 books to a black readership. "My books are like seeds," she said.[35]

Librarians were another source of encouragement for readers, although some found that the day-to-day practice of librarianship fell short of their ideals. Like Carol Kennicott in Sinclair Lewis's *Main Street*, both poet Marianne Moore and novelist Nella Larsen were excited about their library jobs but became disillusioned with them. Moore was assistant librarian at the Hudson Park Branch of the New York Public Library. Larsen was an assistant librarian in the city.[36]

Moore, one of the most influential poets of her time, needs no introduction. Larsen, on the other hand, is unfamiliar to most of today's readers. Larsen's novels provide some valuable material for studies of identity and race. Her biracial female characters problematize distinctions of white and black. She was born in Chicago in 1891 and became part of the Harlem Renaissance. Her father, Peter Walker, was Afro-Caribbean, and her mother, Marie Hansen Walker, was Danish. The racially mixed family was met with discrimination in Chicago. Nella studied nursing at Lincoln Hospital in Manhattan and went to work as a nurse for the Tuskegee Institute in Alabama. She returned to Lincoln Hospital, working through the flu epidemic of 1918. She married Elmer Imes, a black physicist, in 1919. They moved to Harlem in 1920, and she became a librarian in 1921. She attended studies at Columbia for librarianship and became certified in 1923; however, she took a break in 1925 to write her first novel and then gave up librarianship.

It was during this time that Carl Van Vechten became a friend. In 1928, Larsen published *Quicksand*, a largely autobiographical novel. She created the character Helga Crane, whose background is much like her own. Helga's mother may try to plan her life, but Helga has to find her own way. *Passing* (1929) is the story of two women: Irene Redfield, who lives in Harlem and gives her energy to community development, and Clare Kendry, who is of mixed race and who Irene suspects is having an affair with her husband. The narrative's title refers to racial "passing"—whether one might be part of the white community or the black community. Larsen continued writing for the next few years and then vanished from literary circles and Harlem after her divorce in

1933. She returned to nursing and worked on the Lower East Side, eventually moving to Brooklyn.

Along with the potential influence of librarians, there was the influence of fellow readers whom people met in local reading circles. Books also reached readers through new marketing schemes. In 1926, Harry Scherman began the Book-of-the-Month Club, which selected books for readers and marketed and distributed those books to them. The Literary Guild followed in 1927. Neither was really a club. Members never met in person. As is the case today, they were sent their monthly selection and an array of other books that they might choose from, bringing selected books to the attention of many readers.

ONSTAGE AND ON THE PAGE

Some people preferred to appreciate the vicissitudes of human behavior in stage drama and musicals. Theaters—almost seventy of them—occupied New York by the mid-1920s.[37] Movie studios like Warner Brothers took on mass-production methods. In 1915, D. W. Griffith's *The Birth of a Nation* launched the use of innovative film techniques. The American film industry prospered after the Great War. Film entertainment burgeoned as talkies emerged. In the 1920s, New York was still responsible for about a quarter of the movie business, with studios in Astoria, Queens. Meanwhile, New York publishers developed strategies for advertising and promoting books. The idea of featuring "best sellers" emerged between 1900 and 1920, as a term to market popular books. The Book-of-the-Month Club began in 1926 and the Literary Guild in 1927, to feature popular books for potential buyers. Advances in print technology helped pulp fiction and confession magazines prosper.[38]

Playwright Arthur Miller once said that "modern drama documents human frustration."[39] In the 1920s and 1930s, Eugene O'Neill, Elmer Rice, Maxwell Anderson, Thornton Wilder, and Lillian Hellman critiqued the modern world in their plays. Miller's work arose in the 1930s from social drama. Tennessee Williams's lyrical drama came from the South, where he had written a few short stories in the 1920s. Expressionism in O'Neill's theater followed Ibsen and Strindberg. To this, he brought experimentalism, an ear for dialogue, and a curiosity about

Freudian analysis and the psychodynamics of his characters. In the 1920s, such modernists as Luigi Pirandello, Bertolt Brecht, Jean Cocteau, and Eugene O'Neill took the theater in new directions. The theater of realism transformed into expressionist theater. Pirandello's *Six Characters in Search of an Author* initiated a movement toward the theater of the absurd. His play implies that human life might be much like living as characters in a play: People were trapped on a stage, as in a theater.

In the 1920s, theater turned to the bare stages and scaffolding of expressionism. Artists questioned photographic realism. The scientific rationalism of the late nineteenth century was met with new discoveries at the beginning of the twentieth century. World War I disrupted naïve notions of progress. Freud's investigations of unconscious drives and repressions opened new perspectives on human motivation and behavior. Einstein's theory of relativity told people that space and time were continuous and that speed exists only in relation to where one stands. By now, sociologists like Durkheim and Weber had explored social conditioning, group behavior, and modernization. In his novels, Theodore Dreiser pondered the inescapable struggle for survival in Darwinian terms. He marveled at the vigorous energy of the financier and business titan, while critiquing the world of the exploiter and the exploited. His world was one of people as objects moved by impersonal forces and inexorable natural laws. Other novelists asserted the uniqueness of individuals and essential human qualities: consciousness, will, and love. Dramatists, for instance, O'Neill, Rice, and Wilder, showed people as trapped in social arrangements, economic situations, historical environments, and their struggle to fulfill their dreams. These were limited characters, never as powerful as the protagonists of Greek tragedy, who fought against the darkness with dignity.

Of course, most Americans could not afford to travel to New York to see Broadway theater. For them, drama came on the silent film screen or through a variety of stories. Most 1920s readers were not exclusively reading the works that became American classics. They read popular mass-market fiction, newspapers, and magazines. The printed page provided them with entertainment, information, and news from faraway places. Zane Grey westerns were popular during the 1920s. Every cliché of the western seemed to be set by Grey. *Riders of the Purple Sage* (1912) had become a classic western during the previous decade. Grey's novels appeared steadily throughout the decade. The West was a moral battleground of heroes and villains. There is *The Man of the Forest* (1920), *The Mysterious Rider* (1921), *To the Last Man* (1922), *The Wanderer of the Wasteland* (1923), and *The Call of the Cougar* (1924), all adapted into films. Along with the narratives of Grey there were westerns in magazines. Pulp fiction fare included *The Frontier* (1924), *Cowboy Stories* (1925), *West* (1926), and *Wild West Weekly* (1927). George T. Dunlap has provided figures for sales of westerns. Grey's *Riders of the Purple Sage* sold 835,506 copies. John Fox's *The Trail of the Lonesome Pine* sold 808,506 copies. Grey followed with *The Lone Star Ranger* and others, and Owen Wister wrote *The Virginian*. As of the close of 1936, Grey had sold 11,245,278 copies of his books.

The sale of some 2 million Grey novels demonstrates the reach of the popular novel in the 1920s. Edna Ferber published *So Big* (1924), about a girl named Selina De Jong from a farm near Chicago. It became a silent film. Her novel *Show Boat* (1926) became a classic musical, and *Cimarron* (1929) was a popular western about the opening of the Oklahoma Territory (it also became a film). Rafael Sabatini, who was born in Italy, was on the U.S. best-seller lists with *Scaramouche* (1921), set in the French Revolution, as well as with *Captain Blood* (1922), a story about pirates. His romantic adventure stories were popular between 1920 and 1924, and his earlier novels, *Mistress Wilding* (1910) and *The Sea Hawk* (1915), were reissued. Gene Stratton-Porter, a feminist, photographer, and writer of romantic stories, wrote *Her Father's Daughter* (1923) and the best seller *Keeper of the Bees* (1925). Stratton-Porter, whose limousine collided with a trolley in 1924, did not live to see the huge success of her novel. It is the story of an American soldier who renews his life by turning his attention to helping other people. It appeared at the same time as the American classics *The Great Gatsby* by F. Scott Fitzgerald and *An American Tragedy* by Theodore Dreiser. Neither of these enduring works was a best seller.

PUBLISHING FOR THE POPULAR MARKET

The 1920s marked the beginnings of new publishing firms that began to thrive by responding to popular culture and the rise of the middle-class reader. Harcourt Brace was new, and so was Farrar and Rinehart and the firm of Simon and Schuster, which soon published its first book: *The Cross Word Puzzle Book*. Crossword puzzles became a craze, and the company was soon well-situated to make a growing impact on the industry. Alfred and Blanche Knopf, beginning their firm in 1915, launched new business methods to promote European and American literature. They chose to develop a list rich in literary fiction. Random House was also founded in the 1920s. Doubleday, which moved to Garden City, New York, and the new firms of Farrar and Rinehart and Simon and Schuster emerged forcefully. Meanwhile, editor Maxwell Perkins became legendary for his close editorial involvement with authors. Hiram Haydn of Crown Publishing and Saxe Commins of Random House likewise edited manuscripts and engaged in authors' careers.[40] The Book-of-the-Month Club began offering readers books by mail in 1926, and it grew to more than one hundred thousand members by the end of the decade. The mass production of the paperback book would come in the 1930s, with Penguin Publishing in Britain in 1935 and Pocket Books, funded by Simon and Schuster, in 1939.

Publishing had become an increasingly uniform and standardized commercial venture by the turn of the twentieth century. Books had become more readily available to all regions of the United States. Advances in printing technology and increasing advertising revenue for periodicals prompted the growth of the national magazines. The sale of hardcover books was assisted by more clearly defined channels of distribution. The concept of a best seller emerged in 1895. With the 1920s came what might be called a "golden age" of American fiction.[41] The mass-market magazine carried the work of Sinclair Lewis and F. Scott Fitzgerald, among others. During this time, 1919–1936, Fitzgerald earned $225,784 for his short stories, yet only $66,588 for his novels.[42] *This Side of Paradise* was published on March 26, 1920, and 3,000 copies were sold in three days. There were twelve printings in 1920–1921, and 49,075 copies were sold. Fitzgerald earned $6,200 in 1920.

Harcourt Brace began in 1921, immediately preceded by Harcourt, Brace and Howe in 1919. Alfred Harcourt states that the influx of immigrants to the United States between 1890 and 1914 urged publishing to be cosmopolitan. New York became a Jewish, Italian, and German city, he notes.[43] Indeed, it was increasingly Irish and Slavic as well. Huebsch, Knopf, and Liveright were among the new publishers, and

these companies fostered the trend to publish young authors who had
"broken away from Victorian point of view."[44] Harcourt adds that Scribner's, Putnam's, Appleton's, E. P. Dutton, George Doran, and Doubleday had all begun as publishers' salesmen.[45] A general trade publisher
was offered 1,000 to 3,000 manuscripts a year. According to Harcourt,
"As far as I know, he [gave] careful consideration to them all."[46] The
firm published the Bloomsbury Circle: Virginia Woolf, Lytton Strachey,
and Clive Bell. A week after Hogarth Press published Woolf's *Orlando*
(1928) on October 11, Harcourt Brace also published the novel on
October 18. They published W. E. B. Du Bois, Sinclair Lewis's satire
The Man Who Knew Coolidge, and *Hunger Fighters* by P. de Kruif.
Only in 1931 did the firm begin placing the words "First Edition" on
the title page.

In 1918, the George H. Doran Publishing firm moved to 244 Madison Avenue, at the corner of 38th Street, where the Havermeyer man-
sion had been.[47] The Morgan mansions were across the street, and the
Morgan Library was to the north. In 1919, Doran's daughter married
Stanley Rinehart, who teamed with John Farrar to edit *The Bookman*.
Doubleday built their plant in Garden City and later absorbed Doran
and Company in 1927. By then, Farrar and Rinehart had started their
own firm.

In 1925, B. W. Huebsch merged his imprint with the newly formed
Viking Press. That same year, Charles Scribner's published Fitzgerald's
The Great Gatsby. For Boni and Liveright, 1925 was a good year. Donald Friede recalls that Boni and Liveright editor T. R. Smith had to cut
one hundred thousand words from *An American Tragedy*.[48] In 1925,
the firm published Sherwood Anderson's *Dark Laughter*, Gertrude
Atherton's *The Crystal Cup*, and Loos's *Gentlemen Prefer Blondes*.
They also published the first novel by William Faulkner, *Soldiers' Pay*;
however, the profits were not extraordinary. The auditor's list, Friede
reported, "[showed] just under $1 million and a net profit of exactly
$8,609.12."[49] Friede said that Liveright turned down Hemingway's
work against the wishes of the company's editors. He became the agent
for the motion picture sale of *A Farewell to Arms*, which sold for
$150,000.[50] Pascal (Pat) Covici and Donald Friede were brought to-
gether by artist Alexander King, who won a contest initiated by the
company in 1926. They illustrated the 1927 Boni and Liveright catalog.
Covici had run a book store in Chicago and published Ben Hecht and

the *Chicago Literary Times*. They set up offices in a building on West 45th Street. Covici would later be involved with the work of John Steinbeck, following the publication of *A Cup of Gold*.

Mass-circulation periodicals were another fact of 1920s life. Middle-class consumer magazines included the *Saturday Evening Post*, in which stories by F. Scott Fitzgerald, Sinclair Lewis, and Ring Lardner appeared. In February 1922, De Witt and Lila Wallace started *Reader's Digest* as a way for readers to manage the increasing amount of information they were being exposed to. *Time* magazine began in March 1923, with Henry Luce and Briton Hadden offering a general news publication featuring business development and short, easily read items on culture. Also circulating was *American Life*, which would later transform into *Life*, the photojournalism magazine. Women could read *Good Housekeeping, McCalls, Harper's Bazaar, Vogue, Women's Home Companion, Ladies Home Journal*, or *Delineator*. *Ladies Home Journal* was targeted at married, white, middle-class women and provided stories, recipes, decorating ideas, and cosmetics and clothing ads. The intellectual set could turn to *Vanity Fair*, the *New Yorker*, or to H. L. Mencken's *American Mercury* and *Smart Set*.

Today print newspapers are a dying breed. Many people get their news electronically or through television broadcasts. In the 1920s, the newspaper industry was a thriving business. Hearst and Scripps and Howard owned vast newspaper chains. News items originating in a major newspaper were reprinted in dozens of others. As salesmanship and advertising entered the field, news media recognized the public's desire for sensational stories, which they began to cater to with tabloids.

GENRE FICTION: CRIME MYSTERY AND SCIENCE FICTION

Perhaps public interest in sensationalism in the 1920s was the flip side of the coin from images of the wasteland. The public's taste for the sensational was responded to by popular pulp fiction periodicals. These magazines had a lasting impact on the detective story, science fiction, and the western. Printed on cheap paper, they were fast-paced, trendy, and mass produced. They featured hard-boiled detectives in lurid settings, beautiful women, and tough cowboys. The publications were richly illustrated and sold for anywhere between five and twenty cents.

Fiction noir depicts a shadowy side of culture and has an array of damaged hard-boiled detectives who try to set the world back in order. Dashiell Hammett, Raymond Chandler, and Erle Stanley Gardner were among the authors who published in *Black Mask*. *The Maltese Falcon*, by Hammett, ran as a serial from September 1929 to January 1930. Readers in the 1920s saw the appearance of *Real Detective Tales and Mystery Stories* (1925), *Clues* (1926), *Crime Mysteries* (1927), *Tales of Magic and Mystery* (1927), *Secret Service Stories* (1927), and *Gangster Stories* (1929). War stories produced for pulp magazines recalled World War I. They dwelled in nostalgia and repeated stories of heroism: the kind of stories that Howard Krebs, Hemingway's character, found so difficult to tell and felt that no one listened to. About ten years after the war, there were such magazines as *Battle Stories* (1927), *Over the Top* (1928), *Under Fire* (1928), and *Soldier* (1929).

Science fiction appeared in that genre's almost legendary magazine, *Amazing Stories* (1926). This periodical created a community of readers. Its pages included a reader's column where readers could contact one another. *Amazing Stories* included the first stories of Isaac Asimov, as well as the stories of Robert Heinlein and other masters of science fiction. The horror genre displayed the chilling imagination of H. P. Lovecraft, and *Weird Tales* (1923) and *Ghost Stories* (1926) circulated to this audience. Among those readers was a fourteen-year-old boy, Thomas Lanier Williams, better known to later theater audiences as Tennessee Williams. He contributed a short story to *Weird Tales* in 1928, expressing the imagination that he would soon put to good use in an extraordinary career in the field of drama. Many writers got a start in these publications, which opened the world of fiction to a popular readership that expanded tremendously in the 1920s.

5

MIDWESTERN VISION AND VALUES

Sherwood Anderson, Sinclair Lewis, Willa Cather

In the 1920s, the American "Midwest" was becoming a state of mind, says Frederick Hoffmann in his book *The Twenties*.[1] It was also becoming the geographical source of some of the most incisive writing on American society. From England, Ford Madox Ford called "Middle Westerness" an "enormous awakening." Yet, this was no accolade. It registered a kind of cultural deprivation. The fictional protagonist who grew up in a rural Midwest town usually wanted to escape from it. This character wanted to break out of convention and broaden his or her horizons. Social criticism of this type was one of the strongest trends in American fiction in the 1920s. Community in this Midwest was presented by such writers as Sherwood Anderson and Sinclair Lewis as conformity, a moral zone that was suffocating. The protagonists in their stories seek action and love. Some crumble under the constraints of life, while young people dream and seek to make a journey to the wider America. Meanwhile, Willa Cather viewed Midwesterners as an antidote to modern machinery and greed. Cather opposed the claims of modern gadgets and gimmicks, and she preferred the pioneer hardiness, grace, and natural balance of Midwestern people. American fiction of the 1920s, in many respects, hinges on the tension between appreciations of wholesome hardiness and social criticism of conformity and limitation.

There were many beauties in the Midwestern landscape, and there was sturdiness in the people, as Cather recognized; however, Lewis satirizes the provincial qualities of the Midwest in *Main Street* and *Babbitt*. Sherwood Anderson uncovered odd grotesques: the sad, warped, inarticulate folks that fill his fictional *Winesberg, Ohio*. Robert McAlmon wrote the satiric "Village," set in North Dakota, in which a nomadic individual seeks to overcome incompleteness. The *Apple of the Eye* (1920), by Glenway Wescott, recognizes beautiful farms and simplicity, and a flight into complexity. Carl Van Vechten set *The Tattooed Countess* (1924) in Iowa to present the rural reception of the return of a countess who had lived abroad. Hemingway imagined Nick Adams in Michigan, seeking restoration after the war years. Fitzgerald's Nick Carraway runs from Minnesota to explore becoming a bonds salesman but returns home. The Midwest represented the United States over and over again in the fiction of this era.

In the 1920s, Robert and Helen Lynd offered up a sociological study of a typical town in the American Midwest: Muncie, Indiana. They called their study "Middletown." We may ask how typical Middletown was of America's Midwestern locales. American writers portrayed the region from Ohio and Michigan to Wisconsin and Minnesota in a variety of ways. Indiana, Illinois, Iowa, and Kansas came under the gaze of writers of fiction. Wisconsin was home to three memorable novelists of the 1920s: Glenway Wescott, Zona Gale, and Edna Ferber. The images of family and small-town life fill Wescott's fiction, most of which he wrote while abroad in Paris. Gale's "Friendship Village" offers a picture of rural life in Wisconsin, which some critics have disparaged as too idyllic, since the wholesome image contrasts with darker portrayals like Anderson's *Winesberg, Ohio*. In Ferber's early fiction, we see Milwaukee in the first decades of the twentieth century, where Ferber was, for a time, a newspaper reporter.

Today almost no one reads Glenway Wescott, one of the young novelists of the 1920s. Wescott, who was from Wisconsin, was an American expatriate in Paris, like Hemingway and Fitzgerald. Yet, he often seemed to be thinking of his native Wisconsin. The Midwest of Glenway Wescott appears in *The Apple of the Eye* (1924) and *The Grandmothers* (1927), as well as in his essay and twelve stories collected in a book called *Goodbye Wisconsin* (1928). His writing at the end of the decade appeared in *The Babe's Bed* (1930), which appeared in a printed limited edition. Wescott looked at the history of a family in *The Grandmothers*, a novel that won the Harper Prize in 1927. "Backward and forward, two continual motions of the imagination" he writes in his final chapter. These motions reflect the age that he wrote in, as well as the family he refers to. In the last chapter of his novel, the narrator speaks of those who "went back, in imagination . . . their hope, anxiety, and interest went back."[2] Wescott himself went back imaginatively to Wisconsin, to a place he believed represented America. Yet, there he saw a Midwest that had become provincial, a modern world that beckoned to the youths who remained, unable to break away.

Those Wisconsin towns one sees while driving north on I-95 can appear roughened by the winter. Yet, one might think, like Wescott, of fine land, untouched territory, a place of good families, dairy farms, and an abiding faith in life. By the 1920s, Wisconsin seems to him to have changed into a place lacking "poetry," but he had also changed; his story is another "you can't go home again," one different than that of Thomas Wolfe's title. He believed that movies had begun to substitute for imagination and that groupthink had taken the place of courage and integrity. As his story ends, he returns through the cold, believing that some possibility for natural beauty and enchantment still lives in the land that stretches away into the distance.

Wescott's stories in *Goodbye Wisconsin* were written through the eyes of an expatriate in Europe. From within the aesthetic culture of Paris, he cast a jaundiced look at a postwar world where youthful potential seemed to be wasted on the pursuit of wealth, an environment in which creative intellectual activity seemed to be unappreciated. We might see Wescott as a writer who was as disillusioned as a Green Bay Packer fan after a lost game. He remembers his heroes—Starr, Hornung, Favre, Rodgers—and still he seeks hope in the sacred Sunday rite, but he has lost confidence. Likewise, America's great heroes—Washington, Lincoln, Charles Lindbergh—the immortals, have vanished from the new field of play. Civilization is a wasteland. Still, there remains some hope amid the industrial world. One might pack Green Bay toilet paper and Milwaukee beer into trucks and applaud the state's industriousness, but it is the land of Wisconsin, fresh and green with life, that perhaps will catch a ray of hope on a new day.

Zona Gale's fiction has not fully entered the canon of great American works. Perhaps this is partly because most of it appeared in women's magazines from 1904 to the 1930s. Women's magazine fiction, while quite popular, was not well-regarded critically; however, this popular author from Portage, Wisconsin, was the first woman to win the Pulitzer Prize for Drama in 1920, for *Lulu Bett*, her dramatic adaptation of her own popular novel. *Lulu Bett*, as a novel, was a best seller the same year as Fitzgerald's *This Side of Paradise* and Lewis's *Main Street*. Gale followed this with *Faint Perfume* (1923), *Preface to Life* (1925), and *Borgia* (1929). Legend has it that, as a six-year-old, Gale wrote her first stories on brown paper bags in her family home. She later attended Wayland Academy in Beaver Dam, Wisconsin, and the University of Wisconsin–Madison, earning a master's degree. She was a journalist in Milwaukee and New York and then began publishing magazine fiction regularly beginning in 1904. Her first novel, *Romance Island* (1906), appeared soon thereafter. During the next two decades, Gale belonged to the National Women's Party, pursued the 1921 equal rights law in Wisconsin, and supported Robert La Follette as America's Progressive candidate for the presidency.

Gale's image of a small Wisconsin town has sometimes been categorized as conventional. "Friendship Village" seems too idyllic, too placid when set alongside Sherwood Anderson's *Winesberg, Ohio*. Small-town America is scathingly critiqued in Lewis's *Main Street*, where Carol Kennicott is unable to realize her dreams of transforming a locale and is discouraged by its tedious patterns. Gale's Friendship Village is a place that drivers from out of state might simply pass by, like a sign on I-94. Yet, rural Wisconsin was, during Gale's time, as it is now, a world "full of possibilities," and she saw this in the early twentieth century. The customs, habits, and relationships of common people appear in her short story "Friendship Village" of 1908, as well as in its sequels, "Friendship Village Love" (1909) and "Peace in Friendship" (1919). Sometimes she called the place Prospect or gave the rural country towns another name. These are towns where women marry, take their husband's last names, and live what we might call ordinary lives amongst the farmers, the grocer, the jeweler, and the daily newspaper. The plank road through town is known as Daphne Street, a simple thoroughfare perhaps watched over by the goddess of that name. "We are one long street, rambling from sun to sun" begins "Friendship Village."[3] Miss Sprague, Miss Holcomb, Miss Bliss, and Miss Amandy Toplady live here, and among the first images we are given are telephone poles, suggesting the modernizing of communication, and funeral equipment, implying the passage of their lives.

With *Miss Lulu Bett* (1920), Gale provided an alternative to domesticity. The novel recognizes social inequalities for women and urges a response. Her magazine stories suggested a place for the "new woman": an individual emerging into the public sphere. While Lewis's Carol Kennicott was frustrated with her work as a librarian and her days in Gophers Prairie, Gale used her journalistic skills to write "Civil Improvement in the Little Towns" (1913). She was one of twelve novelists who speculated about the future of fiction in a book entitled *The Novel of Tomorrow* (1922). In 1928, Gale wrote about Portage, a town that has named its 279-seat theater after her. The town has preserved her house and study in a museum and celebrates her birthday on the third Saturday of every August.

Edna Ferber was born in Kalamazoo, Michigan, on August 15, 1885, to a Jewish store keeper of Hungarian background and the Milwaukee-born Julia Neumann Ferber. She grew up in Appleton, Wisconsin, a suburb of Milwaukee, and worked for the *Appleton Crescent News* as a reporter, and in the same profession in New York and Milwaukee. Her early novels offer memories of Appleton's stores, hotels, streets, and social life. Ferber is known for her strong female protagonists and lively imagination. Her character Emma McChesney, in "Fanny Herself" (1917), recalls life in Wisconsin, and Dawn O'Hara, who appears in her first novel, *Dawn O'Hara: The Girl Who Laughed*, is involved with newspaper work in Milwaukee. In that novel, comedy meets with tragedy. Soon after we begin reading, we can see that this writer has a difficult time focusing on her story because a woman's work in the house is never done. The narrator tells us, "[I] settled in my cubbyhole, typewriter before me." Suddenly her name is called, and she is asked to "rescue the cucumbers from the ice box," because the ice man is coming and his weighty delivery will crush them. Next, she is trying to write but is thinking of the children's need for food. She looks at her manuscript, but food is on her mind. "What heroine can remain calm-eyed when her creative mind is filled with roast beef?" she asks. The gravy seems to have gotten into gotten into her character's eyes. She has to rescue the burning roast beef from the stove. The she hurries off after the milk man to make sure the milk delivery is made.

Fortunately, Ferber herself avoided these distractions and wrote some of the most popular novels and plays of the 1920s and 1930s. She is author of the Pulitzer Prize–winning novel *So Big* (1924); *Show Boat*

(1927), which became the famed Jerome Kern–Oscar Hammerstein musical; and *Cimarron* (1929), a novel about Oklahoma settlement that was made into a feature film three times. Ferber wrote several Broadway stage plays, including some with George S. Kaufman, when they were both members of New York's Algonquin Club.

In that first novel, Dawn O'Hara returns home to Michigan from her work with a New York newspaper and soon finds work at a Milwaukee newspaper via a German doctor's support. In this novel, Milwaukee is quite German. Dr. Van Gerhard tries to talk her into divorcing her insane husband, Peter, but she worries about Peter and will not divorce him or succumb to the doctor's advances. The narrative contains Milwaukee scenes that are finely drawn. The narrator says, "Winter in a little town! I should go mad. But Winter in the city!" Then we are given a description of Milwaukee's shop windows, and it is as if West Wisconsin Avenue is appearing before us: "rows of lights like jewels strung on an invisible chain; the glitter of brass and enamel as the endless procession of motors flashes past." The scene is "taking on a mysterious beauty with the purple dusk."[4] The passersby intrigue her, and she wonders who they are: "people I'd like to know," those "unknown friends." She guesses at who they might be: "Mister Red-headed Man, I'm so glad your heart is young enough for Dickens, I loved him too—enough to read him standing at a book counter in a busy shop. . . . Girl with the wide, humorous mouth, and the tragic eyes." Does she write or paint or act? She has a hole in her shoe that she has inked out, and the narrator urges her (as if she could hear) to "please keep laughing."[5]

So Big appeared with an orange cover and was priced at two dollars. Its title comes from that phrase that is often said to little children who are rocked in their parents' arms: "How big is baby? So big!" Selina Peake De Jong intends to be a teacher in a farming area. She stays with the Pool family at their farm, where she encourages Roelf Pool to create his art. She marries Purvis, a Dutch farmer, and they call their child Dirk, or, affectionately, "So Big." When Purvis passes away, Selina has to take over running their farm while she is raising Dirk. Her protégé, Roelf, goes away to France to study and practice his art. Dirk, as an adult, becomes an architect; however, he soon only wants to make money and has forgotten, or set aside, the claims of art. His mother is crestfallen when he becomes a stockbroker. Artist Dallas O'Meara tries to persuade him to recognize the value of fine art and not be so attached to monetary gain. Roelf eventually becomes a great sculptor. Dirk sees the value of his mother's wise advice and the merit of bringing beauty to the world. He ends up unhappy, sitting in his luxurious apartment, having given up architecture and his mother's sense of values, which he now realizes will lead to a sense of meaning in life. The message of following one's authentic desires rather than the lure of money might be usefully placed alongside those important works of the following year, 1925: Fitzgerald's *The Great Gatsby* and Dreiser's *An American Tragedy*.

The first silent film of *So Big* was directed by Charles Brabin, with Colleen Moore in the lead role. William A. Wellman directed the 1932 remake, starring Barbara Stanwyck, George Brett, and Bette Davis. A 1953 remake starred Jane Wyman and Sterling Hayden. By the time of the silent film, Ferber had already seen the production of her play *Minick* (1924) in a theater where bats swooping down upon the audience from the chandeliers and dome of the building had cancelled a performance. *The Royal Family* (1927), her collaboration with George S. Kaufman, was staged without bizarre interruptions. Her theatrical sense also filled her new novel, *Show Boat*, which was adapted into a renowned musical. *Show Boat* turns south to Mississippi and the *Cotton Blossom*, a riverboat theater during the Reconstruction Era. The action then goes to Chicago and later to New York, during the Roaring Twenties. Paul Robeson's singing of "Ol' Man River" provides one of the classic moments in this enduring production, with music by Jerome Kern and lyrics by Oscar Hammerstein II.

Ferber wrote her novel in France and then New York, looking back at the United States with a story in which romance met with racial issues. This includes miscegenation, which remained controversial. Julie Dozier is half black and Steve Baker is white, although love urges him to claim that he too is black, recalling that "one drop of Negro blood makes you Negro in these parts." He has sucked blood from Julie's hand to prove it. The novel also follows the life of Magnolia, the daughter of a retired riverboat captain. It spent about twelve weeks on best seller lists. Louis Kronenberger of the *New York Times* called Ferber's novel "first-rate literature" and an "irresistible story."[6]

Cimarron explores the land settlement of Oklahoma in the days of the rush for unassigned lands. This territory had been mostly Cherokee lands and the lands of the Sioux: the Cherokee outlet of 1893. Ferber gives her readers a lesson on U.S. history in a historical epic. The first edition appeared with an attractive, light cover dotted with illustrations, with the title in white lettering in a black square. RKO Pictures bought the film rights to *Cimarron* for $125,000, a hefty sum in those days, and spent $1.5 million during the Depression to make it. Director Wesley Ruggles developed Harold Estabrook's screenplay with a cast that included Richard Dix, Irene Dunne, and 5,000 extras. At the Jasmin Quinn ranch outside Los Angeles, twenty-nine camera men filmed the movie, working with cinematographer Edward Carnaper, who closely followed Ferber's landscape descriptions. Native American Cherokees were portrayed with greater dignity in the 1960 remake of *Cimarron*. After all, it was their lands that were at stake. This is the version of *Cimarron* that gets broadcast on television, although the 1931 version has been considered by many critics to be better.

Ferber had stretched imaginatively to the American West. Readers back home in Wisconsin could also see the West through the writings of Wisconsin-born historian Frederick Jackson Turner, who wrote in the 1890s that the frontier at the center of American development was fading. Rural readers in Wisconsin became acquainted with other authors as book and periodical distribution expanded throughout the state. In 1922, Charles Rounds of the Milwaukee Normal School brought together a team that wrote *Wisconsin Authors and Their Works*. The project included anyone who could be identified with Wisconsin. Writers included Zona Gale, Hamlin Garland, Frederick Jackson Turner, and Edna Ferber.

Reading in Wisconsin was promoted by the Wisconsin Free Library Commission. Starting in 1896, it helped create local libraries in Wisconsin and launched traveling libraries to bring books and periodicals to rural areas. In *Reading Places: Literacy, Democracy, and the Public Library in the Cold War*, Christine Pawley offers us many valuable insights into the formation and operation of these libraries. Whereas public libraries tended to follow an East Coast "Yankee" heritage, traveling libraries reached readers in ethnic groups who spoke other languages. One of the key proponents of this expansion was Lutie Stearns, who, in 1928, called these readers the "great unreached."[7] From 1896 to 1914, Stearns helped establish 1,400 traveling libraries and fourteen county traveling libraries. She sometimes delivered the books herself, wearing a bearskin over a muskrat coat and driving a sleigh filled with books through the Wisconsin winter.[8] Changes in postal regulations after 1914 made it easier to send books to rural areas by mail. Readers like Ben Logan, whose autobiography Pawley cites in her book, could look forward to books for Christmas. Logan would forever associate *Bambi* with winter in Wisconsin.[9]

Progressive Era institutions had an immediate impact on Wisconsin before the 1920s. Schools, libraries, and women's clubs contributed to fostering literacy. In women's clubs, reading groups turned to Shakespeare and English and American writers. Yet, differences remained amid the counties of Wisconsin, which was filled with a variety of ethnic groups, a state that Pawley notes was "etched by immigrants" who held contrasting views on books and their importance.[10]

What was considered acceptable for the collection in each Midwest library had much to do with the area's culture and the cultural guardians of its libraries. Wayne A. Wiegand points out that Theodore Dreiser's *Sister Carrie* (1900), after being banned for many years, finally reached the shelves of the Bryant Library in Sauk Centre, Minnesota, in 1927; however, it was not accepted in other Midwestern libraries until much later. In 1929, the Moore Library of Lexington, Michigan, had 21 titles by Horatio Alger, 26 by Olivia Optic, and 40 Bobbsey Twin titles. The Rhinelander, Wisconsin, library had two Alger titles. The Bryant Library in Sauk Centre, Minnesota, had many Alger books but none featuring the Bobbsey Twins.[11]

SHERWOOD ANDERSON'S *WINESBERG, OHIO*

Sherwood Anderson's legacy largely resides in his memorable work *Winesberg, Ohio* (1919). This golden age of 1920s American literature may be said to have begun with this pivotal work, which appeared in the months before 1920. Anderson's *Winesberg, Ohio* examines the isolation of individuals in a small American town that is a site of separation rather than one of community. Anderson's protagonist, George Willard, is a reporter who interviews these people. With these encounters, Willard gains sympathy and insight. These individual lives ultimately appear connected, for life, Anderson claims, is a loose, flowing thing. *Winesberg, Ohio* portrays the human spirit of lives that are lonely, quirky, and struggling in America's Midwest. Anderson's sympathetic and sometimes caustic interpretation of this society had a far-reaching influence on the next generation of American writers.

Perhaps it was fortuitous that Hemingway and Faulkner each connected with Anderson. Hemingway, as a young reporter from Illinois working for the *Kansas City Star*, may have reminded Anderson of his fictional character Willard. Anderson's work suggested to Hemingway issues of communication like those we see in Hemingway's story "Hills Like White Elephants," in which laconic, uneasy dialogue between a man and woman implies some tension between them about the woman's pregnancy. In a letter from Anderson, Hemingway was introduced to Gertrude Stein in Paris. Anderson's short story collections offered Hemingway a model for his first short story collection, *In Our Time* (1925).

For Faulkner, Anderson was a bridge to the publishing industry and the publication of his first novel with Boni and Liveright in New York. Elizabeth Prall, Anderson's wife, was the proprietor of a bookstore in New York where Faulkner worked for a short while. When the writers were later introduced in New Orleans, Faulkner and Anderson had a conversational relationship, with Anderson doing most of the talking. Anderson's focus on a specific town likely suggested to Faulkner that he could focus his attention on characters in Jefferson, a town in a place he called Yoknapatawpha County. Anderson embraced imagination as an "other world" that provided a sense of meaning through the creation of fiction. He offered Hemingway and Faulkner models of a young man's awakening in self-discovery and gaining a mature grasp of life's circumstances. [12]

Winesburg, Ohio is a series of interlinked stories in which Anderson achieves what he called a "new looseness" of form. The Anderson Papers, housed in the Newberry Library in Chicago, make it clear that this work was conceived of as a single project, not a series of short stories or sketches. [13] Anderson's work in this book is less autobiographical than some of his others. This is a book in which he goes beyond himself into the inner workings of human lives in a town filled with anguished lives and dislocations of the human spirit. Anderson created this town as typical, a place filled with types of people that one might find most anywhere. The isolation of these lives from one another is the central issue of the narrative. *Winesburg, Ohio* seems to say that we live in a society of industrialism (or, in our time, what has been called postindustrial society), in houses and apartments, within our separate and unique stories and struggles. This isolation is often a kind of separation for convenience or privacy. Yet, Anderson appears to imply that we are interconnected. In revealing this, *Winesberg, Ohio* becomes an American fable.[14] This collection of lives, this scrapbook of alienation, thwarted promise, and incompleteness, attests to the beating heart of ordinary life and urgent longing for love. As Herman Melville once wrote, we are all "isolato," and Anderson, believing this, reflects on atomized individuals, on what he calls "common everyday lives."[15]

Some critics called *Winesberg, Ohio* a critique of the small town. Others viewed it as an interrogation of middle-class morality. But the book's main concern is human isolation and the need for communication. As Irving Howe points out, this is less a social fiction or an inquiry into abnormal psychology and more a lyrical and nonrealistic view of "lonely eccentricity." Winesberg is a place of "oddities and wrecks," the "buried ruin of a once vigorous society," where men and women seek life.[16] This is indeed a book of "twilight and darkness," as Howe says. The people of Winesberg sense the youthful freshness of George Willard and recognize his ability to listen to their longing and the failure in their lives. By telling him about their pains and problems and revealing their stories, they can survive with their truths and find some restoration of their humanity.

Waldo Frank calls *Winesberg, Ohio* "a prophecy and an illumination."[17] He recognizes it as a story cycle with a nonlinear form, as in music. Edwin Fussell points out that during the years in which Anderson was writing the stories (1915–1916), American culture was moving toward an awareness of depth psychology, and Anderson probed beneath surfaces and appearances to see beneath the surface of lives. Anderson was a lyric realist of "loneliness and incompletion."[18] Hoffmann, who wrote about Freudian influences, believed that Anderson's work was uniquely his own investigation of the human spirit and ran parallel with that of Freud.[19] Howe says that these grotesques needed to draw life from George Willard. Yet, Fussell insists that these townspeople had something to give. Howe saw in *Winesberg, Ohio* nostalgia for a lost, more pastoral America. In Edgar Lee Masters's *Spoon River*, Howe contests that Anderson must have seen how a study of local life might be organized. He believed that Anderson's use of the common language of Midwestern people was much like Mark Twain's use of local speech. His reading of Twain was similar to that of Van Wyck Brooks, who portrayed Twain as an artist baffled by the "shrillness" of America.[20]

In *Winesberg, Ohio*, Anderson goes beyond autobiographical writing into the inner workings of this town. This is a place where people are emotionally dislocated. Anderson creates this town as typical. It is a place filled with the types of people that one might find most anywhere. The isolation of these lives becomes the central issue. They live in a society of industrialism, in houses and apartments. George wishes to understand these people. He works for the community newspaper, the *Winesberg Eagle*. He is a sign of the supposedly healthy, well-integrated community that Winesberg actually is not. He listens to people and allows them to tell their stories. This gives them an opportunity to speak again and regain human communication. George does not really understand these people, but, for a while, he is there for them.

"The Book of the Grotesque" begins with the suggestion that the lives of people in Winesberg have been uniquely warped, knocked off-balance, or spiritually distorted. For some characters there is an experience of alienation that elicits a reader's sympathy. An old writer has retired, and he watches people and seeks to teach them how to move toward understanding. People live "snatched up" truths that have made them "grotesques," not realizing self-actualization as people. They are incomplete and imperfect. These individuals need to express themselves and find understanding. "Hands" asks how a person can communicate feeling. "Paper Pills," which follows, seems to ask how one can communicate thought. "Mother" asks how one can express love. Characters feel or know something, yet they are unable to speak about it or make it available to others. Anderson's story is about the distances between people and their common humanity that go beyond social distortions.

In "Hands," George wonders at the hands of old Wing Biddlebaum. Perhaps those hands hold a secret that one never learns. As a teacher, Wing was once accused of making homosexual advances at students because he once tousled their hair. He now tries to hide his hands. The sketch suggests that he has been misinterpreted. George wonders about being misunderstood. In "Hands" we see a "poor, little man, beaten, pounded, frightened by the world into something oddly beautiful."

In "Paper Pills," Dr. Reefy is limited in his ability to communicate. He feels a need to express himself without being misunderstood, so he creates "paper pills," that is, he makes little notes that he rolls up and stuffs into his pockets, little balls that he can toss at people. Sometimes these are wordless scraps, isolated puffs of paper he may toss at a friend. In "Mother," George is concerned with his own mother, Elizabeth. Can love be communicated as she takes over the family business, a hotel, from her husband, George's father? George's father does not like her taking charge, but he is no longer able to run the business. Perhaps George can fill this incompleteness that she feels.

George is a symbol of the supposedly healthy, integrated community. He serves the function of listener and gives people an opportunity to speak and perhaps regain some ability to communicate. Yet, there are limitations to this communication. Materialism isolates people. Still, Jesse Bentley's Calvinism sees a sign of salvation in material wealth. In "Adventure," Alice Hindman runs naked into the rain and finds no one, no love in her life. In "The Strength of God and the Teacher," Reverend Hartman sees loneliness as a sin. He looks at school teacher Kate Swift in her room and feels damned for doing so. She was George's teacher, and she takes him into her arms rather than advising him. In "Respectability," a family story, Wash Williams is tricked by his mother. In "Awakening," we meet Belle Carpenter. When George embraces Belle, a bartender, Belle hits him. George realizes that he must go beyond the conventions of this place. In "The Thinker," Seth Raymond is unable to communicate with Helen White, the banker's daughter. In "Drink," Tom Foster is an outsider. George rejects his dreams of Helen. Later, in "Sophistication," Helen is a symbol of spiritual fulfillment whom George has loved from a distance.

Anderson's stories are about the distances between people and the human need for relationships, connections, and community. George's gathering of stories suggests that there are common features of humanity that go beyond social distortions. The natural speech of Midwesterners enters these stories, which imply that the kind of social communication this society offers is not enough to sustain people in their lives. Nonetheless, it may be possible to find understanding and realize fellowship and love. Rather than acting as a critical expose of society, as did his first novels, *Winesberg, Ohio* provides a reflection on the effects of an age of materialism on the people of a town. The novel is a sympathetic portrayal of humanity and an inquiry into how love and sympathy might help a person overcome feeling lost, lonely, or isolated within a community.

Anderson's *Winesberg, Ohio* has had lasting importance, even while regard of his other works has slipped in critical estimation. David D. Anderson considers the author's major contribution to be an inquiry into the meaning of the American experience.[21] Sherwood Anderson sought to look past appearances, place the ideal alongside the real, and argue against the ways in which some of America's ideals were subverted by a materialistic ethic. His work, like that of Dreiser, Fitzgerald, or Dos Passos, presents a variation on the theme of the American dream.

Anderson's first novels are filled with images of his own pursuit of fortune in Chicago, where he began a business career and later an advertising career. Anderson's first novel, *Windy McPherson's Son*, portrays a small town beset by modernity. It is a place that Sam McPherson, Windy's son, rejects and leaves in search of a career. *Marching Men* was Anderson's next novel. It is an autobiographical work in which his main character, Beaut McGregor, breaks from his mining town in Pennsylvania and travels to Chicago to pursue his fortune. It is in the Windy City that he becomes accomplished in the material world but feels a need to seek meaning.

Anderson's own search for meaning evidently led him to probe the imagined life of a small town in Ohio. A reflection on the effects of the second great wave of industrialism in the latter part of the nineteenth century led him to imagine this distorted local life. Yet, rather than a critical expose of society, like his first novel, *Winesberg, Ohio* would be an affirmation of the human spirit. People can be a little odd at times, Anderson suggests. They may be affected by modern pressures in society or experience isolation and loneliness, but one can overcome loneliness and isolation.

In his own life, Anderson broke with his career in advertising and Chicago commerce as he became a full-time writer. The themes of *Windy McPherson's Son* and *Marching Men* were reworked in subsequent novels like *Winesberg, Ohio*, and the natural speech of Midwesterners entered his fiction. Anderson's reputation is largely based on *Winesberg, Ohio*, for it is a sympathetic portrayal of humanity.

Anderson began to look back at the American past with nostalgia for a world that was not so complex as the one he was experiencing. Like Willa Cather, who by now was seeking those strong pioneer values and a way of life apart from commercial city values, Anderson was perhaps hoping for a setting where people were not being dehumanized. A town's passage from an agricultural base to an industrial economy is again seen in *Poor White* (1920). In this novel, Anderson explores the Midwest and its history, drawing on Mark Twain and a Mississippi River setting. The story begins in Missouri, with Hugh McVey, whose father, like Huck Finn's, is an alcoholic. The railroad gives Hugh a way out, and he dreams of achieving success. Anderson repeats this familiar motif of an individual breaking out of small-town life in search of something he believes will be better.

In *Poor White*, Anderson unfolds a cautionary tale, for Hugh's inventions contribute to the industrialization of Bidwell, Ohio. Through this character, Anderson asserts that the American dream has been co-opted by materialism. Behind him is the ideal of Abraham Lincoln: a practical dreamer, a frontier man who sought political freedom and to invent a new society. In contrast, Hugh invents for profit and participates in industrialization, which causes isolation. Bidwell becomes the scene of isolating factory work, mechanism, and the rise of materialistic goals and values, which can result in a brutal world of disconnection. Yet, there is also the possibility of some positive change—a reclaiming of values when society is not influenced by greed.

Poor White was met with slow sales. Anderson expected to have to continue his work in advertising. He then journeyed to Europe for a time, returning in October 1921, at the age of forty-five. He wrote a series of stories that would be collected as *The Triumph of the Egg* (1921). These stories would have an impact on Ernest Hemingway, serving as a model for his short story collection *In Our Time*. The first story in the volume is "I Want to Know Why," a narrative about adolescent initiation. A boy who is fond of race horses goes to Saratoga. The contradictions of society can be seen through his perspective and inability to understand emotions. "I Want to Know Why" is followed by "Seeds," in which an artist and a psychologist engage in dialogue. They ask whether the scientific approach can result in understanding or if the artistic approach is better.

In "Brothers," an old man is labeled insane. In "The Door of the Trap," a college professor feels misunderstood and withdraws from life. Anderson repeats the pattern of fleeing small-town life to go to city in "Out of Nowhere into Nothing," in which a girl seeks freedom in the city but returns home disenchanted after finding the city dehumanizing. Yet, once she returns home she runs off into the night. The story suggests that people can only desperately run from life with "fleeing, harried minds." *Dark Laughter* draws on Joyce's *Ulysses*. But Anderson's "virtues" are not those of prose rhythm, says Hoffmann.[22] Rather, he was a writer of imagination who paid much attention to his craft.

Anderson was something of a writing coach to his younger contemporaries: Hoffmann refers to him as a literary analyst of human loneliness.[23] He was a historian of the transitional period that immediately preceded the 1920s.[24] This was a time of a new wave of industrialization, a period of realism and naturalism in the novel. Faulkner and Hemingway drew on Anderson but also caricatured his writing. It is clear that Faulkner's Yoknapatawpha, for all its difference from Anderson's Winesberg, provides a local focus for a variety of stories. In *In Our Time*, Hemingway mirrors Anderson's own preoccupation with the innocent confronted with a violent education in the world and a resulting loss of innocence and isolation. We see this in such Hemingway characters as Nick Adams and Howard Krebs. Yet, Hemingway's *Torrents of Spring* (1926) parodies Anderson's style in *Dark Laughter* (1925).

Anderson could see that rapid social change was occurring, and the twentieth century was becoming increasingly complex; he sought new forms in his writing. Hoffmann considers Anderson's "appraisal of . . . American life" one that engaged "several voices."[25] Anderson's concern for Americans and his rebellion against dehumanization was central to his work. In Hoffmann's view, while Anderson's life was contemporary with those of Joyce, Hemingway, Pound, Stevens, and Eliot, his writing was not. Anderson's chief accomplishment, in Hoffmann's view, was "[defining] the misery" experienced by those who were viewed to be eccentric.[26] Human sensitivity and self-consciousness met the crude, material realities of this industrial and commercial life. Anderson imagined these tragic lives and probed the human mind and heart.

SINCLAIR LEWIS, AMERICA'S FIRST NOBEL PRIZE WINNER

In 1930, Sinclair Lewis became America's first Nobel Prize–winning author. This recognition came on the strength of his 1920s novels, *Main Street* (1920) and *Babbitt* (1922), *Arrowsmith* (1925), the controversial *Elmer Gantry* (1927), and *Dodsworth* (1929). His play *Mantrap* (1926) and the satirical *The Man Who Knew Coolidge* (1928) were also works of the 1920s. Lewis's work from this time period appealed to a variety of readers. It received critical acclaim and a wide popular readership.

Main Street was written by Lewis before 1920 and refers to the first decades of the century. It was during this time that Lewis was in contact with one of the premiere novelists of the period, Joseph Hergesheimer, a writer who has largely been forgotten. In 1918, Lewis was vacationing in Chatham on Cape Cod when he wrote to Hergesheimer asking him to travel with him and "see America."[27] Lewis went to Manhattan, where he lived in William Woodward's apartment on West 79th Street. Woodward has commented that Lewis "seemed depressed" and never showed his novel to anyone.[28] During this time, Lewis met with Arthur Harcourt and wrote four Hollywood film scenarios, including *Prairie Gold*, which was later filmed. He returned to Chatham at summer's end and did further work on *Main Street*.

Main Street describes the way of life in Gopher Prairie, what this place looks like, and how it feels to live there. Lewis's powers of observation render these images clearly. Carol has always wanted to transform a small town, to make it beautiful. She meets Dr. Will Kennicott at a Minneapolis party. He is sincere and loves her, and they get married and move to Gopher Prairie. Carol does not like her new home. She doesn't fit in. She finds that "conversation does not exist in Gopher Prairie." Her ideals are met by a town that frustrates her. She works for a time at the library, where the librarian does not encourage lending or reading books, as she believes that the library is for preserving them like museum pieces or artifacts. The women in the Jolly Seventeen club find Carol a little too uppity and too much like a city girl. Erik Valberg, a Swedish tailor, arrives in town and becomes an interest. He concludes that broad plains do not mean broad minds. He has to get out.

In early 1920, Lewis mentioned in a letter to James Branch Cabell that he wrote *Main Street* with "complete dissatisfaction" and had revised most of the 30,000 words that he had shown him.[29] Cabell was working on *Jurgen*, his soon-to-be controversial novel. The Society for the Suppression of Vice would serve a summons on the publisher, Robert McBride. Lewis supported Cabell's novel as a work of "extraordinary merit."[30] Lewis's own novel *Free Air* was then circulating. Harcourt's publication of *Main Street* was slated for one year after that novel. In March, Mrs. Lewis went to Pompton Lakes, New Jersey, and Sinclair embraced the seclusion of writing *Main Street* in a rented room. He received about $900 for each story he sent to the *Saturday Evening Post*: "Bronze Bars" in October and "Habeus Corpus" in November. He wrote a series of articles for the magazine for $2,500 and worked diligently on the novel.

On July 17, 1920, Lewis finished *Main Street*. Harcourt had set up a promotional campaign and had expectations of selling as many as 20,000 copies, but the novel sold much more quickly than they had estimated. In 1921, it became a best seller, with 180,000 copies sold in the first half of the year. An American classic, *Main Street* has since sold millions of copies in hardcover and paperback.

Main Street took shape in Lewis's mind because he was critical of what he saw as the standardization of American life. He believed that the desire to appear respectable manifested itself in sameness and conformity. Whereas television in 2014 celebrates the zombies of *The Walking Dead*, for Lewis in 1920, the "quiet dead," in their "restless walking," were to be criticized for living in "dullness made God."[31] Lewis chimed in with such critics as H. L. Mencken in speaking out against "savorless people" who listen to mechanical music and say mechanical things.[32] Lewis would not be at home in Simon and Garfunkel's "My Little Town." Middle-class convention, evangelical religion, and the bureaucratization of business culture were targets of attack for him. For him, the sociology of Middletown that the Lynds investigated in the 1920s was a source of satire.

Lewis had his finger on the pulse of his times. It is hard to understand why such critical and satirical fiction would otherwise be so successful. As Mark Schorer points out, his plot is usually the same: a young woman or man has a dream and wants to escape a life-limiting environment.[33] In *Main Street*, Carol maintains this hope, and that dream shared by some readers is perhaps one of the things that made the book so widely popular. Lewis's vision contrasted sharply with the more or less idyllic Midwest of Booth Tarkington's popular fiction. Lewis's novels are in the Midwest tradition of Edgar Lee Masters's *Spoon River*, William Dean Howells, Floyd Dell, and Zona Gale. Yet, the critical thrust of his *Main Street* lies closer to the colloquial speech and social critique of Mark Twain or the incisive stories of Sherwood Anderson in *Winesberg, Ohio*. The picture of the Midwest that emerged from Lewis, as from Anderson, was ambiguous. On the one hand, most people there were sensible and authentic. On the other, middle-class life was narrow, and many people's lives felt incomplete. [34]

Main Street quickly became part of public conversation. On February 9, 1921, in the *New York Tribune*, under praise of Henry G. Aikman's "Zell," appeared verses by C. W.:

> I admit I am not a Main Street fan
> I don't love how a Main Street man
> In his Main Street home with his Main Street wife
> Took a Main Street outlook on his life. [35]

Schorer, Lewis's biographer, suggests that the writer changed the tone of American literature in the 1920s. It might just as well be said that the cultural mood of the nation was changing at this time. The noisy indictment of provincialism that Schorer points to was indeed the start of a "decade of literary revolt." [36] Yet, a point that has been understated is that there was a receptive audience for this. *Main Street* had exceptional sales that were completely unexpected by Harcourt Brace. For *Main Street* to sell so well or F. Scott Fitzgerald's first novel, *This Side of Paradise*, to be so popular, the time had to be ripe. The "revolt" lay within a significant portion of this generation of readers, as well as in the writers.

So why did *Main Street* sell so well? Did people see themselves in it? Were they willing to be that self-critical? Or was it other people they saw or a trend of their time they saw in it? Its argument is that small-town life during this time was shallow. People like Carol dreamed of a fulfilling life, a beautiful and exciting life. Yet, they lived amid limitations, which included their limited sense of history. Sinclair Lewis, Edith Wharton, Ellen Glasgow, and Willa Cather all stared into the glass of history and manners and critiqued those habits and limitations. [37] With *The Great Gatsby*, Fitzgerald reversed the frontier thesis of Frederick Jackson Turner. Now, as Hoffmann says, "The young man had to go east instead of west." [38] One sought freedom, prosperity, cul-

ture, sophistication, and style; however, as Schorer points out, this goal
to find in the east what was unavailable in the west was "exposed as false
and fruitless."[39]

Lewis delivered his manuscript for *Main Street* to Harcourt Brace
on July 17, 1920. The hope was that the novel would sell 20,000 to
25,000 copies.[40] On December 1, Lewis wrote to Harcourt, stating,
"Actual sales of *Main Street* are within 400 or 500 copies of 20,000."[41]
By December 15, he was writing, "Dear Alfred, the sales are glorious!
35,000! And a start in England!"[42] In *The Bookman*, John Farrar mentions the novel's extraordinary sales.[43] Vachel Lindsay had encouraged
the book's publisher to saturate the Midwest with review copies, and
they did. In the first months of 1921, rapid sales of the novel continued.
Schorer records that within six months it had sold 180,000 copies.[44] The
Bismarck Tribune (April 27, 1921) in North Dakota told its readers that
Main Street had put Lewis on "easy street" by selling "nearly two hundred thousand copies in the first five months."[45]

We may ask if women saw themselves in the character of Carol
Kennicott. Women wrote to Lewis saying that he saw their situation.[46]
"I'll do everything for you," an anonymous female fan wrote to him,
"and when I say everything, I mean everything." Dorothy Thompson,
Lewis's wife, responded to her that as for "everything," she took care of
that.[47]

The novel came out at a time when Americans were reading popular
novels like *Moon Calf* by Floyd Dell, *Miss Lulu Bett* by Zona Gale, and
The Brimming Cup by Dorothy Canfield. These became associated
with *Main Street*.[48] When William Dudley Pelley's *The Fog* (1921) sur-
faced featuring characters in winter hats and coats in a small New
England village, it was immediately cast alongside *Main Street* in a *New
York Tribune* review.[49]

There were mixed reactions to the book from common readers.
Some people in the town that Lewis hailed from, Sauk Centre, Minnesota, thought·Gopher's Prairie was based on their town. Lewis wrote to
the *Sauk Centre Herald* that his novel was in no way based on actual
people there. Some residents disagreed. Alexandria, Minnesota, near
Sauk Centre, banned the book from its library.[50] But in Missouri, when
the Jefferson Mother's Club contributed children's books to their town
library that spring, they included a copy of Edith Wharton's *The Age of*

Innocence and Sinclair Lewis's *Main Street* for the adult "rental shelves."[51]

Some people in small-town America thought that Lewis was way off course. He was a critical maker of American images. He witnessed the vanishing of villages and growth of cities. He recognized that the small town, the "Friendship Village" of Booth Tarkington, was not always as pleasant as that writer portrayed it. Novelist Floyd Dell writes that *Main Street* is no work of fiction; it is an argument.[52] Thomas J. McCarthy, editor of *Devil's Lake Journal* in Bismarck, North Dakota, took exception to Lewis's portrayal of the small town. Lewis had stopped in Bismarck two days before, and McCarthy argued back, writing in his column "Missing Links," "We tried our best to read Sinclair Lewis's *Main Street*, but like taking one drink of Scotch too many, it wouldn't stay down." McCarthy describes Lewis's effort as that of a high school boy "trying to write a newspaper story." He asserts that Lewis appeared to want to tell a story, but he really had no story to tell. He was likely responding to Lewis's tendency to write in set pieces rather than produce a strongly plotted work of fiction. "Main Street starts off all right, but it should have ended there," McCarthy says. "Had he lived the real life of a small town and become a real 'Main Streeter,' he would have at least been more charitable to the people in these communities."[53] McCarthy insists that city or rural, people are all human and should be treated with respect.

Haywood Broun wrote in the *New York Tribune*, "I don't think Sinclair Lewis confines his attack to the small town; I think his small town is really a symbol for all America."[54] Carol's predicament was the problem of other young Americans. William Allen White, in *The Emporia Gazette*, concludes that small-town life in the United States was probably no different than small-town life most anywhere in the world. "They are very human, very like people you know," the *Bismarck Tribune* told its readers. The Reverend Dr. Pace had preached about Main Street "last Sunday evening."[55] Sherwood Anderson, who had imagined *Winesberg, Ohio*, thanked Lewis for his novel and suggested that it would "find most of its readers in the cities."[56] Lewis responded on December 6 that he had reread *Winesberg, Ohio*. He called it an "authentic text."[57] Anderson recognized the great sales Lewis's book was achieving. To Hart Crane he wrote that Lewis sold more copies in a week than *Poor White* had sold altogether.[58]

In Nebraska, on April 14, 1921, the *Red Cloud Chief* reported that Lewis read the works of Nebraska authors and called Willa Cather's *My Antonia* "one of the greatest novels in all American literature." The newspaper reported that Lewis's novel had sold 1 million copies in the United States. To readers the editor wrote, "You must persevere with it. It is very long. People talk through its pages in the most incredible language—the American tongue."[59] In a letter to Lewis, British novelist John Galsworthy praised the novel. He observed that the critical attitude had not recently been present in the American novel and said that the novel would start a "national mood."[60] F. Scott Fitzgerald marveled at the "sheer amount of data" Lewis had compiled.[61]

By this time, Lewis had written another novel, one that would be equally stirring and almost as popular: *Babbitt* (1922). Washington, DC, area residents who opened their papers on Sunday morning, September 17, 1922, saw the *Washington Times* headline that declares, "Lewis's Babbitt Is an Even Better Novel Than Main Street." Under the subtitle "Sinclair Lewis Picks on U.S. Americans Again," Ames Kendrick writes that Lewis had fun depicting 100 percent right-thinking forward-looking individuals such as exist in our land" and "disposing of cultural pretentions" in small-town America. He concludes that *Babbitt* would not be as popular as *Main Street* had been. The Babbitts in the land are not going to enjoy this, he says.[62]

That same day, readers of the *New York Tribune* saw the announcement that Lewis had written a "Mirror of Mediocrity." The paper recognized *Babbitt* as a social satire. Readers also saw an ad for the book that appeared in a square box. Next to this, in the "Review of Books" section, was an explanation that *Babbitt* was about to join a best-seller list that included *If Winter Comes* by A. S. M. Hutchison (Little Brown), *Gentle Julia* and *Alice Adams* (Doubleday) by Booth Tarkington, *Maria Chapelaine* by Louis Hemon (Macmillan), *Brass* by Charles Norris (Dutton), and *To the Last Man* by Zane Grey (Harper).[63] The *Philadelphia Evening Public Ledger* cast the novel as "Fiction That Entertains and Irritates," adding that the "book as a whole is as untrue as a burlesque sketch of a team of vaudeville actors."[64]

Lewis wrote some of *Babbitt* while in France, Rome, and London. He dedicated the book to Edith Wharton, who, in *The Age of Innocence*, critiques the society of New York's elite of the last decades of the nineteenth century. *Babbitt* welcomes us to the city of Zenith, where

George Babbitt, age forty-six, is a realtor who wants to succeed and fit in. He wakes up with a hangover, although Prohibition had been established a year earlier. He lives a banal life, recites slogans and clichés, seeks gadgets, joins organizations, and seeks objects for social status. There is little plot to drive the story and a series of set pieces. George becomes a public orator for the realtors, supports a Republican mayor in an election, and tries to move upward socially and fails. Zenith has become a place of skyscrapers, billboard ads for movies, factories, and drug stores. George has only one friend, Paul, whose life falls apart. George then suffers a midlife sexual crisis. He has not been adventurous and goes on to meet Mrs. Tanis Judique, with whom he has an affair. He also meets Seneca Doan, a town radical who supports a strike. The town turns against George.

For Lewis, George F. Babbitt was the average American, a man trying to make his way. He joined clubs. He bought new gadgets. He was a good, practical man who sought to be a "solid citizen," although he was probably more like the "Unknown Citizen" that W. H. Auden wrote about in one of his poems. Whereas Mencken could be harsh in casting the American middle class as the "booboisee," Lewis's Babbitt was not all boob. Rather, Lewis humanized his character. Beginning as caricature, George grows as a character who is concerned about his family. He yearns to "seize something more than motor cars and a house before it is too late."[65] He concludes by admonishing his son to live a life different from his own. Readers get the image of an individual. In the end one can come to the consensus that while George is a bit of a boob, he is sometimes loveable.

The first third of Lewis's novel presents the vacuity of George's life: his mundane rituals, routines, and assumptions—dressing, starting the car, driving through downtown Zenith, the ceremonies of daily life, fashion and cultural conventions. Can that epoch translate into ours? Does Lewis also show us how we live? When he recreates the period from 1910 to 1920, can we recognize and experience this life? The temper of the times brought a satirical style that appears to have been derived, in part, as a response to the postwar era. It is a time that conceives of itself as free from convention and the restraints of tradition. Analysis of middle-class life moves from laughter to sharp critique.

We might ask whether George was representative of his era. Does his noisy, restless way of life typify some features of American life in the

1920s or even today? In Maxwell Geismar's review of the novel, he calls George's Zenith "our native Inferno." Perhaps it is as fantastic and morally damning as Dante. But for Schorer, George provides a "sociology of middle-class life" in the first, carefully planned twenty-seven chapters.[66] In the tradition of the business novel, his story points to "emotional and aesthetic starvation."[67] Living amid conventions and social mores, George becomes increasingly discontented with his life. He sees Paul Riesling, a friend he admires, become imprisoned for shooting his wife. He tries to find belonging with the "Bunch." Then the Good Citizen's League pressures him. As George unravels, readers may see that his superficial values need to change. The depth of love and the importance of family and kindness are the things he begins to realize. George has always desired belonging and to be loved; however, his acquisition of things and futile quest for power and prestige in his little local puddle of a world is not enough. He also has to learn to seek "tolerance, justice, and integrity; beauty; intellect."[68] Babbitt is indeed pathetic until he begins to learn what is essential.

Harcourt Brace printed 80,500 copies of *Babbitt* and anticipated strong sales. Newspapers in Minneapolis, Duluth, Cincinnati, Kansas City, and Milwaukee claimed that their city was a model for Zenith. Other people were upset with Lewis's caricatures. A column in the *New York Times*, "Topics of the Times," tried to console them by pointing out that there were Georges everywhere.[69] Exploring the local controversies the novel provoked, Schorer mentions Dr. Emanuel Sternheim's address at the Cleveland Kiwanis Club and a review by Minneapolis attorney C. C. Champine in the *Realtor*. Real estate broker Norman F. Emerson indicated that Lewis must have been thinking of a member of their real estate board.[70] From London, T. Owen Jacobsen wrote to the *New York Times* that he and his friends were practicing American phrases and working them into their conversations.[71]

During this time, Sinclair Lewis was reading copies of *Broom*, a small magazine published by Harold Loeb, whom he met with in Rome. Many would consider Loeb (sometimes called "low ebb") the prototype for Robert Cohn in Hemingway's *The Sun Also Rises*. Loeb was assisted in editing the publication by Alfred Kremborg, and *Broom* was read by such modernist poets as Ezra Pound and William Carlos Williams, among others. The interesting thing is that Lewis was reading modernist journals while writing middlebrow fiction.

As Lewis drew further public attention, he supported his books with lectures at halls, libraries, bookstores, and churches. He praised the work of Theodore Dreiser and Sherwood Anderson. In Milwaukee, he spoke of Zona Gale, who set stories in Wisconsin. He paid tribute to Willa Cather in Omaha, Nebraska, and in Indianapolis he recognized both Booth Tarkington and Dreiser. Schorer observes that Lewis was "selling contemporary American literature."[72] For his lectures, Lewis chose as his topic "The American Novel as an Invitation to Life." He later insisted to the *New York Evening World* that the United States was filled with Main Streets and that people there are always open to change.[73]

While in Chicago, he met with Ben Hecht, Carl Sandburg, Maxwell Bodenheim, Harry Hansen, and others. He also encountered Paul de Kruif, who would become an important source for his next novel, *Arrowsmith*. Together they set out to conduct research. Lewis's method was to develop biographies of his major characters, giving them a profession or field of work, and then chart out maps of his settings and write a scenario of the action. With de Kruif, he explored the medical background for *Arrowsmith* and the Caribbean setting he would use for part of the novel.

Meanwhile, *Main Street* was being turned into a play. After a run in Indianapolis, it opened in New York at the National Theater. Plans were made for a stage company in Chicago, as well as a road company.[74] *Main Street* was then sold to the movies for $40,000.[75] Lewis sent a message to Alfred Harcourt on January 3, 1922, that he was returning to the United States. *Babbitt* was well underway. Jonathan Cape would publish the novel in Britain, complete with a glossary explaining the American phrases. They would remain Lewis's publisher in England, which Lewis saw as having a leisured and cultivated class of writers, as opposed to American authors, who solely depend on their own resources.[76]

Warner Brothers wanted Lewis's story. Harcourt reached an agreement for film rights in November and reprinted three of Lewis's earlier novels. Lewis and de Kruif made a trip to Barbados, Trinidad, and the Sargasso Sea. The new book would also call for investigations of medical science and laboratories in London. Lewis came from a family of doctors—his father and uncle were physicians. His character would be one who was interested in scientific research. *Arrowsmith*, at 245,000 words on 748 pages, was completed on September 30.[77]

Harcourt Brace planned sales promotions, and March 5, 1925 was set as the date for the publication. Prepublication copies totaled 51,750. Lewis autographed 500 copies. De Kruif arranged for Harcourt to send copies to scientists and physicians. In Paris, Man Ray took a photo of Lewis for publicity in U.S. magazines. Harcourt placed a full-page ad in *Publisher's Weekly* ten weeks before publication.

It is often said that a successful previous book by an author makes way for the next. As such, sales of works of such modern-day authors as John Grisham, Mary Higgins Clark, or Stephen King build on the popular success of the last novel. This was clearly the case with *Arrowsmith*. Reviewers thought it a better novel that *Main Street* and *Babbitt*. It was "truer" says Joseph Wood Krutch in the *Nation*; it was an "authentic fire in which art and science are purified," writes Stuart Sherman in the *Herald Tribune*.[78] *Arrowsmith* was not as critical as Lewis's previous two novels. Harcourt's first printing sold rapidly. F. Scott Fitzgerald, whose *The Great Gatsby* had just appeared, wrote to Lewis that he had read *Arrowsmith* and hoped that his own novel might be the "second-best book of the year." Lewis seems to have had other ideas. He praised John Dos Passos's *Manhattan Transfer* (1925) so lavishly that Dos Passos's publisher turned Lewis's review into a promotional pamphlet.[79]

Lewis's subsequent novel, *Mantrap*, was serialized in *Collier's* between February and May 1926. It was conceived and written quickly, and amongst Lewis's works it is fairly forgettable. His protagonist, Ralph Prescott, has likewise failed to achieve the canonical status of George Babbitt. The book appeared on June 3, and the film followed on July 7, with Ernest Torrence and Clara Bow in the lead roles. Lewis had his mind on another character: a striking, histrionic Methodist preacher like one he had known of in Kansas City. In his mind were now the outlines of his most controversial novel, *Elmer Gantry*. Within months, he would place a copy of a 20,000-word manuscript draft and outline in a Kansas City department store vault. Soon thereafter, he would fan the flames with some controversy of his own. In early May 1926, Sinclair Lewis refused the Pulitzer Prize.

Lewis was busy investigating the preachers of Kansas City—a city roughly at America's geographical center. The idea began in Detroit years earlier with a suggestion by William Stidger, a Methodist minister friend he had met in Terre Haute, Indiana. Lewis admired Stidger, who was now in Kansas City, and returned to visit him in 1925. Through him he met other Methodist ministers and the Unitarian L. M. Birkhead. He had been a Methodist and experienced conversion at a revivalist meeting but was now agnostic. Birkhead became an important source for Lewis's work on his novel.

Lewis clearly viewed some evangelical preachers as charlatans, on the order of L. Frank Baum's *The Wizard of Oz*. *Elmer Gantry* grew into a critique. Published on March 10, it was a selection of the new Book-of-the-Month Club. Harcourt Brace released comments on the material book: its paper and ink, its cloth binding and orange cover. *Elmer Gantry* was advertised on billboards—perhaps the most famous fiction to grace a billboard since Fitzgerald's T. J. Eckleburg. The appearance of the novel was proclaimed on billboards by the General Advertising Company of New York and later similarly promoted in Kansas City, a clear indication of the rise of advertising in the 1920s.[50]

With *Elmer Gantry*, Lewis crafted a persistent cultural symbol of the revivalist preacher. These controversial evangelists have drawn both praise and derision. Followers see them as holy men through whom the Holy Spirit speaks. Detractors call them charlatans, with quite worldly motivations. In 1960, Richard Brooks brought *Elmer Gantry* to film, with Burt Lancaster and Shirley Jones.

Kurt A. Edwards contends that Billy Graham was a clear figure behind the film portrayal. He acknowledges that Aimee Semple McPherson and Billy Sunday were Lewis's models in the 1920s. He then makes a convincing case that Graham, who sought "performative manners" to refrain from being perceived like Elmer Gantry, was a model for Richard Brooks and Burt Lancaster. Graham has evoked a long line of preachers, from George Whitefield and the Great Awakening and Dwight Moody and the social gospel to Charles Finney and Billy Sunday, a major figure of the 1920s. In 1950, he reacted to the *Atlanta Constitution*'s pictures implying the "fleecing" of a congregation. After much soul-searching, he sought to continue to evangelize, while distancing himself from the unscrupulous image of Elmer Gantry.

Billy Sunday drew large crowds to his revival meetings. For years he had played baseball with teams in Pittsburgh, Chicago, and Philadelphia. He became a Christian through the Harry Monroe mission in 1886, and refused to play ball on Sundays. He soon left the big leagues and went to work for the Y.M.C.A. Sunday began pitching sermons from makeshift wooden platforms. He preached fire and brimstone from temporary pulpits. A bombastic, plain-talking showman, he was sometimes likened to P. T. Barnum: flamboyant, dramatic, rousing emotion in his audiences. Critics opposed his emphasis on personal salvation, asserting that it lacked a social dimension. Others, for example, H. L. Mencken, were harsher. He called Sunday a "gymnast for Jesus," the "calliope of Zion."[81] For critics like this, Sunday became a caricature. Lewis pounced on it.

Lewis also found a target in Aimee Semple McPherson, one of the most famous preachers of her day. In 1926, she disappeared into Mexico and claimed to have been abducted. She had actually run off with a married man. The affair resurfaced memories of Reverend Henry Ward Beecher's highly publicized affair in the nineteenth century. Today the Elmer Gantry figure may suggest such problematic televangelists as Jimmy Swaggart and Tammy Faye Bakker. Congress subpoenaed the economic records of church leaders Benny Hinn, Kenneth Copeland, Eddie Long, Joyce Meyer, and Paula White. Behind the suspicions lay Elmer Gantry, a lasting cultural type created by Lewis in 1927. This was reinforced by Patrick Keaney's theater adaptation, which opened on Broadway on August 7, 1928.

In 1945, Lewis reviewed Richard Brooks's novel *The Brick Foxhole* for *Esquire*. The director of *Lord Jim, Cat on a Hot Tin Roof, Blackboard Jungle*, and *The Professionals*, Brooks was well-established when he turned back to the property of Lewis's novel. Brooks's *Elmer Gantry* takes the story out of 1927 and brings it into 1960. He only made use of the first two-thirds of the book. The film received five Academy Award nominations and eventually won three Oscars. Burt Lancaster won for best actor for his portrayal of Gantry; Shirley Jones, who played prostitute Lulu Barnes, received the award for best supporting actress; and Brooks was awarded for his screenplay.

Lewis has by now faded from view, although not entirely. He "seems to have dropped out," Gore Vidal observes in "The Romance of Sinclair Lewis."[82] He points out that phrases like "it can't happen here," images of "main street" and terms like *Babbitt* still have some resonance. Lewis is still spoken of in Sauk Centre, where there is a memorial to him. He is also read by graduate students, for instance, Elin Arnestrand of Norway, who chose Lewis as the subject of her master's thesis at Oslo

University. This graduate student's goal was to explore the United States in the 1920s through Lewis's novels. After all, Lewis was quite popular during that decade and was awarded the Nobel Prize in Scandinavia in 1930. Arnestrand begins by observing that Harry E. Maule and Melville E. Cane point out that Lewis had a "profound influence" on the United States during his time and helped people better understand America.[83] But Arnestrand soon recognizes that Lewis's novels are satires, not objective accounts of the Roaring Twenties in America. A novel is a work of imagination and is not strictly mimetic, nor is it primarily a sociological study or an ideological brief. Rather, a novel is principally an act of storytelling.

Yet, even so, fiction can prompt reflection on the present or open a window to the past. A novel may be quite suggestive of an era's social patterns and cultural consciousness, as well as make an impression on the popular consciousness. This seems particularly true of the popular novel. Lewis was one of the few authors whose major works received both popular acclaim and critical recognition. Arnestrand perceptively argues that "an author cannot escape his context."[84] Because Lewis was a product of his time, we may ask how his personal experience and detailed research affected his readers. Several of his readers rejected his portrayal of the small-town life of Gopher Prairie in *Main Street*.

Main Street was a publishing sensation, John Updike points out in the *New Yorker*; however, he wryly asks what Lewis had done lately to merit another biography of 554 pages from Richard Lingeman (2002).[85] In the end, one would think that Schorer's monumental tome would have been the last word. Updike notes that best-selling does not make for a classic and that *Babbitt* comes closer to this than *Main Street*. Lewis's novels are by no means contemporary classroom standards like Fitzgerald's *The Great Gatsby*. Writers "slightly younger" than Lewis— Fitzgerald, Hemingway, Faulkner—have more currency with us. For Hemingway, in his time, Sinclair Lewis was already forgettable. Hemingway was after a different kind of fiction. Schorer is critical, calling Lewis "one of the worst."[86]

Perhaps some of this is true; however, what is also is true is that the 1920s and American literature cannot be understood without Sinclair Lewis.[87] He created no school of writing and no imitators, but Lewis was among the best-selling novelists of the decade.[88] His influence was on public thinking, not writing style. The Harcourt Brace edition of

Main Street and the cheaper edition from Grosset and Dunlap sold more than 2 million copies. *Babbitt* followed with strong sales. *Elmer Gantry* created a stir in 1927, with its critique of an evangelical preacher. *Arrowsmith* and *Dodsworth* also sold reasonably well. Lewis's books were made into movies, attracting a broader audience. While contemporaries like Zona Gale and Dorothy Canfield Fisher have largely been forgotten, Lewis hangs on—although most people today have not read him.

In the 1920s, the novels of Sinclair Lewis were popular entertainment. They were meant to be widely read. In those days, magazines were filled with fiction. Since then, Vidal claimed, we have "no time to read." We have movies to watch and television. Those *Saturday Evening Post* stories are now mini-series and television serials. Nonfiction fills magazines. Writing on the occasion of the Library of America volume of Sinclair Lewis's works, Vidal commented on the energy and "Balzacian force" of Lewis's writing and recognized that he was a master of the polyphonic novel, in Mikhail Bakhtin's sense. [89] That is, Lewis created a dialogical fiction of many voices. In the 1920s, Sinclair Lewis was one with his readers; he was much like them.

WILLA CATHER AND HER READERS

Nebraska, further west, in the American heartland, was the home of Willa Cather, one of America's finest writers of the 1920s. Recent criticism has highlighted some of the modernist qualities of her fiction and brought her further into focus as one of the important writers of the Roaring Twenties. For years, many of Cather's personal letters were not available to researchers, but they have become increasingly accessible through the University of Nebraska's collection of letters, drafts, manuscripts, and other items. The Willa Cather Collection at Drew University in Madison, New Jersey, also sheds light on the work of this notable writer. [90]

Cather's work has increasingly been studied by critics throughout the past several decades. She often wrote of pioneer fortitude, as in *O Pioneers!* She wrote of the diligent work of farmers in *One of Ours*, immigrants in *My Antonia*, and the people of the southwest in *Death Comes for the Archbishop*. Cather maintained a broad audience, broader than only the fine readers she evidently sought with her well-crafted fiction. Her letters and documents in the Cather collections at Drew University and the University of Nebraska help extend our reevaluation of this writer's work. Some readers may find questions about how her sexual orientation affected her writing interesting, as have some recent biographers. Others will give their attention to her craft in the fiction itself.

Cather's attention to the history preceding 1920s America ought not suggest that she had no interest in the life of her own times. Indeed, she did. In her preface to *Not under Forty* (1936), she says that the world had broken in two in 1922 or thereabouts. Change had come to American life. Although Cather lived in New York for many years, she preferred solid rural values to the relativistic ones she believed were in the city. She looked at what she felt was superficial culture and the need for something deeper and more enduring: an America with roots. In writing her novels, she listened for American speech and sought something she believed was authentic.[91]

Each of Cather's novels of the 1920s is different from the others. On May 20, 1923, her Pulitzer Prize for *One of Ours*, a story she said affirms life, was announced.[92] *One of Ours* recalls World War I but is not a war novel. Most of Claude Wheeler's story takes place on a Nebraska farm, where his work is dutiful, his father difficult, and his marriage empty. Next came the novel *A Lost Lady. The Professor's House* soon appeared as a crafted novel about an aging historian who, upon receiving a monetary award, builds a new house. Tom Outland becomes the professor's protégé or alter ego, an individual willing to go on a quest. So too were several of her other characters. Those in *O Pioneers!* (1913) cross the country. Those in *My Antonia* (1918), part of the immigrant experience, travel the cultural horizons of the United States. In *Death Comes for the Archbishop* (1927), respect and integrity came too, as the priest who would become a bishop crosses cultures in the American southwest amongst the Native American Indians. As Bernice Slote references, in her attention to the environment, to multicultural America and ethnic individuality, Cather was not only looking back in history, she was looking forward with concerns that are relevant even in our time.[93]

One of Ours received many favorable reviews; however, one by the *Washington Herald* in September was less so. "The end of the book . . .

is silly," the reviewer writes, also complaining that Claude "always manages to find nice, heroic things to do and charming people to do it with."[94] Cather makes use of a third-person limited point of view in the book. Claude acts as a viewpoint character, and through him we see the war. Hemingway claimed that Cather took her battle scene from D. W. Griffith.[95] But as JoAnn Middleton points out, Claude's vision leads readers to fill in the blanks and supply images.[96] In a 1921 interview with the *Omaha World-Herald*, Cather called Claude a "red-headed prairie boy." She attested to her lack of "descriptive work" and "pictures."[97] Yet, there is memory and storytelling at work when Cather has Enid lock Claude out of their stateroom on the Denver Express. In *Willa Cather: A Literary Life*, James Woodress writes that Cather recalled in her novel an incident that actually occurred in Pittsburgh with a young man who was similarly locked out of his room.[98] The alienation Claude experiences in his marriage is perhaps more poignant than his encounter on the battlefield.

A Lost Lady was a 1920s best seller. Critics evidently liked the novel as much as Cather's common readers. Krutch calls it "nearly perfect."[99] The novel is comprised of two parts of nine chapters each. These sections are set ten years apart. Cather began *A Lost Lady* several times, shifting point of view. She had used omniscient point of view for *Alexander's Bridge* and *O Pioneers!* She would later use it for *The Song of the Lark, Death Comes for the Archbishop*, and *Shadows on the Rock*; however, in *My Antonia*, Cather makes use of a frame narrator and Jim Burden's first-person story. Nellie Birdseye is a first-person narrator in *My Mortal Enemy*. Selective omniscience is used in *One of Ours* and *A Lost Lady*. In *A Lost Lady*, there is a unifying narrative voice, a consciousness that provides continuity, but the novel becomes dialogical, as Cather uses multiple points of view and brings readers into Niels's thoughts. Niels is an observing consciousness. His consciousness is given to us in limited third-person point of view, and we see through his perspective.

Marian Forrester is Cather's central character. Marian's decline appears to be equated with the decline of the pioneer spirit. Cather shows concern for this decline and that of the "old ways" of Midwestern life, which she believed gave integrity to American life. She follows Marian's "blind, directionless course."[100] Marian is married to Captain Forrester. Her complexion is described as one of the innocence of white lilacs.

Wearing jewels and earrings of garnet and pearl, she has an affair with Frank Ellinger. Her evident charm is related to the sound of her laughter. This "long-lost lady laugh" may have influenced Daisy Buchanan's laugh, which has the sound of money in Fitzgerald's *The Great Gatsby*.[101]

In Cather's *The Professor's House* (1925), Godfrey St. Peter has won the Oxford Prize for History for his *Spanish Adventurers*. With his prize money, he builds a new house, where he retreats into history. Cather makes use of the past, or history, to reflect on the present and situate the traditional values she upholds. In contrast to modern commerciality are her strong figures of settlers and immigrants. In *My Antonia*, Cather gives readers the story of an earnest search for a new home and life, and a story of resilience. She includes noble characters that dream patiently, work faithfully, and endure, with a firm belief in the possibilities of the land. For Cather, the prairie states still held the virtuous and authentic life of the old world. In Cather's work, notes Hoffmann, the cities are not communities but rather places of isolation. Antonia Shimerda has moral courage and a "strong sense of what is proper."[102]

Cather is generally not identified with the high modernists; however, she did engage in experimentation with technique and point of view. Eudora Welty spoke of a "rare sureness" in Willa Cather's subject matter.[103] Middleton makes a case for Cather's modernism in her various uses of point of view and use of excision, that is, like Hemingway later, Cather leaves out certain details, and yet these spaces in her narrative imply a great deal that the reader is able to fill in.[104] The reader is an interpreter with the power to create and interpret. In her work *On the Art of Fiction*, Cather suggests that part of art's process is to cut away, to practice excision, "so that all that one has suppressed and cut away is there to the reader's consciousness as much as if it were typed on the page."[105] The idea is the same as Hemingway's: The writer evokes things by leaving things out. The reader comes to a work's suggestions. Jo Ann Middleton observes Cather's experiments in form and uses the term *vacuole* to suggest the gaps, or what is left out but implicit in Cather's fiction and Cather's "means of suggestiveness."[106]

Cather's awareness of the response of her readers is modernist, Middleton argues. Cather gives attention to the "fine reader," rather than the "cinema public."[107] This is a reader who can be engaged in an act of creation. She points to David Craig's observation that modernism

sought to create a distance between "quality" and the "popular."[108] This
was sometimes marked by difficulty, urging readers to work at a text.
Even so, Cather invites her readers to have sympathy.[109] Cather was
quite aware that shifts in point of view will affect a reader. In *A Lost
Lady*, readers create their own sense of Marian.[110] Cather was conscious that a novel is an interaction between a writer's text and a reader.
The author should respect and anticipate the engagement of the reader's imagination. Middleton points to Cather's sympathy with her material and to the reader who develops sympathy with her subject matter.[111] This is what Wayne Booth calls "keeping company."[112]

The readers Cather sought were those who were like friends. She
distinguished between amusement and art, observing that they serve
different purposes.[113] In her essay about Sarah Orne Jewett in *Not
under Forty*, she remarks that some writers seek a "sense of pitch" in
writing and language. People like a writer as they like individuals, "for
what he is, simply."[114] During this period of experimentation that we
call modernism, art crossed media boundaries into intermediality. Literature combined with techniques from the visual arts, music, and film.
The filmmaker is a storyteller who uses technical skills to create a film;
however, Cather was never impressed with the filmmaker's art and
never cared for what filmmakers did with her fiction. Warner Brothers
got the rights to *A Lost Lady* for a reported $10,000. Irene Rich ap-
peared in the January 1925 premiere as Marian Forrester, catapulting
the novel onto the best-seller list. Nevertheless, Cather disliked cinema
and especially did not care for adaptations of her novels. In 1934, Barbara Stanwyck played Marian Forrester in a remake. Cather disliked
this one so much that she refused any further films to be made of her
work.

Cather may have recognized that like the novelist, the filmmaker is a
storyteller who uses technical skills in a primarily visual medium to
communicate meaning, but a film cannot easily capture shifting points
of view in the same manner that Cather seems to have intended for *A
Lost Lady*. Rather than creating images or characters for a movie actor's
portrayal, Cather appealed to feeling. She respected the imaginations of
her readers enough to allow them to create these characters, in the
mind's eye as it were.

Readers always bring their lives and past reading experiences to
their reading. A reader helps create the characters of a novel by visual-

izing them in his or her mind. Aware of this, Cather attempts in *A Lost Lady* to convey a "single impression." She wanted an emotional response from her readers.[115] A unifying narrative voice and consciousness provides unity in a novel, but Cather's narrative disrupts the flow of events. She makes use of point of view for character development and imagery to help her novel cohere. Her use of Henry James's method of indirect presentation is often commented on.[116] Niels is an observing consciousness, and we see the action through him. The method here is like that of Fitzgerald's use of Nick Carraway as his narrator for *The Great Gatsby*. Niels's consciousness comes to us in a third-person limited point of view.[117] Faulkner's modernist novels *The Sound and the Fury* and *As I Lay Dying* would challenge consistent point of view.

Readers in Cather's locale in Nebraska were often told the news of their well-known author in the local newspaper, the *Red Cloud Chief*. When Sinclair Lewis, author of the popular novel *Main Street*, visited Nebraska in April 1921, he acclaimed Cather as a "greater author than [he] ever dared to be, although her books have had no phenomenal sale." He added that Cather, with Edith Wharton and Frank Norris, represented the "highest type of fiction written in America." The *Red Cloud Chief* reported that Lewis called Cather's *My Antonia* "one of the greatest novels in all American literature." When *One of Ours*, Cather's story of World War I, appeared, Lewis added, "Willa Silbert Cather is greater than General Pershing."[118]

Cather was clearly interested in appealing to the values of simplicity, resourcefulness, and independence. These were among the strengths she saw in America's rural communities. On November 3, 1921, she told the *World Herald* that she saw the smaller cities of America imitating the larger cities. "And she [plead] for development of individuality," notes the article that was reprinted in the *Red Cloud Chief*. Five days later, the *Alliance Herald* announced that the Alliance Women's Club would meet at 2:30 on Friday, November 11, at the city library. The subject was "Nebraska Writers." Mrs. Bogan was scheduled to give a speech entitled "Life Sketches of Willa Cather and Bess Streeter." Mrs. Alberta Reynolds planned to review "The Squirrel Cage" by Dorothy Canfield, and Miss Amy Sturgeon was going to read a poem by Neihardt.[119]

Publisher's statistics show the book's sales record and production costs. It is possible to show year by year how well Cather's books sold and suggest the growth of her audience in quantitative terms. One may also gain a grasp of the geographical distribution of Cather's books by investigating the records of Alfred A. Knopf, for example. Her readers are far more elusive. They were each situated in a personal history. In Nebraska, Cather's readers lived in specific rural communities and had different religious affiliations and family experiences. Who were Cather's "fine" readers? Clearly they were not only literary critics and journal editors. People in Nebraska were particularly interested in their homegrown author.

We know that people in Nebraska read *A Lost Lady*. The audience in Nebraska heard Cather speak about modern culture. Less is known about how they read her books. Newspaper commentary focuses on the author rather than her audience at these speaking engagements. Cather clearly sought what Middleton calls the "fine reader" of fiction. Yet, unless we can begin to find the autobiographies, letters, and journals of those individuals, their comments in letters to newspaper editors, or library records in Nebraska, their responses are lost to us. As Robert Darnton states, to move "from the *what* to the *how* of reading is an extremely difficult step."[120] Cather's audience might make for an interesting case study.

6

SOUNDS OF THE CITY

Theodore Dreiser, John Dos Passos, Anzia Yezierska,
Langston Hughes

American cities grew swiftly in the 1920s, with immigrants arriving from overseas and people seeking jobs in the industrial north. Cities rose upward with the construction of buildings to daring heights. The United States transacted business in its cities, hauled its products through them, broadcast its first radio programs from them, and recorded the pulse of life in city-based newspapers. This extraordinary growth of the nation's urban centers is highlighted in the fiction of the period. Many novels give us a look at the shape of cities, as they emerged as centers of American life. *Manhattan Transfer* by John Dos Passos, in particular, provides a sense of the fragmented vitality of New York. Likewise, the writers of the Harlem Renaissance give us a view of features of African American life in Harlem and beyond. The city of Chicago is portrayed in the fiction of Theodore Dreiser, Ben Hecht, Sherwood Anderson, and others, and it found its troubadour in the vigorous poetry of Carl Sandburg. Meanwhile, the writings of novelists from ethnic backgrounds, for example, Anzia Yezierska, offer us images of immigrant life in the city. Immigrant reading also emerged in the 1920s. Literacy and education amongst the young fostered a new generation of American readers.

THEODORE DREISER'S *AN AMERICAN TRAGEDY*

Theodore Dreiser gives us the city—not in any detail, but more as a place where striving young characters, shadowed by a kind of luckless ambition, meet one another. Early in *An American Tragedy* (1925) we hear of cities, as the narrator lists the missions that Clyde Griffiths's family passed through in Grand Rapids, Detroit, Milwaukee, Chicago, and Kansas City. St. Louis is mentioned, as is the idea of moving to Denver, suggesting a mobile society, the growth of urban centers, and the idea of opportunity. Clyde Griffiths, the protagonist of the novel, looks up at a twelve-story hotel made of glass and iron at 14th and Baltimore, where taxis are always waiting. There are stars hovering above a dark street, taxis and old-time carriages, and sounds of doors opening and closing. [1]

We are told of Clyde's contact with "some rough usage in the world."[2] He meets Hegglund from Jersey City. Ratterer has been in Buffalo, Cleveland, and St. Louis. Hortense, the "crude shop girl," looks at herself in a mirror. Perhaps she is a woman who catches a glimpse of her reflection as she passes by a dozen shop windows. In the midst of this scene, a "young negress" remains nameless; she is subject to erasure.[3] Amid this swelling, surging prose, bald statements appear that tell us such things as "Clyde had a soul that was not destined to grow up."[4] Peoria, Chicago, and Milwaukee are the sites of odd jobs Clyde and others can do: grocer's clerk, dishwasher, shoe salesman, Chicago delivery wagon driver.[5] From a life of deliveries to the Union League Club at Jackson Boulevard and work at the Great Northern, he escapes to upstate New York—Utica, Albany—where he meets Roberta. It is a fateful meeting, for once with him she soon drowns at a lake, and Clyde is pressed by a trial and collapsing dreams.

Dreiser participated in this abundant phase of American literature with a worldview developed during the late nineteenth century. On the one hand, he paid tribute to the business energy and ingenuity of the gilded age. On the other, he recognized that there was a Darwinian cast to its rapacity and ruthlessness. Dreiser's naturalism flowed from the age of realism and found its way to the American city, where the psychological and moral dimensions of humanity appear lost amid urban necessity and power. In *An American Tragedy*, we are drawn into the consciousness of Clyde Griffiths. We travel from the drifting world of his youth with his evangelical family to the naïve promise of his young adult years as he discovers the city. It is a world that has been secularized: a zone emptied of its vitality, where people live in compartments. He is drawn like a moth to the flame of gaudy ads and lights. Clyde is fooled by glitz and glare, the tawdry showiness that suggests privilege: gilded ceilings, the laughter of unsophisticated women dressed in undress like Victoria Secret models. He seeks the ideal woman, like Pygmalion wanting to carve perfection but unable to live with reality. The boy who rejected evangelical religion now worships idols. He worships Sondra Finchley, a "seeking Aphrodite" who wishes to be "free of any entangling alliance or compromise."[6]

Clyde's dream of business success in the employ of an urban hotel is like a sixty-second commercial that promises transcendence and then evaporates. He heads to upstate New York, where the river runs past the town of Lycurgas, the red and gray of its brick factories and a dreary life broken up only by his affair with Roberta Alden. Yet, even here the naturalness of sex and possibilities for love are defeated, and nature, in the form of a lake, becomes a site of death rather than renewal. Roberta longs for affection and Clyde's approval; however, once she becomes pregnant, Clyde does not want the birth of a child. Rather, he wishes to find a way to obstruct that birth because it will inconvenience him. Without any regard for moral questions and no ethical compass, he plots to overcome this burden. He finally decides not to kill Roberta but does so anyway in a boating accident on the lake.

Clyde has not changed. He is arraigned on a murder charge, and the remainder of the novel describes his trial. His mother's Christianity, or that of the minister who visits him in prison, cannot save him now. The forms of traditional faith cannot break through. The final chapter suggests that another boy, Russell, is out there and will repeat the cycle: He seeks to flee his family into the restless, incomplete story of another American tragedy.

JOHN DOS PASSOS, *MANHATTAN TRANSFER*

John Dos Passos wrote of life in the city with a critical pen. With his story of settlement in New York, he gave us a large, innovative novel intended to engage American society in reflections on the dreams of people arriving in New York. Dos Passos, in one sense, took the approach of a realist, giving an altogether real setting to his story. He used newspaper headlines and snippets from songs and wrote with numerous technical innovations. In his *U.S.A.* trilogy, biographies are dramatically integrated to capture a cross-section of America. This work tends to focus on social concerns even more than *Manhattan Transfer*, where we see both the lucky and the unlucky, the successful and the idealists, and those who play the game. In *Manhattan Transfer* there is, however, a strong sense of fatalism. In the 1930s, people were less concerned about the social structure than asking why things in the United States were not working.

The social and political aspects of the novels of Dos Passos are rather unyielding. He insisted on forcing readers to ask questions about the lives of people in different strata of American society. Like John Steinbeck in *The Grapes of Wrath*, Dos Passos focuses on the down and out, on social injustice. But whereas Steinbeck concentrated on character complexities, Dos Passos was apparently not as adept at creating three-dimensional characters. For instance, in *Manhattan Transfer*, Ellen Thatcher becomes a glittery character with magical, attractive qualities, and she is probably the most complex character in the book. Jimmy Herf is always dreaming of being elsewhere, yet he seems to lack psychological depth.

Manhattan Transfer is a point in New Jersey, one like Secaucus, where those attending the 2014 Super Bowl transferred to get to the game. In this novel, New York City has become a symbol of human striving, immigrant energy, and a force that might suffocate the individual; it is a place where bad choices can be made to derail a life. Dos Passos's characters are prompted into action by their desires. Jimmy observes it all: Ellen seeks conquests of men, money, and fame in the theater that leave her unfulfilled. Bud Korpening fears the city and falls into ruin. Stan Emory, an alcoholic architect, ends his own life, and Joe Harland likewise becomes an alcoholic, dead within life. Armand Duval, called Congo, seems to be the only character who succeeds in becoming an individual.

In *Manhattan Transfer*, Dos Passos makes use of montage techniques. He often spoke to interviewers about his interest in film and how it affected his fiction; however, the films of Sergei Eisenstein or Dziga Vertov were not available in America until after Dos Passos wrote his novel. The montage technique introduced by Eisenstein could only have influenced Dos Passos during a later period of his work on *U.S.A.* Yet, visual art and film clearly influenced the author's approach to *Manhattan Transfer*. Dos Passos sought the simultaneity of cubism and montage. From the time of *Three Soldiers* he had sought form, and it is there that we encounter the impressions of John Andrews. Dos Passos was painting at this time and living in Greenwich Village. He had been writing "The Moon Is a Gong," an experimental drama for the theater. He developed a synesthesia, drawing on many of the arts. The city was the subject for such painters as Charles Sheeler in *Aucassin and Nicollette* (1921), Charles Demuth in *Machinery* (1920), and George Ault in *Brooklyn Ice House* (1926). Charles Sheeler and Paul Strand created the short film *Manhatta*. Dos Passos brought all of this to bear on his fiction.

Immigration to the city created cultural energy. Dos Passos drew on cubism, futurism, and the motion of narrative and sought a theme of fragmentation. Lionel Trilling calls *Manhattan Transfer* an "epic of disintegration."[7] Dos Passos pursued in his writing something organic, voicing humanity in a 1920s culture of billboards, ads, subways, and Times Square. The center of this novel is the city itself: its movement and lives. Dos Passos gathers fragments of news clippings, voices, songs, and the elements of popular culture. His notebooks show that the various sections were written separately. He intentionally broke the sections into parts and then edited them, as a filmmaker would do.

Manhattan Transfer is a busy jungle of a place, full of traps that can eat one up. This place can dash one's hopes or grind down one's life, as Dos Passos shows. This is a New York City of revolving doors. Those who make the system work for themselves do so by whatever means are at their disposal. Those "succeeding" do so by cheating, manipulation, and fakery. Dos Passos shows a place that stomps on those who are vulnerable. What results is a seething gutter of human life in a struggle for survival. This is a dark vision of flawed lives that bump together. It is a nightmarish vision of New York in ferment, ready to explode. One has to ask to what extent this is a realistic picture of Manhattan. Or is this Dos Passos imposing his own apocalyptic worldview?

The author provides us with his comments on life in this environment in the form of character types. One of the primary fakes, cheats, and manipulators is Congo Jake, a pragmatic individual who is simply out to enjoy the good life. He ironically ends up on Park Avenue. Gus McNeil, out of the money he got for his injury while dreaming of leaving New York City, ends up as a Tammany Hall fixer. Dutch, who can't make it by getting a job after he leaves the army, ends up involved in crime and is sentenced to twenty years in prison. James Merivale plays the game and goes through the motions; he smugly passes judgment on others while escaping personal hardship. George Baldwin is committed to no woman but wants them all, married or not, and he is consummately ambitious in his law practice. Baldwin is quick to seduce women. He has a fascination with Ellen. It is clear that in his relationships, as in his legal work, he has no scruples.

At the center of Ellen Thatcher—if she has a center at all—is the question of identity. She is a chameleon actress who can become whoever people want her to be: Elaine, Ellie, then Helena. Her identity keeps changing, but there is an inconsistency about her. Ellen frames the novel. She is the baby at the story's beginning, afraid as she lies in her bed. She later leaves her own baby, Martin, in his crib and tells him not to be afraid. Ellen is attractive but lives something of a stage life.

Juxtaposed is a scene of Ellen with Jimmy Herf in which he says he will honor her choice to keep the baby. Ellen proceeds to get an abortion. Jimmy makes an effort to break from the city but struggles to do so. It is the psychological turmoil of these characters in which we get caught up. Dos Passos expresses a psychological truth as he portrays anguish.

With the lives of Jimmy and Ellen serving as the focal point of the novel, readers hear of their histories and emotions and how they respond to the city and a corrupted ideal of success. Ellen learns to dance so she can capture her father's affection. She becomes a dancer, actress, fashion periodical editor, and superficial success. Jimmy, returning from abroad with his mother, sees the Statue of Liberty in the harbor. He wants to join the July 4th celebration and waves his little flag, exiting near the immigrants who are arriving. As an adult he will not enter the family banking firm to perpetuate its version of success. He refuses to be caught in a revolving door or grinded out like meat.[8]

Ellen marries John Oglethorpe. She gets into theater, performing in musicals and advancing her career by flirting with producers and rich men. She falls for Stan Emory, who commits suicide and leaves Ellen pregnant with his child. She then conveniently marries Jimmy, but they divorce. Jimmy is a news reporter. In this role he sees urban corruption and collects bits of news stories. We see Ellen's distance and her loss of humanity in a "metal green evening dress."[9] We hear of her "dollself" and loss of authenticity. Jimmy becomes disillusioned with his news work and contemporary uses of language. Reporters, he concludes, are "parasites on the drama of life."[10] Journalism has become dehumanizing work and made him feel like a "traveling dictograph" and an "automatic writing machine."[11]

Manhattan Transfer includes a critique of the public press and journalism. In contrast are the "old words" of immigrants, American ideals, and something that exists above technology and machines. Jimmy symbolizes the United States and questions the values and fate of the country. The foundational formulations of 1776 are deemed important, not superficial materialism. Amid the skyscrapers, Jimmy seeks to reclaim the "old world." Typewriters rain confetti in his ears: He says, "If only I had faith in words."[12] He wishes to get out of the city machine and become whole again. Illustrating Jimmy's life, Dos Passos seeks a new language in visual art and film. He uses cubism to recognize simultaneity in time and the variety of city life, something not static but always in motion.

The first section is called "Steamroller." It is the human confrontation with deterministic forces. Ambition resides in Ellen. She goes with Oglethorpe to Atlantic City for a honeymoon and discovers that he is bisexual. They change trains at Manhattan Transfer: the railway station in New Jersey, where trains arrive on electric power. To get ahead "she'd marry a trolley car" says an actress of Ellen's ambition.[13] Her goal is to be "glamorous." Jimmy's story and Ellen's story are brought together via time shifts and cuts.

Bud Korpenning, from Cooperstown, appears in the first five chapters. He goes to New York to be "at the center of things."[14] He is exploited and cheated and lives in a flophouse, unable to sleep. A Bowery bum tells him to get out of the city while he can, but he has been the victim of domestic abuse. He walks over the Brooklyn Bridge, a "spiderwork of cables."[15] This is a callous city, and his death comes from this.

The novel is not one of narrative order. There are juxtapositions and structural schemes and images. Dos Passos presents a mechanical world, one spilling forth immigrant energy, caught in urban industrial life, seeking love and meaning in the web-like cables of the bridge, the shadows of skyscraper aspirations. Dos Passos rejects systems, seeks to reshape words and form—to humanize, to find power again in words, the human spirit, to save humanity. Utilizing cinematic techniques, he offers human consciousness in the city, a radical politics and theater in which the larger a nation is reflected in a city mirror.

For D. H. Lawrence, *Manhattan Transfer* was a "very complex film" about New York City.[16] T. Austin Graham points to the Cinderella tradition in musical theater and Dos Passos's transformation of the Cinderella myth into "something considerably less inspiring" in Ellen Thatcher.[17] Dos Passos was inclined to believe that experimental theater might revitalize the 1920s stage, and he critiques the musical theater enterprise, which had become increasingly commercial by 1925. The reader looks behind the scenes at the New York theater, at Ellen, who has become a representative figure and been called a star. "Dos Passos suggests that performers have grown dramatically and unhealthily disconnected from their audiences."[18] Ellen, who is always performing, has become a victim of this "system of cultural commerce."[19] Dos Passos hoped that audiences might shift their attention to other ideas of theater and popular culture.

Throughout *Manhattan Transfer*, the author uses fragmented narrative structure, a polyphony of voices. Ellen is a central figure amid this variety of characters, and like the other characters, she is terrified but hides it well. Graham calls her "a vortex, a body around which the others swirl . . . a common point of reference" amid this disconnection.[20] So too is Jimmy Herf, who falls for this stage symbol, this star of the gossip columns, an insincere user of whoever will advance her career. She is the shallow center of a media swirl: Her face is splashed across magazines. The movie actress lives amid the rumors of tabloid entertainment shows that take viewers behind the scenes. Her dress is featured in an empty affair of dazzle: a bold creature whose celebrity is built by sounds, imagery, and advertising.

In Dos Passos's view, the culture of musical theater is a fraud. His novel is only a step away from Nathanael West's 1930s critique of Hollywood in *The Day of the Locust*. The fantasy Ellen is at odds with is the isolated character she has become. Glamour falls into degradation. Willing to sleep with powerful businessmen and producers, the would-be starlet manipulates them to rise in an artificial world and comes crashing down, devoured by the industry, left with the reputation a fellow actress sees clearly: "Why that girl'd marry a trolley car if she thought she could get anything by it."[21]

Ellen represents the public's interest in gossip, an interest that, as Graham notes, came to define 1920s celebrity culture.[22] Yet, this woman uses coldness to escape reality; she is callous, pretentious, and paranoiac. For her, "It's not so easy never to be able to have friends."[23] She is always self-conscious, always onstage. Jimmy associates her with the Ziegfeld Follies girls, whose dancing becomes mechanical and whose aura is given over to mass production and marketing.[24] In this sense she is dehumanized and objectified, the kind of individual the band Foreigner would call "cold as ice." Dos Passos brings his reading audience less to sympathy and more to disgust with this manipulative woman, who, without any real relationship, is utterly alone.

The aural, polygot quality of the city is characterized in *Manhattan Transfer* by competing music from different apartments: "Apartment round about emitted a querulous Sunday grinding of phonographs." Heard are "It's a Bear," the sextet from *Lucia*, and songs from *The Quaker Girl*. In Sinclair Lewis's *Babbitt*, we hear of the "song of labor in a city built—it seemed—for giants." In *Main Street*, the word *phonograph* represents a talker who speaks in clichés.[25] In *Three Soldiers* (1921), Dos Passos writes that the "same dull irritation of despair droned constantly in his head, grinding round and round like a broken phonograph record."[26]

In his introduction to *Manhattan Transfer*, literary critic Alfred Kazin writes that Dos Passos captures with his novel the rhythms and energy of twentieth-century America. The enterprise of expressing the voice of the people found in Langston Hughes's poetry and fiction is also very much present in the work of John Dos Passos. In *Manhattan Transfer*, Dos Passos attempted to make objective the novel's action, while experimenting with fragmented structure. With *The 42nd Parallel*, which begins his *U.S.A.* trilogy, he takes this fragmentation a step further. Dos Passos sought to make the energy of the United States palpable in his fiction. He was a modernist in his experimentalism. Yet, with populist fervor, he created fiction in which he toiled to overcome what he called the "schism between Highbrow and Lowbrow."[27] His trilogy, like *Manhattan Transfer*, expresses the United States as an urban nation.

In *U.S.A.*, he offers a conservative statement. He had traveled the political spectrum, beginning as a leftist. With this change he tended to leave his socialist ideals behind. Dos Passos, like most writers in the post–World War II world, retreated from the large social canvas and focused more attention on the individual, the self.

Yet, overall, Dos Passos is excessive. His canvases are large. His writing is splashy. In contrast with Hemingway, who deals in subtlety and is somewhat impressionistic, Dos Passos is expressionistic. He deliberately exaggerates intensities, in a louder-than-life manner. Hemingway gives us concrete things and actions. Dos Passos gives us an intense attitude about what he is showing; a feeling is injected into the language. Hemingway concretizes things with nouns, moves things along with verbs, and underplays adjectives. Dos Passos runs strings of adjectives that lend a coloration to everything in his story. In Hemingway, meanings are implicit; we have to search for them. In Dos Passos, everything is spelled out. While Hemingway brings us into the worlds of first-person narrators, Dos Passos uses the third-person omniscient point of view. Hemingway exercises restraint and selectivity, Dos Passos uses "loaded" language and extroverted breadth.

Kazin comments on how Dos Passos's prose rhythms and images captured the rhythm and energy of twentieth-century America. To express the voice of the people is central to the work of Dos Passos. He once described his project as an effort to take in his times, across the broad range of life.[28] He wished to close the distance between high culture and popular culture. In *Manhattan Transfer*, Dos Passos applied techniques from modern art, film, and experimental theater. As a painter, he was keenly aware of innovations in visual art during his time. He was involved with experimental theater for several years, and critic Edmund Wilson remarks that this had much to do with shaping the style of Dos Passos in his *U.S.A.* trilogy.[29] The new art of film also caught Dos Passos's interest, and he learned from Russian film. In 1928, he visited the Soviet Union to look at the Moscow theater and work of dramatist V. E. Meyerhold. He became interested in Sergei Eisenstein's technique of montage and synthesizing, and aware of Dziga Vertov's concept the kino-eye. Film would continue to be an important contribution to this visually oriented novelist's work. In his *U.S.A.* trilogy, "Camera Eye" becomes the viewer, much like one who is watching a film.[30]

As the political perspective of Dos Passos shifted throughout his career, so did the perspective of his writing. In the 1920s, he was a liberal voice in fiction and experimental theater for "industrial and white-collar working classes."[31] He later became a conservative. During the 1920s, he was a writer who was interested in socialism, although he remained independent of the Communist Party and eventually became suspicious of it. His setting was the thriving city of working people and new immigrants. His theme was human freedom and authenticity. His works announced the human struggle against institutions that dehumanized people. In the mid-1920s, Dos Passos got involved with set design for the stage. At the same time that *Manhattan Transfer* was being published, an article by Dos Passos, "Is the Realistic Theatre Obsolete?" appeared in *Vanity Fair*, suggesting alternatives to Broadway theater. For *The New Masses*, Dos Passos wrote "Toward a Revolutionary Theatre" (December 1927), in which he discusses the limits of iconoclasm in political theater, as well as "Did the New Playwrights Theatre Fail?" (1928).

In his fiction, Dos Passos placed fiction and history in dynamic connection. He worked through an individual's perspective to comment on the changes taking place throughout history. The media of his day—newspapers, advertisements, radio, and film—became central to this project. In 1925, *Manhattan Transfer* made a start in this direction; however, it was in the 1930s and thereafter, in the *U.S.A.* trilogy, that Dos Passos's new style came into its own. "Newsreel" scatters fragments of headlines, news stories, tabloid announcements, and pop songs on the page. "Camera's Eye" provides slices of life, angles of vision. The result is a montage of items that might be likened to our evening news: a collection of images, sound bites, and news stories.

The first novel of the trilogy, *The 42nd Parallel*, looks at the years before World War I and American culture at the beginning of the war period. Women had recently won the right to vote. Yet, in Dos Passos's view, they were still under the control of cultural forces that hearkened back to the Victorian era of the late nineteenth century. For Ellen Thatcher in *Manhattan Transfer*, sex appeal was a form of power, something she could use to manipulate her way into achieving the kind of success she dreamed of. Ellen substituted a notion of sex and power for real relationships. Her dreams were ones of shallow materialism seeking respectability. Still, the alternative was obscurity and vulnerability to the large forces of a male-dominated world. Dos Passos argues that the modern world made mechanical beings of people. Civility seemed to break down in the mad rush along the road of modern life.

In *The 42nd Parallel*, "Mac" McCreary, a printer, enters the politics of unions and the labor movement. Mac is a working man who might suggest today's middle-class worker waving an "Occupy Wall Street" sign. Monopoly capitalism is emerging, and Mac is troubled by it. He is also a Fenian, an Irish nationalist, a man with an immigrant background looking back at his heritage; however, his feisty spirit of reform faces the harsh forces of nature and culture, which limit him. He seeks the promise of the American dream but soon retreats from it and participation in the labor unions.

In contrast with working-class men like McCreary and the middle class are Wall Street tycoons like J. Ward Moorehouse, a man born on July 4th. He has gained success in manipulating sales images. In his view, World War I is America's "great opportunity" for economic advancement.[32] Dos Passos portrays Moorehouse as a seeker of power and wealth who cares much about profits and little about the patriotism of the young men who have fought overseas. He represents a betrayal of the principles of America's founding fathers and reflects the politician who seeks power rather than liberty, justice, and freedom for people he is supposed to represent. Dos Passos's critique goes further as Moorehouse's affairs are revealed.

Material success is seductive for Janey Williams and Eleanor Stoddard. Janey is a secretary at a Washington law firm who becomes the executive assistant to Moorehouse. Her goal is material success. Eleanor is an interior designer who seeks taste, culture, and prestige, but she is involved in an exploitative relationship with Moorehouse. The shallow materialism of these women undermines their responsibility, as it does with Ellen in *Manhattan Transfer*, who chooses sex and power over relationship and ethics.

Dos Passos's subsequent novel, *1919*, is a satirical work that reflects bitter disappointment with Woodrow Wilson's plans and competitive capitalism. *The Big Money* completes the trilogy. Jean-Paul Sartre called Dos Passos the greatest American novelist of his generation. One might continue to see the relevance of Dos Passos's style in a postmodern age of sampling, cut-and-paste, and sound bites. He was a multimedia artist who had studied art and culture at Harvard. Recognizing that he was a romantic at heart, inclined to intellectualize, he encouraged himself to follow his other impulses to seize the day in action. He explored his interest in cubism, expressionism, and modern theater with *The Garbage Man* (1926) and *Airways, Inc.* (1928). He also wrote travel books, including *Rosinante to the Road Again* (1922) and *Orient Express* (1927), illustrating the latter, as well as his *U.S.A.* trilogy. Such a voice of distinction might be reclaimed for the political and aesthetic debates of our own time.

IMMIGRANT IN THE CITY: ANZIA YEZIERSKA

In another part of the city, on the Lower East Side, immigrant populations struggling to attain the American dream were being portrayed by such writers as Anzia Yezierska and Pietro di Donato. Yezierska, a Polish Jew, became a voice for the voiceless, a Cinderella figure in popular media whose stories of ethnic identity became widely popular. The writing of di Donato, who hailed from an Italian immigrant family, would emerge in the 1930s, with a powerful tale of workers and families that resonated during a socially conscious time.

Yezierska's readers included middle-class Americans who may have been introduced to her books through film adaptations, for instance, the production of *Hungry Hearts*. She reclaimed her family name after living in New York as Hattie Meyer. When her older brother, Meyer Yeziersky, arrived in New York at Castle Garden, the immigration site that preceded Ellis Island, he changed his name to Max Meyer. Anzia followed when she was about eight or ten years old.[33] The family lived in the tenements, with Anzia's older sisters working in the sweatshops while she was still in school.

Emerging from this experience was a confident, rebellious spirit, and Anzia insisted on going to night school, like her brothers, against her father's wishes. Her brothers became pharmacists, and her sisters left the factories after marrying. Anzia's journey would be a different one. She lived at the Clara de Hirsch Home for working girls while entering the New York City Normal School for teachers. Some affluent patrons had selected her as a charity case of merit and chose to pay her tuition for enrollment in Columbia University Teacher's College. This was indeed advantageous for Anzia; however, her father evidently pointed out the fact that Jewish girls from traditional families were expected to marry rather than advance their careers.

Meanwhile, Anzia's benefactors had set forth a prescribed curriculum of domestic arts that would, in effect, limit her to food preparation and household management. But Yezierska wanted to study literature and philosophy. Accustomed to diligent work, she encountered students for whom college was a "good time," a four-year party. Her own interests tended toward acting and the dramatic arts. While teaching at P.S. 168 on East 105th Street, she took drama lessons and decided that writing would be a better way to make use of her talents.

The notion of marriage eventually entered her life, and Arnold Levitas seemed a good possibility, but she abruptly married attorney Jacob Gordon—and then just as abruptly left him. The annulment stunned her relatives.[34] The May 23, 1911 edition of the *New York American* carried the photo of Hattie Meyer Gordon, whom the newspaper said asserted that marriage was a spiritual friendship.[35] The chutzpah of Anzia Yezierska was already apparent. She soon received her Columbia diploma, reconnected with Arthur Levitas, and set off to work at a settlement house. She also set out to speak with esteemed educator and philosopher John Dewey. Dewey was outspoken about democracy and the strengths that the immigrant population could contribute to American life. His *Democracy and Education* (1916) had recently appeared, and it seemed to Yezierska that she should speak with him about her own quest for democracy, women's rights, and support for the immigrant's American dream. Resolved, she walked into his office. And so began a relationship that seems to have been built on friendship, with occasional romantic overtones.

Dewey was more humane than some of the other educators she had met. He responded to the intense young woman and visited the elementary school where she was a substitute teacher. He may have liked her originality, her spunk, and the way in which she challenged him and the profession of teaching. Dewey read her stories and offered his encouragement, urging her to write about what she knew, her experiences with education, and her encounters with those who had been condescending to her as an immigrant. He advised her not to blame them but to be like an "explorer [in] a strange country."[36]

Yezierska, still known as Hattie, took Dewey on tours of the Lower East Side, at his request. She questioned him about the way he wrote his books. Why did he write so abstractly, like an intellect who was talking to other scholars? She commented, "In your letters . . . you are St. Francis, loving the poor."[37] Yezierska argued that people would understand him better if his writing was conversational. Dewey said that his books were indeed for other scholars and people in the profession. Yet, he also wrote poetry, which he shared with her. She wrote stories that she shared with him. "Soap and Water and the Immigrant" expresses her criticisms of American education. Dewey bought her a typewriter so she could write more stories.

In 1920, Edward O'Brien, editor of *The Best Short Stories* anthology, selected Yezierska's short story "The Fat of the Land" as the best short story of the previous year, initiating a change in reception for Yezierska, whose name was now being recognized. Her stories began to appear in *Harper's*, the *New Republic*, the *Nation*, *Good Housekeeping*, *Metropolitan*, and other magazines.[38] "The Immigrant Speaks," printed in *Good Housekeeping*, is an autobiographical account of her work in the sweatshop environment and her family's efforts to pay rent and buy food. By now Dewey had gone to China, and she tried to make contact with him through the Y.M.C.A.

The publishing firm of Houghton Mifflin, on East 40th Street, encouraged her to write a novel. Editor Ferris Greenslet agreed to publish a book of her short stories, which would become *Hungry Hearts* (1920); however, it was her personal meeting with Dr. Frank Crane, a former minister and syndicated columnist, that brought further results. Crane reported in the Hearst newspapers that a Jewess from the East Side had walked into his office one day and enabled him to look "farther into the heart of Russia and Poland" than he had ever been able to do through his reading.[39]

The film companies of William Fox and Samuel Goldwyn were requesting the film rights for *Hungry Hearts*. Yezierska had received a two-hundred-dollar advance from Houghton Mifflin. She was now being offered $10,000 by Goldwyn for film rights—a large sum in those days. Goldwyn began to crank out publicity announcing the appearance of the East Side Cinderella.[40] Fox, who had Lower East Side beginnings of his own, began to draft a proposal for the movie rights for future works. It was a lucrative offer that Yezierska did not want to be bound by.[41]

When the *Bookman* asked the author to review three books, she added a fourth: Dewey's *Democracy and Education*, which had appeared four years prior. In her first book review, she repeated the comments she had made personally to Dewey. Writers ought to reach the masses, she asserted; they ought to also address people who think with the heart rather than the head.[42] In the meantime, Edward O'Brien asserted that some of the best new literature in the United States would be coming from the "younger elements of . . . mixed racial culture."[43] Yezierska worked in California with screenwriter Julian Josephson on "titles" for the silent film *Hungry Hearts*. She was disappointed by the addition of a rewrite by Montague Glass (a "sleek, smiling man in golf tweeds") and the editing of the film.[44]

Salome of the Tenements, Yezierska's next novel, was written quickly. When Houghton Mifflin passed on it, she offered it to Horace Liveright, whose firm Boni and Liveright published it. The novel appeared in November 1922. Historian James Harvey Robinson advised her to ignore the critics, saying that they have to appear to be all-knowing and wise to keep their jobs and that they are neither. He warned her not to be taken in by their superior air.[45] *The Hungry Hearts* film, which opened on Thanksgiving, assisted the sales of her novel. Grosset and Dunlap produced a movie version with photographs from the film. Fisher Unwin published *Hungry Hearts* in Britain. In 1922, Yezierska met Clifford Smyth, who at that time was editor of the *New York Times Book Review*. He soon left to become editor of the *Literary Digest International Book Review*, and he would soon introduce her to a broader international reading public.

Children of Loneliness (1923) followed, published by Funk and Wagnalls through Smyth's connection with that company. With the title story, a novella, the book gathers together a variety of pieces by Yezierska, who was then at work on her next novel. The *New York Times* critic called her overly autobiographical. In her next work, she responded with a stronger novel, the one that many consider her masterwork: *The Bread Givers* (1925).

The Bread Givers is a work of fiction that recalls a daughter's struggle for a voice and maturity as she tries to find new-world independence from a traditional Jewish father, who is something of a rabbinical scholar. This work of fiction is indeed autobiographical but not factual. The family lives in a dirty tenement, stuffed with her father's papers and books, pots and pans, clothes, and the kind of items one might sell at a garage sale. The sisters are the bread givers who dutifully carry out the father's wishes that they work in the sweatshop and meet men they can marry. They are not permitted to make their own marital choices and are set up in relationships by a matchmaker. The narrator chooses a different direction, escaping from the household.

When the novel was published, Garden City, Long Island, was the site of a garden party given by Doubleday. *The Bread Givers* stirred the critics and attracted readers. William Lyon Phelps writes in the *International Book Review* that the story worked on its readers: "One does not seem to read . . . one is too completely inside."[46]

Before long, Yezierska published another novel, *Arrogant Beggar* (1927), with Doubleday, after consideration by Houghton Mifflin. She continued to deal with the reprint rights clause in her contract with Houghton Mifflin for *Hungry Hearts* In *Arrogant Beggar*, Adele Lindner is a Jewish sales girl cast as the "arrogant beggar." She moves out of her tenement and into a home for working girls. The novel recalls the gift given to Yezierska, and one may wonder why she was not more grateful for the opportunity that led to her enrollment in Columbia University Teacher's College. Yet, it is clear that she did not want charity; she wanted to make it on her own efforts, and, of course, she did.

COMMON READERS IN CLEVELAND

Cleveland is the home of the baseball Indians, Case Western Reserve, and the Rock and Roll Hall of Fame. It is also home to one of the largest circulating library collections in the United States. At night the city is awash in the yellow glow from streetlights along Euclid Avenue. If you take a train into Cleveland toward the Terminal Tower and Public Square, you will pass through an area that was once an Italian neighborhood called Haymarket in the early 1920s. It was from this high-crime district of the Third Ward that "Big Italy," a twelve-year-old boy, walked to the Cleveland Library in 1925. Edward D'Alessandro lived in a cold water–only walk-up on Race Street. It was a fifteen-minute walk from the arcade to the corner of East Third Street and Superior Avenue—and the public library. A future career librarian,

D'Alessandro was already a bibliophile. Teachers suggested that he might need eyeglasses, but he would not tell his parents that.

This boy who grew to love books is an example of a common reader. These are the readers who seldom leave any traces of their reading habits. D'Alessandro was not a notable political figure, writer, editor, or wealthy industrialist whose writings historians and archivists hurried to preserve. Yet, we do have his autobiography. He became a librarian. He was the child of an immigrant family, and his story reminds us of children from immigrant neighborhoods who not only spoke and read the English language but actively sought out books, stories, and ideas. D'Alessandro represents the "average" American who goes to the public library.

Cleveland invested in the construction of a new library in 1923. It became a place where its middle-class workers, laborers, increasing black population, and children of immigrants like D'Alessandro could find books, periodicals, and information. The Cleveland Public Library was like the Holy Grail for the boy. One day a librarian spied him entering the building and guided him toward the Lewis Carroll Room on the third floor, where he saw a wonderland of books. He recalled the knowing smile and blonde bobbed hair of Margaret Phipps, the children's librarian, who selected books for him. He took home four books on a fourteen-day loan and library applications for his family.[47] These were children's books of the 1920s and classics like those on the posters in the Lewis Carroll Room: *Treasure Island* and *Alice in Wonderland*. Within a few years, Edward became the family scribe, writing letters for the family to his brother Nick, who had graduated from John Carroll University in 1924 and was attending the St. Louis University School of Medicine. His brother Sol began working in a shop at East Technical High School and Horn Lithograph Company.[48] Edward D'Alessandro simply wanted to work at the library. From him we get some images of what a valuable city library looked like in the 1920s.

On May 20, 1927, the day that Charles Lindbergh took off on his famous flight to Paris, D'Alessandro, age fourteen, became a library page for the Cleveland Library at the Brownell Junior High School. Inside the three-story brick building, Dorothy Tobin taught him the Dewey Decimal System. In his autobiography, he describes her as a slender woman, about thirty years old, with shoulder-length brown hair, who always wore a jacket and a skirt; however, that autumn he could see the concern on his parent's faces. The family would have to move because a train line was going to be built for the Shaker Heights line. Eviction came in the fall of 1927, and in January, while walking home, D'Alessandro saw his house being razed and felt angry. A worker's gaze met his and looked stunned, staring at the troubled boy.

What the young Cleveland resident later learned was that the Van Swingeren brothers, Cleveland real estate developers, had capitalized on the deal, enhancing their railroad assets. Ironically, one of them would die some years later on a train approaching the Hoboken, New Jersey, station just outside New York City, where much of their company business was centered. When he recovered from the shock of seeing the family house being demolished, D'Alessandro recognized that there was still hope for his family. Although they had been displaced, they had moved to East 116th Street. His father Rocco was a tailor who had always emphasized family values and learning English, and he had found a public transportation route to could get him to his shop for work. D'Alessandro continued to find his way to the main library building on Superior Avenue. His "love affair with books," as he called it, led to forty years of work with the library.

The Cleveland Public Library made itself available to everyone, as did public libraries throughout the United States. Linda Anne Eastman opened the shelves to the public for their own perusal and selection of books. The library purchased Sinclair Lewis's *Main Street*, *Babbitt*, *Arrowsmith*, *Dodsworth*, and *Elmer Gantry* upon their publication, meaning that anyone in Cleveland could read them, as they can now. Today the novels are available in print, on audio books, and in e-book formats. The Library of America volumes of Lewis's fiction are also on the shelves, as are his other writings. The children's library section of the library that D'Alessandro once loved has grown to house a collection of some 130,000 books. On the second floor one can find the literature collection, including novels from the 1920s. There are another thirty branches throughout the city. The library welcomes more than 800,000 visitors each year.

If you go into the library for information about the city, you will learn that the city of Cleveland grew substantially between 1910 and 1920. An increasing number of African Americans traveled north for industrial jobs. By 1921, there were 78 black congregations in the city. In the winter of 1918, there were 44. This number continued to increase in the following years. Of 22,000 Negro church members, 14,000 were Baptists. Antioch Baptist was the largest church in the city. Black urban life in Cleveland was affected when industrial employment was hit hard by the Great Depression in the 1930s, resulting in a general decline of the lodges and a new interest in black folk traditions.[49] Still, the blacks of Cleveland showed a "common sense of destiny" in all socioeconomic classes, says Kenneth L. Kusmer.[50]

Immigrants from Eastern Europe poured into Cleveland before the National Origins Act prohibited further immigration. The population of Cleveland grew more than 300 percent. The public library system responded to the new Polish population with a small selection of materials in their native language. Polish immigrants clustered in neighborhoods near Catholic Church parishes. St. Stanislaus became the largest of these parishes in the Cleveland diocese. Cleveland had sections that could be referred to as Katowa, Warsawa, Krakova, Poznan, and Kantowa. Some tensions arose between Irish and Polish groups, resulting in neighborhood squabbles. Steel and iron workers filled Cleveland, and in 1920, Poles comprised more than 20 percent of the U.S. Steel and Wire Division labor force.[51] In 1920, estimates were that anywhere between 50,000 to 80,000 first- and second-generation Poles lived in Cleveland. The National Origins Act of 1924 limited East European immigration to the United States; however, by that time Polish communities were firmly established, including those in Cleveland.

Italian immigrants also gathered in such Cleveland neighborhoods as Haymarket or "Big Italy" in the Third District. They too had their own newspapers, which fostered awareness in the community. Italian immigrants in Cleveland's Murray Hill section were opposed to Prohibition. Wine was a common feature of many meals at the time that the Nineteenth Amendment was enacted, and Italian involvement in the liquor trade was equally common.[52] In Chicago, Prohibition heightened criminal elements, including the bootlegging escapades of the notorious Al Capone. Italian immigrants in Cleveland resisted associations with racketeers and other criminal activity. *La Voce* printed word of arrests but opposed using any ethnic labels. In 1928, however, the Cleveland House of Corrections continued keeping a list of numbers of criminals by ethnicity.[53]

The meeting of black culture and white culture in Cleveland was epitomized by the sound of jazz and the blues. Jazz in Cleveland arose from the energy of acts that traveled from the jazz and blues scene in Chicago. Ethel Waters sang in Cleveland, accompanied by Fletcher Henderson on piano. Bessie Smith performed at the Globe Theatre. Bix Beiderbecke emerged as a startlingly good player and recorded with Gennett Records, which made its home in the city. In 1923, King Oliver was in Richmond, Ohio, to record pieces like "Chimes Blues," with Baby Dodds on drums, Lil Hardin, and Louis Armstrong, who played his first recorded solo. During the "Dippermouth Blues," Bill Johnson called out, "Oh, play that thing." In the mid-1920s, Gennett Records secured jazz artists from Chicago and grew the company. In 1928, it cut 1,200 masters. By the early 1930s, Gennett was out of business. But people in Cleveland could still remember shows by the likes of Artie Shaw, who played in Cleveland with the Joe Cantor Orchestra and then with the Austin Wylie Orchestra in 1927.

Keeping track of events in Cleveland was Louis B. Seltzer, who became editor of the *Cleveland Press* in 1926 and continued in that role until 1966. In his autobiography, he notes that his love of reading was encouraged by his parents. Seltzer would likely be called something other than a common reader because he made his living as an editor. Charles Alden Seltzer, his father, was among the most prolific authors of westerns in the 1920s, publishing two novels in 1919 and sixteen more in the next decade. It was said that he wrote two hundred stories before he received his first acceptance by a magazine. The editor's memoirs make it sound as if he was always surrounded by paper. Seltzer would buy bond paper for his father from Alderman's Stationery Store. His mother wrapped his father's manuscripts for postal delivery, and the family celebrated his first acceptance by *Short Story* magazine.[54] He claims that as a newspaper boy, at eight years of age, he decided that he wanted to work in the newspaper business. He was soon reading books like *The Three Musketeers*.[55] His mother, who saw him "always reading," cautioned him that he was going to "ruin his eyes."[56] His mother objected to the "trash in the cheap books" they were printing.[57] Instead, both parents encouraged him to read "good books," including the Bible.

At the age of thirteen, Seltzer applied for a job as a reporter and met Victor Slayton, an editor who recognized the name of his father. The city editor, wearing a green eyeshade and glasses, decided to give him a job as an office boy. It was the beginning of a long and distinguished career. By the 1920s, Seltzer was indeed working for Cleveland news-papers. In 1921, he became city editor of the *Cleveland Press*. By 1926, he was editor in chief, a position he held for four decades. The *Cleveland Press* was one of the primary sources of news and information for Cleveland residents in the 1920s. The *Cleveland Plain Dealer* was its biggest competitor.

Seltzer, D'Alessandro, and the immigrant and African American readers of Cleveland represented the thousands of readers throughout the United States who spent time reading the fiction of the 1920s and 1930s. The city of Cleveland, with its thriving library collections, developed one of dozens of well-supported libraries that brought those books to them.

THE HARLEM RENAISSANCE

In September 1921, Langston Hughes stepped out of the subway at 135th and Lenox and walked to the Harlem branch of the New York Public Library up the street.[58] The literary voice that was emerging in that part of the city was extraordinary, and Hughes wanted to get in touch with those African Americans. Miss Ernestine Rose was in charge of the Schomberg Center and assisted there by Catherine Latimer. Hughes was exploring the work of James Weldon Johnson, a writer whose fiction, poetry, and reflections would become central to African American literature and culture in the 1920s. Johnson said, "A people that has produced great art and literature has never been looked upon as distinctly inferior."[59] As if to back up his comment, Alfred A. Knopf would republish Johnson's *Autobiography of an Ex-Colored Man* (1912) in 1927. The Schomberg Center would continue to collect artistic resources and remains a valuable repository of the African American experience.

Hughes, who is better remembered as a poet than a writer of fiction, entered Columbia University as a freshman with plans to write. He began a story that would become his first and only novel, *Not without Laughter* (1930). Hughes was a young man in step with Harlem and its musical culture. He writes that if he had been rich he would have gotten a house with a doorbell that played Duke Ellington tunes.[60]

In *Not without Laughter*, his novel about the 1920s, James "Sandy" Rogers lives in Stanton, Kansas, a fictional variation of Lawrence, Kansas, where Hughes grew up. The story begins when he is nine, nearly ten. The Williams family lives in a house on Cypress Avenue. Presiding over the family is his grandmother, Hager Williams, who can recall slavery in Alabama and has three daughters: Tempy, Annjee, and Harriet. Annjee is Sandy's mother, who married Jimboy, his father. Sandy, like his father, is a bit lighter skinned than his mother and aunts. Tempy is married to Arkin Siles. She works for the Red Cross, assimilates with white society, and believes in Woodrow Wilson. She subscribes to *Ladies' Home Journal* and criticizes her nephew Sandy's tastes in black music. She is a reformer, always trying to "improve his manners and taste."[61] Tempy and Arkin do not live in the same house as Sandy, who criticizes their middle-class pretensions and accommodation to white ideals. Annjee and young Harriet become the focus of the novel's reflections upon protest and accommodation. Meanwhile, Hager encourages Sandy to be responsible and honorable, and to aspire to the greatness of such men as Frederick Douglass and Booker T. Washington.

Early in the story, a tornado rips through town, tearing away the Williams's porch. Later, when Jimboy censures Sandy for buying candy with the coins that Hager gave him for Sunday school, we hear about his creed of honesty. Sandy's father rejects those, white or black, who get rich by stealing, and he passes his ethical worldview on to his son. Hughes, one of the central figures of the Harlem Renaissance, would communicate that worldview to many readers, primarily as a poet.

Hughes arrived in Harlem as the 1920s began. Haarlem was a Dutch name, a section of New Amsterdam. During the 1920s, there was an influx of blacks into the area.[62] Black culture in Harlem became a strong influence on the arts. Black America was working to define itself. James Weldon Johnson used the terms *Afro-American* and *Aframerican*.[63] W. E. B. Du Bois asserted that blacks had a vital culture of their own. This place of brownstones was a black community. Lawrence Levine sees this period as one of the Negro "looking inward," seeking revitalization.[64] In *Harlem Renaissance* (1971), Nathan Huggins writes about black self-definition and "self-determination." In "The Negro Speaks of Rivers" (1929), his first poem to achieve national recognition, Hughes details the historic ancestry of African Americans. Jessie Fauset immediately published the poem in the *Crisis*. In his autobiography,

The Big Sea, Hughes acknowledges the importance of this periodical, edited by W. E. B. DuBois, with Fauset as its literary editor, in bringing his work to a wider public.[65]

Poets like Langston Hughes and Claude McKay faced the difficult heritage of the American Negro. They asserted the determination and resilience of people who faced struggle and by referring to jazz, spirituals, and the blues. In his novel *Banjo*, Claude McKay offers cabarets and parties, pleasure and struggle. In "The Weary Blues" (1926), Hughes portrayed the blues "coming from a black man's soul." We see a piano player with ebony hands on ivory keys playing out his soul.

Hughes's poems are candid about black city life. They are often conversational and reside in a world that is linked with jazz, blues, and gospel music. In 1926, the blues, which he had known and loved his entire life, more vigorously entered into his poetry. In his poems in *The Weary Blues* (1926) and *Fine Clothes to the Jew* (1927), Hughes did not flinch from looking at the less than "respectable" aspects of black culture. The *Chicago Tribune* called the book "a study in the perversions of the Negro." In New York, the *Amsterdam News* called Hughes a "sewer dweller."[66] William H. Ferris, who had edited *Negro World*, claims that this left the bad impression amongst white readers that this is the only way that black folks lived.[67] Benjamin Brawley contends that Hughes, in his rebellion against middle-class complacency, was perpetuating a lower-class stereotype.[68]

The author spoke out about the Harlem Renaissance writers' portrayals of blacks in the *Saturday Review of Literature* and the *Nation*. He viewed racial self-consciousness as a response to segregation. He felt that artistic expression ought to be freed and urged black writers to embrace writing about issues of working-class poverty.[69]

In his poetic attempts to express the black vernacular, Hughes turned to the blues, which would inspire an entire century (and more) of popular songs. Reference to the "blues" appears throughout his writing. We see the children's poem "The Blues," the short story "The Blues" in *Simple's Uncle Sam*, and the short story "The Blues I'm Playin.'" Hughes has given us lyrics to the song "Blues at the Waldorf," composed by David Martin, as well as the song "Blues Montage," composed by Leonard Geoffrey Feather. Along with "The Weary Blues," there are poems entitled "Blues at Dawn," "Blues Fantasy," "Blues in Stereo," and "Blues in a Box." Indeed, blues lie at the heart of Hughes's expression as a poet. He makes use of lyric forms, ballad stanzas, and blues and jazz rhythms in poems like "Reasons Why." He uses call and answer form in poems and gives us blues culture as a subject of such poems as "Cabaret" and "Young Singer." Among his poems are "Barefoot Blues," "Bound No'th Blues," "Crowing Hen Blues," "Down and Out," "Fortune-Teller Blues," "Hard Luck," "Homesick Blues," "Juice Joint: Northern City," "Little Green Tree Blues," "Maker of the Blues," "Mid-winter Blues," "Po Boy Blues," "Red Roses," "Six-Bit Blues," "Red Clay Blues," and "Young Gal Blues." His poem "Curious" is one stanza arranged in six lines of a blues lyric.

Jazz is largely rooted in the blues. The blues and jazz culture enters Hughes's work in many places. *Montage of Dream Deferred* (1951) has jazz flowing through it, as does *Ask Your Mama*, which is a jazz performance piece heavily influenced by jazz. There is "Beale Street," "Cabaret," "Cabaret Girl Dies on Welfare Island," "Jazz as Communication," "Jazz Band in a Parisian Café," "Jazzonia," "Jazz Girl," "Lady in a Cabaret," "The New Cabaret Girl," "Nude Young Dancer," "BeBop Boys," and "Jazz, Jive, and Jam." Hughes later wrote the lyrics for *Street Scene* (1947), a book by Elmer Rice, with music by Kurt Weill. His interactions with music continued. Bebop sounds appear throughout *Montage of a Dream Deferred*. Hughes's gospel musical plays from the 1950s combine gospel songs with a loose plot. He wrote *Ask Your Mama: 12 Moods for Jazz* (1961).

Hughes was one of thousands of African Americans who moved to Harlem between 1910 and 1930. Among blacks there was a sociological shift from the South to the North and from rural environments to industrial work in the cities. In *Black Manhattan*, James Weldon Johnson estimates this at about 1.5 million people.[70] This meant a concentration of African American readers for books, periodicals, and newspapers in America's northern cities. Appealing to this new readership was the *Crisis*, a publication begun by Du Bois, and *Opportunity*, a periodical that had a black and white readership of about 70,000 by 1928.

"Our Literary Audience" (*Opportunity*, February 1930) is Sterling Brown's exploration of the psychology of the African American reading public. Brown begins by saying that "we are not a reading people." He tells readers that as a group they do not read as much as they should. His essay, of course, encourages his readers to read more. Brown considers critical readings, white readers, and characterizations of figures in literature in which the image of black culture is depicted. Fine literary artists like Langston Hughes and Jean Toomer, he says, are criticized for facing reality and showing truth. They ought to be commended. Too often books by black authors are looked upon as sociological documents rather than creative literature. Negro books must be more than "optimistic tracts for race advertisement," he says.[71] Critical thinking is important too. Readers may resent what does not flatter them, and fictional pictures of blacks are not always pretty, nor are they necessarily representative. Black writers cannot evade writing about Memphis dives, southwest Washington, or other difficult areas, Brown relates. If the truth of these environments is represented in fiction, this reality must be faced squarely, for "rushing away from them surely isn't the way to change them."[72]

New voices were beginning to emerge, and Horace Liveright was among the first white publishers to support this new literary movement. Liveright published Jean Toomer's *Cane*, Nella Larsen's novel *Quicksand*, and Alain Locke's essays collected in *The New Negro* (1925). Wallace Thurman followed the lead of Sinclair Lewis in giving attention to female characters in his fiction, for example, Emma Lou in *Blacker the Berry* (1929). Readers could follow Thurman's work in the *Messenger*, begun in Harlem in 1917. Toomer, a light-skinned black who might "pass" as white, wrote to white critic Waldo Frank, saying, "I cannot think of myself as being separated from you in the dual task of creating American literature."[73]

Toomer's *Cane* is a miscellany of styles. There are six short stories in the first section, with interpolated verse. There are seven short stories in the second section and nine verses. The third section is comprised of the novelette *Kabnis*. The stories in the first part are set in Georgia. In the second section, Toomer shifts to Washington and sets one story, "Bona and Paul," in Chicago. Reviewing the novel in the *Crisis* (1924), Du Bois questions how well Toomer knew Georgia. He calls *Cane* a collection of short stories and poems. Alton Locke, in the *New Negro* (1925), calls Toomer's work a novel. Since a central protagonist and plot is not to be found, one may ask if it can be called a novel. Yet, if one considers Sherwood Anderson's gathering of sketches in *Winesberg, Ohio* a novel, one might consider Toomer's *Cane* a novel as well. Like Laurence Sterne's *Tristam Shandy*, it brings together a variety into an organic whole. In 1969, a paperback version of *Cane* appeared, and the novel has appeared in a sturdy edition by the Library of America.

An interest in Harlem's black culture was aroused in white writers, editors, and scholars, who were also supportive. Sherwood Anderson devoted attention to Toomer's work, and Vachel Lindsay was enthusiastic about Hughes's poetry. Zora Neale Hurston, studying anthropology with Franz Boas, was introduced to white literary circles by Fanny Hurst.[74] White writer Carl Van Vechten's own work intersected with the Harlem Renaissance, and he became one of its strongest proponents.

Van Vechten had a lengthy career on the New York literary scene. Soon after he arrived in New York, Theodore Dreiser, editing *Broadway Magazine*, gave Van Vechten an assignment to write on *Salome*. Van Vechten became an assistant to *New York Times* music critic Richard Aldrich in the fall of 1906. By the early 1920s, he was visiting black music clubs on a regular basis. He was ahead of the trend that would bring hundreds of white audience members to the Cotton Club and other locations in Harlem. As Leon Coleman points out, Paul Robeson, Laurence Brown, and Jules Bledsoe sang at Van Vechten's apartment parties in New York.[75] William Rose Benet, who heard them there, writes in the *Saturday Review* that the more spirituals he heard the more moving he felt them to be.[76]

Van Vechten wrote a series of articles on the blues in *Vanity Fair*. He urged Knopf to publish Hughes's *The Weary Blues*. In March 1926, he praised Bessie Smith. He reviewed seven collections of spirituals in the *New York Herald Tribune*, on October 25, 1925, December 20, 1925, and October 31, 1926. Van Vechten encouraged black writers to make use of their folk heritage for self-awareness. Du Bois, however, was not pleased with Van Vechten's novel *Nigger Heaven* (1926), about life in Harlem. There was too much dialect, too much emphasis on what Van Vechten called the "squalor of Negro life, the vice of Negro life."[77] Yet, Van Vechten was a believer in the vitality he saw in the arts in Harlem. Langston Hughes and Claude McKay received honorable mention awards in the Van Vechten Awards of 1927, which he sponsored in *Opportunity*. Dantes Bellegarde won the award for his essay entitled "Haiti under the United States."

Van Vechten believed that black gospel spirituals and the blues were the "most important contribution America has yet made to the literature of music."[78] Writing on black spirituals, he admired their "unpretentious sincerity" and "simple, spontaneous outpourings from the heart of an oppressed race."[79] He insisted that the songs be recorded for preservation.[80] Yet, Van Vechten lamented that many of the songs were not being sung in dialect and was concerned about a loss of authenticity.[81]

James Weldon Johnson was among the closest writer-friends of Van Vechten. He emphasized Van Vechten's assistance in bringing attention to African American writers. On September 28, 1929, Johnson wrote the following in a letter to Van Vechten: "Dear Carl, Has anyone ever written it down—in black and white—that you have been one of the most vital factors in bringing about the artistic emergence of the Negro in America?"[82]

"There is going to be a riot of interest in Negro music," Van Vechten wrote to Johnson, "You now have the upper hand. Don't let anyone else get it."[83] Van Vechten calls Johnson's *Autobiography of an Ex-Colored Man* an "invaluable source book" for the study of Negro life. In his review of Walter White's novel *Flight*, he brings positive critical notice to the work of James Weldon Johnson, Charles Chesnutt, and Paul Lawrence Dunbar.[84] In his review of *Blues* by W. C. Handy, Van Vechten refers to Johnson's strong support of the blues in his writing.

On Thanksgiving Day 1925, Van Vechten met Bessie Smith backstage at her concert in Newark, New Jersey. He and his companion were the only white people in the audience. Hughes wrote to Van Vechten the following January that he had also met Smith backstage in Baltimore. According to Hughes, "She remembered you but didn't seem at all concerned as to whether articles were written about her or not. And her only comment on the art of the blues was that it had put her 'in de money.'"[85] By that time Smith was famous for the hits "Baby, Won't You Please Come Home" (1923), "T'Aint Nobody's Business if I Do" (1923), "Careless Love Blues" (1925), and "The St. Louis Blues" (1925, with Louis Armstrong playing the cornet).

Smith had begun her recording career with the line "Gee, but it's hard to love someone when that someone don't love you." "Downhearted Blues" (February 15, 1923) was the first Bessie Smith recording to be released. It was number one for four weeks and sold 780,000 copies in six months.[86] She was paid a flat fee of $125 per side. The hit record helped to salvage Columbia Records, which was going through hard times; however, Smith was never paid a percentage of mechanical royalties. Al Jolson received 75 cents for every recording of a song released on the Brunswick label. He earned $70,385 for "There's a Rainbow around My Shoulders" and "Sonny Boy," which sold 938,466 copies. When Smith began collaborating on writing songs, she received performance rights as a writer. Although she did not earn royalties on her records, Smith made money from her live performances. As of 1925, she was earning about $2,000 a week, paying her musicians and troupe from her earnings. Porter Grainger, who had written for Smith, recognized that Van Vechten could be of much help to them. Smith went to one of Van Vechten's parties, but only to please Grainger. She felt thoroughly out of place, drank a lot, knocked down Van Vechten's wife, and left early.

Langston Hughes called spirituals and the blues "two great Negro gifts to American music." His book *The Weary Blues* digs deep into that tradition for a language that speaks the blues. Hughes engaged in blues phrasing, voicing, and structure, and brought forth the oral appeal of the blues medium. He writes, "Let the blare of Negro jazz bands and the bellowing voice of Bessie Smith singing the blues penetrate the closed ears of the colored near intellectuals until they listen and perhaps understand."[87]

White audiences were drawn to Harlem by curiosity as much as any interest in jazz. That middle-class blacks were materially successful and some lived in Harlem's spacious brownstones may have been surprising to white visitors, who assumed that most African Americans were destitute. The city was filled with surprises. In *The Great Gatsby*, as Nick drives across the Queensboro Bridge with Gatsby in Gatsby's car, they pass three "modish" blacks—two men and a woman in a limousine—who have a white chauffeur. Here, Nick observes, "anything can happen."[88]

While Hughes's poetry shows the struggle of many blacks in 1920s Harlem, there were others who were well-situated. In Jessie Fauset's novel *Plum Bun* (1929), Angela lives in a rundown place in Greenwich Village, while her sister lives in an upscale brownstone in Harlem.[89] But finding a voice and articulating it in literature was often problematic. Black writers still largely relied on literary models from white writers. In the arts, there were more black music and theater performers than writers. There were many talented black actors and actresses; however, their talents were primarily used by white playwrights, directors, and producers. Publishers were white, as were theater producers. The black theaters, the Lafayette and the Lincoln in Harlem, were owned by whites. *Shuffle Along*, the long-running musical by Eubie Blake and Noble Sissle, attracted mostly white audiences. Yet, their theatrical work was outstanding, as was the acting and singing of stage artists like Paul Robeson, whose career emerged from the singing of gospel spirituals. He had been a ballad singer in cabarets. During that time he acted in Eugene O'Neill's *Emperor Jones* and *All God's Chillun Got Wings*.

African Americans inevitably made their most visible impact in the arts in the blues and jazz. Johnson depicts the jazz band as a "playing-singing-dancing orchestra, making dominant use of banjos, mandolins, guitars, saxophones, and drums in combination."[90] Louis Armstrong, King Oliver, Sidney Bechet, Fletcher Henderson, and Duke Ellington were among the jazz musicians who provided the soundtrack of their time. From New Orleans to Kansas City, St. Louis, Chicago, and on to New York, the music migrated. On April 6, 1923, Oliver's "Chimes Blues" was recorded with Armstrong on cornet, Honoré Dutrey on trombone, and Johnny Dodds on clarinet. The piano parts were played by Lil Hardin, who would become Lil Armstrong. Bill Johnson added some banjo and Baby Dodds played the drums. "Cake Walkin' Babies Blues" came two years later, with Bechet playing alongside Armstrong. Bechet was brilliantly individual in his playing but a difficult personality, and he soon took off from New Orleans for Europe. Meanwhile, Armstrong, on cornet, was becoming legendary. He changed music by insisting on its potential for soloing and daring improvisation.

Louis Armstrong pushed the ensembles he played in. He gave rhythmic energy to King Oliver's group in 1922 and, by 1924, was soloing fluently in Fletcher Henderson's band, prodding the band to swing and encouraging saxophonist Coleman Hawkins to develop his art. He was one of the greatest improvisers and trumpet artists of all time. His brash melodic lines soared; he twirled on glissandos, crafting solos with rhythmically punctuated riffs, and played seemingly impossible notes sustained with vibrato. In Chicago, Armstrong assembled his Hit Five: Johnny Dodds on clarinet, Lil Hardin on piano, Johnny St. Cyr on banjo, and Kid Ory on trombone, playing "Heebie Jeebies," with Armstrong contributing the vocals. By 1927, he had moved from cornet to trumpet and added Pete Briggs on tuba and Baby Dodds on drums, replacing Kid Ory with John Thomas on trombone and creating a Hot Seven for "Potato Head Blues" and other tunes. He opened "West End Blues" on June 28, 1928, with a stunning nine-bar cadenza, backed by Earl Hines on piano. He featured his unique phrasing in "Tight Like This" on December 12. Armstrong recorded Fats Waller's "Ain't Misbehavin'" on July 19, 1929, quoting George Gershwin's *Rhapsody in Blue* and pieces from known melodies. When "Black and Blue," by Fats Waller and Andy Razat, was recorded in the same sessions three days later, Armstrong's vocals suggested that to be a black man is to be black and blue. Such a protest lyric by black composers and a black vocalist was unusual in 1929, although the issue was soon highlighted in fiction by William Faulkner. W. C. Handy's "St. Louis Blues," three minutes on a 78 rpm record, was one of Armstrong's last recordings of the 1920s (December 13).

The Great Depression shook the music industry as much as it did other areas of life. Armstrong, however, was tapped as an entertainer and a gravelly voiced singer. Singing popular songs in the 1930s, he turned to greater commercialism. He performed for white audiences, appeared in such movies as *Rhapsody in Black and Blue* and *Going Places*, and became a trickster figure who played with minstrelsy. Ralph Ellison compared Armstrong to an Elizabethan clown, and jazz trumpeter Miles Davis complained that he grinned too much. Yet, no one could dispute the innovative art in his playing in the 1920s, and he often rose to the occasion with artistry throughout the next several decades. It would take Charlie Parker, Lester Young, John Coltrane, Miles Davis, and Ornette Coleman, among others, to elevate improvised jazz solos to other extraordinary levels. Ellison's invisible man would feel displacement as he listened to Armstrong's trumpet. Louis Armstrong had by then become Satchmo, crystallizing his career with humor and sentimental vocals that proclaimed "What a Wonderful World."

T. S. Eliot's *The Waste Land* is a kind of jazz, Wyndham Lewis once said—although what he meant by jazz is anyone's guess. F. Scott Fitzgerald once wrote that the jazz age was first sex, then dancing, and then music. One might suggest that for Fitzgerald, drinking, writing, and Zelda might also be placed before the music. For Fitzgerald, the jazz age was a generational, cultural signifier. The term was not a commentary on musical style but, rather, connoted a sense of the energy and aura of the age. Jazz was about a perceived freedom, a kind of being in the moment with the courage to improvise. One could be primitive, youthful, and daring and toss off the constraints of Victorian propriety. For Eliot, jazz may have been a modern voice, a jazzy minstrel voice that he could weave into his poetic reflections, as David Chinitz, T. Austin Graham, Michael North, and Ann Douglas have suggested. For Wallace Stevens, William Carlos Williams, and Hart Crane, it provided inspiration. Langston Hughes would write the blues into such poems as "The Weary Blues."

Musically, jazz was something else. It was blues meeting syncopation, an aching soul giving voice to pain and celebration, a community of individuals listening, speaking in rhythm and melody, improvising together. Duke Ellington once said that he would call jazz "Negro folk music" if pressed to put a label on the art form to which he gave orchestration.[91] Jazz, he said, was his mistress. Whatever jazz was, Fitzgerald did not really "get it" musically. Still, he astutely recognized jazz as the soundtrack of his time and an apt symbol for a new development in American culture.

In the 1920s, this wonderful world included all of the beautiful things Louis Armstrong sings about. It also included the urban energy restated by George Gershwin in *Rhapsody in Blue* and John Dos Passos in *Manhattan Transfer*. Jazz was at the roots of the Harlem Renaissance: a black cultural expression that became a feature of the urban pulse of the time, intersecting with the world of white audiences and bringing newfound wealth and social energy to the men who recorded, promoted, and distributed it.

7

HISTORY AND MYTHMAKERS

Edith Wharton, William Carlos Williams, Stephen
Vincent Benet, John Steinbeck

In the last pages of *The Great Gatsby*, the narrator, Nick Carraway,
reflects on the promise that Dutch explorers once saw in the vistas of
the New World. Thus, Fitzgerald concludes his story of Jay Gatsby with
a reflection on the American dream. It is a story that, in an age of sound
bites, downloads, Facebook, iPods, and iPads, will continue to prompt
reflection on the dream that one is pursuing and why. To pick up a
novel of the 1920s is to discover a new way to look at the American
dream. It is to see again the ambitions and dreams of individuals and
the choices they have made. Patience is indeed a virtue when one picks
up a long Theodore Dreiser novel or the stories of John Dos Passos or
William Faulkner. Yet, if we slow down and truly take those stories in,
their meanings become part of our lives. The works of Ernest Hemingway, Willa Cather, Zora Neale Huston, and Sinclair Lewis address fundamental human qualities, questions, issues, and hopes. Through these
American novels we can begin to make better sense of our own lives
and time.

With *The Great Gatsby*, F. Scott Fitzgerald creates an enduring
myth and dissects a dream at the center of the American ethos. His
novel, like other novels of this period, was part of the nation's story and
reflects its life. A person who picks up these novels of the 1920s may
find how one fits into history and the American dream of today. Several

American writers of the 1920s turned to history and social experience to create fiction with a mythical scope, much like Homer did when he gathered together the epic tales of the ancient Greeks.

Readers in the 1920s were curious about how they fit in. The historical novel was quite popular during this time, as Ernest Leisy's *The American Historical Novel* demonstrates.[1] Library records show that book borrowers were drawn toward reading history. Circulation ledgers in the New York Society Library for this period show a steady pattern of borrowing books on U.S. and European history. H. G. Wells's *The Outline of History,* in which the author talks of progress, was a best seller; however, Oswald Spengler's earlier *Decline of the West* runs counter to Wells's optimism. Translated by Charles F. Atkinson, this history, in two volumes, asserts that history is made up of cycles, contrary to the progressive orientation of both Marxism and liberalism.

The same sense of both optimism and crisis occurs in 1920s fiction. Perhaps this can be likened to the hopes and concerns of our own time. The sensationalism of the 1920s is not unlike the sensationalism in some of our own media. The 1920s was an age of celebrity, a period of fads and conspicuous consumption, a time of dreamers and frauds. The challenged ethics of the 1920s Teapot Dome Scandal politicians and Prohibition period bootleggers are comparable to the lack of regard for human life exemplified by those who perpetrated dot-com schemes. Dos Passos, Dreiser, and Fitzgerald offered their readers dreamers, risk-takers, and heroes—like Amory Blaine, who sometimes were only legendary in their own minds. They gave readers characters who were living ethical lives and opportunists who acted out ambitions contrary to the dreams of America's founders.

During a period of rapid change, American writers were concerned with how the present fit in with the past. Such writers as Edith Wharton, William Carlos Williams, and Stephen Vincent Benet looked back at history, knowing that what was considered progress in the present needed to be anchored in ideals and values. Many of the novels of the 1920s take a backward glance: Anderson's *Winesburg, Ohio* recalls the beginning of the century, Lewis's *Main Street* portrays the 1910s, and Wharton's *The Age of Innocence* reaches even further back to upper-class culture in New York in the late nineteenth century.

American literature's portrayal of the vitality of the immediate present was echoed by the progressive historians of the 1920s. In *The*

Mind in the Making (1921), James Hervey Robinson writes of the prospects of liberal hope. Vernon Parrington's *Main Currents of American Thought* (1927–1930) offers a glimpse into the American past, with a hopeful Jeffersonian ideal for the future. Charles Beard examines the economic origins of America's foundations. Meanwhile, literary critic Van Wyck Brooks inquires about American culture in a series of books that sharply critique the country's cultural experiment. In *The Ordeal of Mark Twain*, Brooks asserts that Twain became a case of arrested development because of the limits of American culture. In *The Wine of the Puritans* he insists that art and the life of the mind was not valued in the United States as much as practicality and profits. The result was a lack of sustenance for artists like Mark Twain.

Fitzgerald, for example, has often been described as a writer who was caught between his interest in his craft as a novelist and material prosperity—the quest for money, for which he churned out short stories and went to Hollywood. Van Wyck Brooks underlines this dichotomy in *America's Coming of Age*, where he argues that the idealism of transcendentalists faced Benjamin Franklin's emphasis on Puritan practicality and opportunism. William Carlos Williams was even more critical of Franklin in his alternative history *In the American Grain* (1925). Williams, like Brooks, believed that the Puritans had damaged the national culture. The Puritans became a target of the social critics. Religion had become a scapegoat in the critique of an outmoded morality connected with the Victorian Age and, further back, the Puritans. Charles Beard, seeking to correct the record, asserts in the *New Republic* (December 1, 1920) that the term *opprobrium* was used for anything that interfered with the "new freedom." In contrast, in *Religion and Capitalism*, R. H. Tawney connects Puritan thinking with economy and business efficiency, which served as an engine for modern industrial development.[2]

During the same year that William Carlos Williams wrote his impressionistic history of the United States, Gertrude Stein offered up *The Making of Americans* as a reflection on families and generations. Her history is one of a continuous present in which human actions unfold. Fitzgerald wrote to her in June 1925, to say that he was anxious to get her book and learn from it.[3] But there were others whom he could have learned from as well. After missing the opportunity to see Edith Wharton one day in May 1924, Fitzgerald wrote to Thomas Boyd that she was a "very distinguished grande dame who fought the good fight with bronze age weapons."[4]

Wharton seemed to him to express a style of the past, and Fitzgerald sought to be alone so he could work on *The Great Gatsby*. He told Boyd, "I am going to read Homer and Homeric literature—and history 540–1200 AD."[5] With confidence that he was writing the Great American Novel, for those moments, he mused about finding an imaginative space removed from the business of contemporary life where he too could fight the good fight.

EDITH WHARTON, *THE AGE OF INNOCENCE*

Edith Wharton's family was from old money, and money meant a lot to F. Scott Fitzgerald, who read her fiction. The culture of old New York may be what his character Jay Gatsby aspires toward but, with his ostentatious display, can never quite reach. The energy of the new era was still decidedly bound by the vestiges of nineteenth-century commerce, but the 1920s saw the extension of credit and a new emphasis on commodity production and marketability. "Keep up with the Joneses" was the rallying cry of the new consumerism. Edith Jones had no need to heed this. She was already one of the Joneses, a prosperous family of old New York. By the time she married Edward "Teddy" Wharton at Trinity Chapel in 1885, she had lived most of her childhood and adolescence in Europe. The phrase can allegedly be attributed to her family, whose wealth and property in Manhattan and Newport, Rhode Island, provided her with considerable means. Nonetheless, Wharton did not settle for Victorian notions of an elite debutante's role—one that did not allow women to work. For her, this was trumped by a commitment to writing and exploring society in her stories. Women at all levels of society were often denied opportunities to develop a career, and they could not vote in the United States until 1920. Wharton, treated by Dr. Weir Mitchell as a young woman, was encouraged to write, in contrast with Charlotte Perkins Gilman, who wrote despite the "rest cure" prescribed to her. She had an obvious talent for storytelling and never stopped writing.

Edith Jones Wharton experienced the culture, pretense, and mores of the stratified society that she portrays in her 1920 best seller *The Age of Innocence*. She received the encouragement of Henry James to focus on the culture and society that she knew and became one of our great novelists of manners. In her short stories and longer fiction, she critiques social behavior and values, while upholding principles of conduct and moral awareness. Wharton deals with marriage and relationships, the behavior of people amid social pressures, and issues of the artist and society. She offers the viewpoints of men, for example, Newland Archer in *The Age of Innocence*, and women, for instance, Lily Bart in *The House of Mirth*. *The Age of Innocence* gives readers a nostalgic view of upper-class society in old New York. Newland takes an interest in the young Ellen Olenska but stays with his wife, May Wellend.

The Age of Innocence received the Pulitzer Prize in 1920, after the committee withdrew its recommendation for Sinclair Lewis's *Main Street*. At the time, Wharton was living in France. Following a divorce in 1913, she made France her home. When World War I began, she dedicated much of her time and attention to war relief efforts, traveling to the front five times, raising more than $100,000, and setting up funds and assistance for Belgian orphans displaced by the conflict. In *Fighting France* (1915), Wharton urged the United States to join the war effort in Europe. She also wrote the novel *The Marne* and later *A Son at the Front*, about a father's response to his son's sacrifice in the war. In "Writing a War Story," she challenged writers who merely wrote about the war rather than getting involved in it. With "Coming Home," she portrays a French citizen's antipathy for Germans who had left a path of destruction throughout France.

Wharton's novels are moderately paced and richly textured. Patience with the slow narrative journey of a Wharton novel has its rewards. As she develops characterizations, she offers an insightful panorama of a social scene, inviting her readers to view and listen to the proceedings. In *The Age of Innocence* we meet an elite class that is so regulated by propriety that they almost seem trapped. The scene of an opera becomes a public event much like the Golden Globes: a place for gowns and gestures—and to be seen. The attendees are hyperconscious of one another's presence; however, it is not at all clear that they like opera. Wharton's narrative critiques their superficiality, while creating the well-rounded characters of Newland and Ellen.

When *The Age of Innocence* was filmed in 1992, it became a box office hit, and the book once again became a best seller. Still, for contemporary audiences to enter the narrative requires a patience that our Internet world of instant "facts" may be attenuating. Wharton's writing is more like that found in a nineteenth century novel than today's genre page-turner. Readers enter a context and an experience, not a welter of rapid information. Her novels are coherent portraits of society of the past that call us to be reflective about our lives and the world around us. Wharton looked back in time, but her work is timeless. The pace of *The Age of Innocence* is slow and rather stately in comparison with some current works. It can be read with the sense of irony favored in much contemporary writing. Yet, it is far from a television drama. Wharton explores the characters and ethos of a particular time, place, and society, and asks us to witness, think through, and allow ourselves that willing suspension of disbelief by which we imagine and experience another time—perhaps an age of innocence, but also one that speaks of human society throughout time and beckons us to reflect on our own age.

Wharton was indeed of an older generation than the youthful writers of the 1920s, Fitzgerald or Hemingway, who also published with Scribner's; however, their respect for her work is evident. Fitzgerald may have become identified with genius and dissipation, charm and waste, but throughout the boom of the Roaring Twenties he was an observer of culture, as was Wharton. He remained a conscious craftsman of fiction, and Wharton was among his models. When Fitzgerald met Wharton in France there was an awkward shyness about him. His comments were always deferential. There is little record of Hemingway talking about Wharton's fiction, but he was clearly aware of her work. Several of her books were in his library.

Wharton belongs to the age before World War I. Her sensibility is closer to that of Henry James than a young Fitzgerald or Hemingway. Wharton wrote of the past and its values. She lived in Europe in the 1920s and only returned to the United States briefly in 1923, to receive an honorary doctorate awarded to her by Yale University. Her major works, for instance, *The House of Mirth* (1905) and *The Age of Innocence* (1920), concern themselves with a time before the 1920s. Her novels of the 1920s appear to reach for a popular female audience. *A Son at the Front* (1923), *A Mother's Recompense* (1925), *Twilight Sleep* (1927), and *The Children* (1928) lack the power of her earlier works. The stories of *Old New York* (1924) contain far less vigor than *The Age of Innocence* (1920), Wharton's most poignant and well-crafted work of that period.

The Age of Innocence is a masterwork in which the imaginative Ellen Olenska is everything that a heroine ought to be: resourceful, inquisitive, independent. Although she is descended from one of those first families of the elite, she has no love for pretense or propriety, nor does she care for the opera, occupying one's box, and attending parties in the proper manner. She marries a Polish count and then leaves him. She wears a velvet gown to the opera and sits next to May Wellend, her cousin, who is always obedient to convention. Newland Archer likes Ellen's vitality but marries May because it is proper. The family encourages him to dissuade Ellen from getting a divorce. Responding to this charge, he falls in love with Ellen. He is doomed to face a New York high society that thinks he and Ellen are lovers, when they are not. Newland has accepted the propriety and duty of his society rather than break free from it. In his acceptance of his social role, he is its victim, a man with a truncated life, a lost love, and all the right conventional social behaviors.

WILLIAM CARLOS WILLIAMS, *IN THE AMERICAN GRAIN*

Picture a car from the 1920s slowly climbing a hill that leads to 131 West Passaic Street in Rutherford, New Jersey. A row of Victorian frame houses stand on a residential street a few miles walk from the town center. At the house where William Carlos Williams was born, steps lead to a wide front porch. The front door opens into a spacious front room, where, it has been said, Williams's mother once performed séances. William Carlos Williams wanted nothing to do with his mother's Caribbean mysticism or the church across the street. His religion was Keats and Whitman, and the human compassion and scientific training that came with becoming a doctor. Ezra Pound visited the Williams home on Thanksgiving Day 1910. It is here that Pound would later stand on a chair to kill a mosquito. H. D. (Hilda Doolittle) went with him to meet Flossie, the girl Williams would marry. On February 13, 1911, Williams and Pound walked together in what was then called Kipps Woods, an area now filled with residential homes. This would be the last time Williams would see Pound for another thirteen years.

Pound went to London on February 22 and soon made an impact on T. S. Eliot and other modernist artists.

Williams met Pound at the end of September 1902 in 303 Brooks, a freshman dorm at the University of Pennsylvania. On Tuesday, September 30, while in his room after dinner, Williams may have been looking out the window at the botanical garden when he heard someone playing the piano in the next room. He picked up his violin and began to imitate the melody. Morrison Robb Van Cleve knocked on his door. When Williams conceded that he was not really a musician and was mostly interested in poetry, Van Cleve suggested that he meet the crazy poet he knew and went to go get him. And so began a sixty-year friendship between William Carlos Williams and Ezra Pound—one that would greatly influence modern American poetry.

In the 1920s, Williams's poetry came forth in small magazines and such volumes as *Spring and All* and *Kora in Hell*. Kenneth Burke, a friend, points out in an earlier review that Williams gazed intently at surfaces and concrete things and had a "complete disinterest in form."[6] Meanwhile, in his short stories, Williams described life amongst his patients. He began a novel and also wrote plays for the Rutherford Little Theatre. One of his most interesting works of the mid-1920s is *In the American Grain* (1925), his account of American history.

Dr. Williams was not a historian. He was a man who was fascinated by the nation's past and what he thought it said to the present. With poetic imagination he crafted a book in which he reflects on what he saw as the subconscious features of the American experience. In *In the American Grain*, he considers key figures of a mythical cast: Leif Erikson, Spanish conquistadors, Benjamin Franklin, Daniel Boone, Sam Houston, Abraham Lincoln. His series of sketches is an impressionistic gallery of improvisations in which he seeks the American mind and the American character. Williams was concerned with places; he believed that history occurred in daily life, within locales, and that each of us has our place in history. His sketches are more like fiction than the logical, analytical pieces of historians. He takes great liberties with his history, as when he offers a fictional journal from Sir Walter Raleigh; however, if history is also stories and anecdotes, one might say that this book can be read for Williams's style and insights more than his historical grasp. The modernist twist Williams brought to his work may make this a somewhat challenging read. Nevertheless, it is an interesting look at what has been called the "American experience."

For *In the American Grain*, Williams engages a rather peculiar range of characters, from Leif Erikson to Edgar Allan Poe. Like many other artists of his time, he believed that Puritan attitudes thwarted modern progress and that the Puritan legacy was "like a relic of some tribe."[7] There is courage in his attack on Benjamin Franklin, in whom he saw the manifestation of Puritan values. Williams also presents his unconventional assessment that American wealth grew out of fear.

As a poet, ever an innovator, Williams lived in Rutherford. As a doctor, he was an obstetrician at Passaic General Hospital in nearby Passaic, where he tended to the needs of an immigrant population, as well as the immigrants in East Rutherford, Lyndhurst, Wallington, and Garfield. It is an area that dips into the New Jersey Meadowlands, within sight of the skyline of Manhattan.

Williams's father was English. His mother was Puerto Rican and came from a mixed background of French, Creole, Spanish, Dutch, and Jew. While attending Horace Mann High School in New York City, he remained focused on poetry. In John Keats he saw elegant phrasing and a sense of poetic craft. In Whitman he felt the pulse of the American idiom: a raw, cosmic vision presented in natural speech. Williams would follow his lead and break with form to refashion through imagination a direct treatment of objects: the thing in its local conditions. He started with the material he knew: the lives of his patients or the red wheelbarrow he saw in a neighbor's backyard. So much depended on seeing things for what they really were. He followed life into those ordinary places and wrote quickly, scribbling notes on prescription pads. His typewriter rattled in the office during brief breaks with patients. When he moved into a house at 9 Ridge Road, close to the center of town, he tapped on his typewriter into the evening in an upstairs room.

Williams was a full-time doctor, one who made house calls, but few of the locals knew that he was also a full-time poet. He listened to local people's voices and the sound of their speech, hearing something common, earthy, and clear-sighted. Williams became a poet of Imagism, seeking concrete images and language. *Spring and All* (1923) looks at the American landscape, finding the potential of spring birth in the industrial rumble. In contrast with Eliot, Williams wrote of hope, in the spirit of Whitman and self-reliance. Wastelands with footnotes were not for him. Imagination would break through like the clear cut of the river winding past East Rutherford.

Williams's writing on early spring in the Meadowlands and the Paterson environs were written at the same time as T. S. Eliot's *The Waste Land*. Perhaps they are, in part, a response to Eliot, with whom Williams disagreed. In a quite different style, Williams suggests hope for rebirth "on the road to the contagious hospital."[8] He saw this landscape on a daily basis as he drove his Ford Coupe toward the Meadowlands or on Union Avenue and across the bridge to Passaic.

After completing *Spring and All*, Williams mostly wrote prose for the rest of the decade. His focus throughout this period was America, historically and mythically remembered in *The American Grain* (1925) and locally in his stories. As he remarks, *In the American Grain* is his search as a child of immigrant parents to see what the America of his "more or less accidental birth must signify."[9] It was his search for the American dream. Williams also wrote *A Voyage to Pagany* (1928), based on his trip to Europe in 1924, as a traveler looking back at the United States. By 1924, several young American writers had gone to Europe, to Paris, where some of them remained for quite some time. Williams merely visited. His practice and business was in Rutherford and to Rutherford he returned.

Williams had begun a novelette in 1921, while feeling skeptical about the American progress that was being touted by the newspapers. He wrote *The Great American Novel*, or so he called his story of eighty-one pages. William Bird published it in a short-run for Three Mountains Press, the same firm that had first published Hemingway. He printed 300 copies of Williams's novelette in the spring of 1923, along with Ford Madox Ford's *Women and Men*, Ezra Pound's *Indiscretions*, and stories that would be in Ernest Hemingway's *In Our Time*. The book did not sell well.

The novels of William Carlos Williams that followed never made any real impact. Williams's novels form a trilogy: *White Mule, In the Money*, and *The Build Up*. While writing these works, he was also writing *Paterson* and other poems and delivered about 2,000 babies. In the midst a busy practice, on scraps of paper, the doctor continued to make brief jottings—glimpses of life, fragments. They showed objects and corners of life in northern New Jersey. Williams knew that the broad reach of a novel was something else. A novel was more like distant thunder and lightning that lit up an entire landscape. Poems were like crystals, but novels required plots. Dare he imitate the focus of Joyce's *Ulysses* on Dublin by looking at New York or a nearby place like Paterson? He would use the natural speech of Americans, the American idiom. He would find sure words and the feeling of contemporary America: news and letters, flappers and jazz, and silent film.

Williams steadily worked on *In the American Grain* for a year and a half. In a letter to Monroe Wheeler he says that he wanted to work on the "Americana pieces."[10] The poet-doctor took notes for some of this work at the New York Public Library. He took the train from the Rutherford station, as he had done regularly while attending school years earlier with his brother. He had a secretary in Rutherford who helped him with some of the typing; however, to complete his personal history of America he knew that he needed some time off from his busy medical practice. He chose to take a hiatus from the summer of 1923 until the summer of 1924.

Williams lived with his wife Floss at 54 East 87th Street off Central Park with their friend Louise Bloecher. He and Floss later traveled to Europe. Their sons, Bill and Paul, were nine and six. Lucy, a black maid, watched over the children at 9 Ridge Road. Razor Watkins, the Rutherford football coach, assisted Dr. Albert Hoheb, a cousin on Williams's mother's side, and his wife Katherine Rader Hoheb in running the practice. They had a room at 9 Ridge Road. Katherine was busy completing her residency at Passaic General Hospital. She would eventually become head of obstetrics there. Their child, Albert Carlos, was born in 1925 and lived in Rutherford.

The Williams children were thus treated to the attention of some interesting guardians while their parents were away. Watkins had played halfback at Colgate University and been named to the All-American team in 1917. He was an aviator in World War I and graduated from Colgate in 1920. While coaching in Rutherford from 1923 to 1928, his team won two state championships. In 1927, the team was undefeated, and he returned to Colgate to coach in 1928. The following year his team was not only undefeated, they shut out every team they played against.

Williams made regular trips to the New York Public Library on 42nd Street to look for letters and journals and explore U.S. colonial history. Investigating Alexander Hamilton and Aaron Burr, he developed a revision of the story of Aaron Burr in his section "The Virtue of History." He lived privately and focused on his work. Only Kenneth Burke and a few others had his phone number. [11] By the fall, he was making arrangements to travel to Europe. In November he wrote to Burke, saying, "Hemingway is a star, I think. . . . Who is he anyway?" [12]

From Williams's work on *In the American Grain*, an idiosyncratic study of the American dream, emerged *Paterson*, a long poem that some have called an epic, which can, of course, be debated. What is clear is that the poem is a diagnostic look at the modern world and the everyday speech of Americans within it. Preparation for *Paterson* involved reflecting on several key questions: Who are these people? What is this place? What language of life is spoken here? His own locality was highly significant, and Williams asserted "the whole world is about me." He knew that his readers were a small following, readers of modernist journals. Only a few of the locals would ever read his work. They were busy striving, struggling, and raising families. Literature was not their thing. This was the voiceless crowd, the inarticulate roar of the river to which he was trying to give voice. The central image of *Paterson* is of a man lying on his side, filling the place where his thoughts reside. A prominent symbol is the Passaic River, which is intended as a primal river and reflects the flow of human life and language. Paterson itself is an industrial prototype. It was the place where Alexander Hamilton once envisioned a manufacturing economy issuing from the rushing water power of the Great Falls. Like Fitzgerald's Long Island or Whitman's *Manhatta*, it was a symbolic image of the American dream.

STEPHEN VINCENT BENET, *JOHN BROWN'S BODY*

Twice a Pulitzer Prize winner, Stephen Vincent Benet, like William Carlos Williams, is better known as a poet than a writer of fiction. Yet, as a young man, he wrote stories to make a living and support his craft as a poet. Benet was a contemporary of Fitzgerald and Hemingway; however, unlike them, his time spent overseas in Paris was brief, and he was not a fellow traveler with high modernism, which likely had some impact on his subsequent reputation. Benet was intensely interested in American history and folk tales and myths that illuminated the

American experience. In his stories, myths, legends, and dreams are intertwined with America's history.

Benet's first public work of fiction, *The Beginning of Wisdom* (1921), is a college novel of the young generation that never caught on like Fitzgerald's *This Side of Paradise*. While working on his novel, Benet was quite conscious of that of Fitzgerald. He insisted that his work was less gaudy. It was also less popular. The *Bookman* printed the story in three installments, and Henry Holt published the novel in hard cover. Benet attempted a couple of other novels during the 1920s. His magazine stories were often written under the pressure of deadlines to make money so that he could focus on his poetry. This attention to poetry resulted in one of the great poetic works of the decade, *John Brown's Body*, which became a best seller for Doubleday and won the first of two Pulitzer prizes Benet would be awarded for his poetry.

The imaginative, mythical strain to Benet's fiction often found its ground in American history. His fiction is notable for his recovery of native material and close identification with the United States. Poet Archibald MacLeish once said that Benet was more conscious of being an American than anyone he had ever known, which may have had something to do with Benet's family heritage. He spent some of his childhood at the Watervliet Arsenal near Troy, New York, where his father was the military superintendent. He was also the grandson of a brigadier general. Stephen had been unable to enlist for military service because of poor eyesight. He served in the State Department, and his brother William Rose Benet was an officer in Washington for the Air Force Corps. For Stephen, an office job was "hell without grandeur."[13]

Immediately after the war, in 1919, Benet began writing for the Yale literary magazine and *SN4*, a small magazine in New Haven. By 1920, Benet stories, including "The Blood of Martyrs," "Schooner Fairchild's Class," and "The Professor's Punch," had begun to appear in nationally published magazines. In "Elemental," a nonfiction piece printed in *Cosmopolitan*, he asserts on behalf of teachers the "ludicrousness of the contrast between the salaries paid American teachers and the energy, personality, and wide knowledge expected of them."[14] His poetry, meanwhile, was winning awards. Benet shared the 1922 Poetry Society Award with Carl Sandburg for *Smoke and Steel*.

It was during this time that he met Rosemary Carr, who would become his wife. She had been a Phi Beta Kappa honor student at the

University of Chicago, and her mother was one of the first female physicians in the Chicago area. Carr became a prolific writer for the *Herald Tribune* and several periodicals. Benet also began the most important professional relationship of his life at this time, when Carl Brandt became his literary agent. Brandt was a man with a keen sense of readers and the literary marketplace. He asserted that if Benet's primary goal was to be a poet, then he should churn out marketable short fiction to make a living. The best way to do this, Brandt said, was to write serials. Serial fiction, with its "to be continued" endings, was, in the 1920s, much like today's television series that build on an audience's acquaintance with characters and previous shows. Brandt showed Benet how to use a series of episodes with "hangers" to provide momentum. He encouraged him to use a chase scene, to fashion each installment as a complete unit, and to not get his hero and heroine into bed too soon. This was a far different world of fiction writing than Benet had been used to with the Yale and New Haven magazines.

Benet continued to try to write novels. *Young People's Pride* (1922) examines what was going on in contemporary society. Benet was criticized in the *New York Tribune* by Thomas Caldecott Chubb for his descent into potboiler sensationalism. In the meantime, in his short fiction, he was beginning to create nostalgic American myths. He would later write the classic story *The Devil and Daniel Webster*, featuring the great American orator. But first there were other mythic figures to explore, and Benet's keen history was beginning to show.

Poet Elinor Wylie sharply criticized *Young People's Pride*, saying that Benet's techniques used the "sleepy, meretricious fabrics of the scenario and the mystery story."[15] Soon thereafter, she became part of the Benet family, marrying William, Stephen's brother. When she died in December 1928, Stephen was away in France.

Benet was not an overtly political man. Yet, he was deeply concerned about the America of his times. When Benet looked at the early 1920s and the Harding administration, he saw a period of disenchantment. He wanted to speak in magazine fiction of the good in America. He sought to face the uneasy present with a sense of a national tradition. To do this, he created folk stories—colorful, imaginative, fanciful pieces in which he sought to entertain people while making money. Upon writing "The Ballad of William Sycamore," an unpopular poem written in a folk tradition, he was sure that an audience would follow it.

After reading Benet, a Kentucky reader named Jesse Stuart said, "I knew this writer, and he was my friend."[16] Benet followed with a poem called "King David," which appeared in the *Nation* (February 14, 1923). Edgar Lee Masters called it a "miracle."

For a time in 1923, Benet wrote articles for *Time* magazine. He also wrote book reviews for the *Bookman*, which was edited by his college friend John Farrar. Farrar drew Benet toward the theater when he wrote the play *Nerves*, published by Samuel French in 1922. When *Nerves* was produced, Humphrey Bogart, who was in the play, received one of his first public reviews. Farrar's play encouraged Benet to write a stage play, *That Awful Mrs. Eaton*, for which rehearsals were held in a building with glass skylights in Fort Lee, New Jersey, before the George Washington Bridge had been built there. When the play moved across the river for a production in New York, it did not do well. Benet decided that theater would not be profitable and directed his attention into other areas of writing. Nonetheless, Farrar, who soon joined with Stanley Rinehart to start a new publishing firm, later commented that he believed that Benet's theater interest contributed to the radio plays he penned in the early 1940s. In 1929, Benet also wrote four versions of scripts for a D. W. Griffith film that was never made. He did not stay to work on a film about the Alamo.

The readers of Benet's fiction were the popular audiences of the magazines in which his fiction appeared. Some critics called Benet's stories of 1923–1924 "mechanical and superficial"; however, his situation at that time must be taken into account in this assessment. Despite the honors he received for his poetry, he was writing to survive. In the winter of 1924, his bank account stood at $35. As a full-time writer with a wife and daughter, this was an uncomfortable time for him. He began a novel, *Spanish Bayonet*, with the hope that Carl Brandt could find a way to serialize it in magazines. It was a racy, energetic tale based on history, intended to be popular. He looked to William Makepeace Thackeray's *Henry Esmond* as a model. He grew a mustache and took walks along Second and Third avenues, as well as in Central Park.[17] It may have been during these walks that he thought of a new project. He began writing in verse about the legendary abolitionist John Brown.

"We have our own folk gods and giants and figures of earth in this country," Benet once asserted.[18] John Brown was one of the notorious ones. The raid he conducted on the Harper's Ferry military installation in 1859 set off a firestorm that contributed to national tensions before the Civil War. Benet reflects on his story, as well as that of America, in *John Brown's Body*.

Benet and his wife went to Paris in 1926, and their child was born there on September 28. From Paris, he looked back at the history of the United States as he wrote his poem. The American Library at the Rue de l'Elysee got its books from New York publishers. Benet read about Abraham Lincoln and John Brown. He read Proust and Hemingway's *The Sun Also Rises*. "Life abroad has intensified my Americanism," he said.[19]

In the fall of 1927, Benet was writing short stories. "The Giant's House," "Johnny Pye and the Fool Killer," and "Candleshine and Green Christmas" appeared in *Ladies' Home Journal*. *John Brown's Body* was ready in 1928. Dan Longwell of Doubleday, formerly a book store manager, became one of its foremost promoters. He had thought Benet's first novel better than Fitzgerald's *This Side of Paradise* and promoted Margaret Kennedy's *The Constant Nymph*, a best seller in 1925. In 1928, Dan Longwell read *John Brown's Body* while at Fisher's Island on Long Island Sound. He soon began to set up an ad and sales campaign for it. He was sure that this was a poem with mass-market appeal.

Doubleday had set up its offices and manufacturing plant in Garden City, New York. There was a first edition of 65,000. Reviewer Herschel Brickell dubbed *John Brown's Body* a "literary event of no small importance."[20] *John Brown's Body* became a major moneymaker for Doubleday. In 1928, it sold 130,000 copies. Benet earned $25,000 in 1928–1929, and the book won the Pulitzer Prize. The poem continued to sell well through the 1930s, with sales of about 6,000 copies per year. There was a trade edition, a high school edition, and a college edition of the poem. There was a great deal of reader interest from the South.[21] There was also a strong response in England. There were forty-four printings throughout the next twenty-five years. About 87,000 copies were sold between 1941 and 1957. The considerable success of *John Brown's Body* suggests that striking quality and promotional savvy met with a receptive, patriotic audience.

John Brown is also the subject of the first major work by Robert Penn Warren, one of America's foremost novelists of the twentieth century. The John Brown story clearly resonated with the American public in 1929. Benet's poem was widely read by northerners and southerners alike. Warren's own work was devised separately from that of Benet. Warren belonged to a southern tradition of American writing that also included the work of Thomas Wolfe, whose novel *Look Homeward Angel* (1929) launched a career that was most significant during the 1930s. Warren was a member of the Fugitive group, or the Southern Agrarians, who were centered in Nashville at Vanderbilt University in the 1920s. The Southern Agrarians are "best visualized as a community," writes Frederick Hoffman.[22] For Allen Tate, John Crowe Ransom, Donald Davidson, and Robert Penn Warren, a sense of place was essential. The community was set on the land, nurtured in a tradition, assured of morals and manners. For these writers, the modern world of industrial progress meant only abstraction, machinery, and the undermining of what Tate called "that quality of life" that could be drawn from a pastoral world passed along to the next generation. Tate looks to the southern past in his "Ode to the Confederate Dead." Warren looked to the past in many of his novels.

From April 1922 to December 1935, these poets and critics wrote and edited nineteen issues of the *Fugitive*. In 1930, they published "I'll Take My Stand, by Twelve Southerners." Davison wrote on how industrialism had disrupted the arts, turning all into commodities or entertainment, and he insisted that humanistic education was dissolved in this sort of culture. His work was what we might call an early defense of the humanities. Concerned with history and myth, his colleague, Warren, wrote *John Brown* (1929), and Tate wrote his biographies of Stonewall Jackson (1928) and Jefferson Davis (1929), as well as his memorable poem "Ode to the Confederate Dead." Ransom wrote *God without Thunder* (1930) and about a "certain inherited way of living." Years before Wilbur Cash's *The Mind of the South*, Tate called the southern mind personal, dramatic, sensuous, and close to nature. Tate and Ransom recalled with nostalgia a heroic tradition of lost innocence, a need to preserve values throughout the generations. Modern men and women, in their present circumstances, must search history for values and traditions, and seek that ideal past, remembered or imagined, that seems to have faded into the harsh present.

The work of these southern writers and Benet suggests that to lose our sense of history is to lose our way. For Benet, a way to preserve and express the American past was through stories and poems. When Benet was born in Bethlehem, Pennsylvania, in 1898, the incident that would be the subject of his Pulitzer Prize–winning epic poem was only thirty-nine years in the past. His father, Colonel James Walker Benet of the Bethlehem Iron Works, had been born in 1857, two years before the incident, which took place in October 1859. On April 28, 1927, Benet wrote to his mother that he would now call his "thing" *John Brown's Body*. The time had arrived for another historical interpretation of one of the most controversial incidents in American history: John Brown's raid at Harper's Ferry. American history would remain central to almost every move Benet made during his career as a writer.

The careful working of his poem makes it clear that Benet was both a fine poet and something of a folk historian. In his search for the America he knew, Benet recalls John Brown as a pivotal figure in American history. Benet liked folk heroes and begins one of his short stories, "A Tooth for Paul Revere," with a narrator who insists that his great aunt wasn't very respectful to the kind of history that gets into the books. What he likes is the "queer corners of it" and family stories.[23] These "queer corners" of history are where Benet began as a writer of fables who looked to America's heritage.

News of the Pulitzer Prize arrived to Benet in Paris by cable from his brother. Soon thereafter, John Farrar and Stanley Rinehart published *The Devil and Daniel Webster*, one of Benet's classic short stories. The 1930s brought two story collections, *Thirteen O'Clock* (1937) and *Tales before Midnight* (1939). *Thirteen O'Clock* includes "The Curfew Tolls"; "The Devil and Daniel Webster"; and "The Place of the Gods," Benet's chilling story of humanity rebuilding after a nuclear disaster, later named "By the Waters of Babylon." *Tales before Midnight* features many of Benet's American folk tales. The author completed his lengthy poem *Western Star* in the 1940s before he died. The poem posthumously earned him his second Pulitzer Prize.

JOHN STEINBECK, *CUP OF GOLD*

John Steinbeck's first novel appeared in 1929. He is most often thought of as a writer of the 1930s; however, he may also be viewed as a writer whose early development was affected by the writing of such turn-of-the-century naturalists and realists as Jack London, Frank Norris, and Theodore Dreiser, and by the writers of the 1920s. Steinbeck was also a writer who "[nudged] readers out of the 1930s into the timeless and the mythic," observes Susan Shillinglaw.[24]

That mythical quality is present in *Cup of Gold*, the first novel by Steinbeck, who was born in Salinas, California, in 1902. He was working at the Spreckles Sugar refinery during the year that Fitzgerald's *This Side of Paradise* appeared and was on his way to Stanford University. Steinbeck never finished college, dropping out of Stanford twice. He worked with a crew draining the swamps and a construction crew building Highway 1. A local editor suggested that he try newspaper work to learn how to present the facts and allow readers their impressions. Steinbeck brought his first attempt at a novel, "A Pot of Gold," with him to New York, where he pushed wheelbarrows of cement as a bricklayer's assistant working on the construction of Madison Square Garden. His uncle arranged a job for him with the *American*, a Hearst newspaper. Steinbeck did not stick to the facts: He wrote stories; embellishing his essays for the newspaper he soon found them cut by the editors. He fell for Mary Ardeth, a would-be actress, and that relationship got cut too. Steinbeck did not have enough money for her, and he would not let go of his literary ambitions, least of all to take a job in advertising.

In 1925, while still in California, author Elizabeth Smith encouraged him to expand his short story "A Lady in Infra-Red" into a novel. He decided to create an allegory of the life of Henry Morgan, a Welsh boy who sought adventure in the West Indies. In *Cup of Gold*, as the novel would later be titled, Henry meets a former pirate, and his mind fills with stories of adventure. Steinbeck's Henry Morgan is an American character with a pirate's last name who is on a quest. While Steinbeck offers lyrical prose that calls attention to nature, he develops a story in which Morgan seeks wealth. After going to the West Indies, he is sold as a servant to a colonial planter. He organizes a pirate band and becomes a buccaneer. Henry hears stories of the most beautiful woman in the world and decides he must find her. He captures the city of Panama and the woman, La Santa Roja, but the pursuit of wealth and power turns him into a bully whose fate is not a good one. While in Jamaica, he tells two pirates that they will die and civilization will split up and he who refuses to split will "go under." At the end of the novel we read that "there was no light anywhere."[25]

In 1927, it seemed that there was no light anywhere for Steinbeck's novel. Guy Holt at the Robert McBride Publishing Company had liked the novel, but he had moved to a job with the John Day Company and McBride, which had rejected the novel. One ray of hope came when Steinbeck's short story "The Gifts of Iban," set in a fantasy land, was published under the pseudonym John Stern. He had spent the rest of the year writing furiously, some three or four thousand words a day, only to once again look at his manuscript with disappointment. Back in California, Steinbeck had another go at the novel, writing longhand in small letters, as he usually did. He needed someone to type his story.

Steinbeck needed a typist. He found a wife. Twenty-two-year-old Carol Henning was a stenographer who took an interest in typing *Cup of Gold*—and Steinbeck. Steinbeck, meanwhile, was rooming with a Stanford friend, Carl Wilhelmson, who was also a writer deeply interested in the writers of the "lost generation": Ernest Hemingway, F. Scott Fitzgerald, and others. In January 1929, Ted Miller, Steinbeck's lawyer-friend in New York, sent a letter: *Cup of Gold* had been accepted by McBride, the firm that had previously rejected the story.

Cup of Gold did not catch the attention of the American public. The cover design features a pirate that appears to have stepped out of Treasure Island. It looked like an adventure book for boys, and some New York bookstores shelved it in the juvenile section. It was not an auspicious beginning for Steinbeck, but it was a beginning. Steinbeck's star rose in the 1930s, when he began to focus on the contemporary California he knew so well and farmers, ranchers, factory workers, and migrants. In focusing on his home state, he finally had his subject, and with that he began to write a series of novels in the 1930s that culminated in the classic *The Grapes of Wrath* (1939).

The Grapes of Wrath belongs to a later period than the one we are studying here. It is a work of the Depression years of the 1930s. Nonetheless, it deserves mention here as one of the great works of fiction that Steinbeck was working toward: a candid expression of ordinary people and their American dream. Effectively expressed through John Ford's film, *The Grapes of Wrath* is a valuable classroom tool for any teacher or student who wants to consider the American dream in the light of the 2000s dot-com bust, the loss of homes or jobs, or issues of immigration, human dignity, and social justice. It reflects the persistence and determination of a group of people in adverse circumstances.

Steinbeck writes with layers of detail, engaging poetic interchapters and a forceful quest-plot. Ford's documentary style, while more sentimental than Steinbeck's novel, shows the struggle of families in Oklahoma. Chock-full of direct images, the book indicts the structures that deprive poor farm workers from Oklahoma of their livelihoods and documents the harsh life of the Depression-stunned 1930s. Steinbeck and Ford bring a searing critique of the forces set in motion by the Depression and those who take advantage of the circumstances.

The impoverished Okies are given a human face in Ford's movie. We are brought into sympathy with them through the Joad family. This sympathy is then extended to include all the families stuck in the disturbing conditions of the migrant camps of California. Their lean faces and the ramshackle conditions tell a story of poverty. In Ford's film, this story is emphasized by many memorable shots: Muley Graves and his family being reduced to shadows on the brown earth and children clinging to a fence, suggesting imprisonment. The American Gothic pose of a man and woman faces us as the Joad family enters one of the camps.

At the beginning of the film, Tom Joad is a lone traveler on a road, and in some of the final frames he appears as a speck against the vast sky. But, we have learned of his dignity and determination, and his "I'll be there" speech still rings in our ears. Ma Joad, ever a sturdy center of strength, rises boldly into action. She sheds sentimentality with the memorabilia she is forced to discard as she sets forth on her family's journey west. Only the recurring tune of "Red River Valley" and a dance with Tom remind us of her strong feeling about home. Women are like a river, she affirms at the end of the film: They wind through things and keep on going. Her final "We're the people" echoes the first line of the Constitution of the United States and the resilience and resolve of Americans.

Ford's grainy black-and-white movie draws our attention to the interplay of light and shadow, hope and darkness, good and evil. The dust and wind at the beginning of Steinbeck's novels are transformed into an eerie sweeping scene in the shadowy recesses of the Joads' former house. Tom, cap on his head, hitches a ride home and encounters Casey, the "preacher," a plain-spoken man who thinks that he has lost his faith but still sings a song about his savior. Casey, whose life is a testimony to justice, exclaims that he is "fit to bust" and that sometimes he wants to just love every one. He asserts, "maybe there's no virtue, it's just what people does."

Joining the Joads on their journey west, he becomes a labor organizer and dies for his convictions. During the journey, we hear gas station attendants in clean white suits condescendingly comment, "Them Okies, they ain't human." Nobody would live that way. As if they have any other choice. We hear of the labeling of committed people who have the courage to speak out against injustice as "agitators" or "reds"—easy, unthinking labels used to dismiss their claim on human dignity. We see a potentially violent mob marching like *Night of the Living Dead* up to the Joads' truck on a dark road to enforce their own right to jobs and "civilization." Thugs are posing as camp guards. We see men hired by owners to manipulate a community dance into a "riot" and the intelligence and resilience of those in the government camp—a shining example of the successes of the New Deal. The film demonstrates how tough economic times can bring out the worst in some people and how some manipulate to maintain their privilege. Steinbeck and Ford's work is a telling documentary of the struggle of people to escape the machines and machine-like interests that would dehumanize them. It reminds us of the heroism of the common man and woman.

Steinbeck received everything from acclaim to death threats for his novel. The book became the topic of newspaper articles, magazine articles, and editorials. It was read and censored and burned. While Associated Farmers turned the pages into smoke, the San Jose, California, library banned the text from its shelves. Readers in Oklahoma were sharply divided over Steinbeck's portrayals of Oklahoma migrants. *The Grapes of Wrath* sold 40,000 copies by the end of 1939 and received the Pulitzer Prize and the National Book Award in 1940. It was called the "Bookseller's Favorite Novel," indicating the novel's appeal to its popular audience. There was an Armed Services edition in 1943 and many subsequent editions, with sales of approximately 100,000 copies per year in the 1980s and 150,000 copies a year in the 1990s.[26] Readers continue to recognize that the American story of the Joads is their own. As we face issues of the haves and have-nots or issues of immigration, *The Grapes of Wrath* remains a significant contribution, reminding us of our dreams, our families, and the imagined community that is America.

The social reach of Steinbeck's novel was enhanced by the film. Upon seeing the film, Eleanor Roosevelt called *The Grapes of Wrath* her favorite book and movie. The film won awards, including an Academy Award for Best Supporting Actress for Jane Darwell's role as Ma Joad. Henry Fonda and John Carradine each went on to brilliant film careers, and John Ford directed some of the most memorable westerns in film history. Although Steinbeck's novel ends differently than Ford's film, Steinbeck said in 1966 that the film stirred him to believe in his book again, that it was "fresh and happening and good."[27]

In *America and Americans and Selected Nonfiction*, Steinbeck suggests that some momentum was gained in moving toward an American literature of international stature in the first years of the twentieth century and further developed throughout the 1920s with the writing of Dreiser, Cather, Lewis, O'Neill, Wolfe, Hemingway, and Faulkner, who "learned from our people and wrote like themselves and created a new and a grand thing in the world—an American literature about Americans."[28] We may add to this list Steinbeck himself. Emerging in the subsequent decade, Steinbeck put forth objectively clear prose describing landscapes and people; he was a writer who often regarded group consciousness as significant, as in his Joad family of *The Grapes of Wrath*.

"Americans do not lack places to go and new things to find," wrote John Steinbeck in 1966. "Far larger experiences are open to our restlessness—the fascinating unknown is everywhere."[29] This is as true of the literature and American people today as it was in the 1960s or the days of the early republic. Our literature is restless and "running," to use Steinbeck's term, and it is always moving toward new horizons. From Ishmael going to sea to Nick Carraway coming East or the Joad family going West, our stories are often about this restlessness. "Our restlessness, perhaps inherited from the hungry immigrants of our ancestry, is still with us," writes Steinbeck.[30] What it means to be American in the twenty-first century is tied up in this restless spirit, and the multicultural voices of our literature express this. Indeed, for Steinbeck, American identity is a multicultural "E Pluribus Unum" of all classes. Steinbeck writes that "our people are of every kind also—of every race, of every ethnic category—and yet our land is one nation also—and our people are Americans."[31] The literature of the 1920s, when it has come from writers attuned to the lives of the people, expresses the voice of America with a kind of truth and integrity.

The restless diversity that makes up this nation and our literature is regionally, ethnically, and racially varied, while also filled with common myths and dreams. Steinbeck reflects on how Americans have been called "a restless, a dissatisfied, a searching people," seeking security, success, and working too hard. "The result is that we seem to be in a state of turmoil all the time, both physically and mentally," he writes. Yet, these "generalities" are part of a paradox. We hold a "strong and imperishable American dream" and "in nothing are we so paradoxical as in our passionate belief in our own myths."[32]

As if to encourage the "myths" that we create, Steinbeck mentions that while he was living in Manhattan he often saw a "stout and benign looking lady" who sought the American outdoors under a beach umbrella on East 51st Street.[33] She rolled out her little lawn on the sidewalk and set out two pots of geraniums, an artificial palm, and a can of Coca-Cola. This was her American dream, one that broke through the painful, exploded dreams of immigrants or concrete limitations of urban life. Her identity in New York was one open to the country: to its beaches, its mountain and fields, its commerce and refreshments, and its myths and dreams. Steinbeck says that "somehow she conveyed her dream to everyone who saw her," and he conveys this image to us. Wishing to "contribute to this sylvan retreat," he gave her a "potted fern and little bowl with two goldfish."[34] As America's literature has come into its own, authors like Steinbeck have given us the images and voices of America's people. In capturing the images, voices, and stories of people like the stout woman on East 51st Street, they have contributed to America's dream of home.

Almost one hundred years have passed since the novelty of car horns blared in Dreiser's Chicago and Fitzgerald's New York. Anderson's *Winesberg, Ohio*, Fitzgerald's *This Side of Paradise*, and Lewis's *Main Street* were written then. Hemingway and Dos Passos, scathed by the Great War, began to create their fiction. Willa Cather wrote of Nebraska and Langston Hughes and Zora Neale Hurston of Harlem and the young immigrant. Anzia Yezierska wrote stories while seeking an education. It was America's voice—from the clean lines of Hemingway to the stylish prose of Faulkner. These were the writers of the 1920s and beyond who contributed to the shaping of the American imagination in the twentieth century. Several of their works still resonate in our cultural life, and we continue to learn about the experience and ideals of Americans as we read them. These writers have provided us with the tapestry of a vital and varied culture and the enduring stuff of our myths and dreams.

Of course, there is also that other reason why the Kindle Fire is on tonight, that other reason why the book is open. Why do we read novels? As Robert Penn Warren once said, it's because we like it.

NOTES

PREFACE

1. Bob Batchelor, *Gatsby: The Cultural History of the Great American Novel* (Lanham, MD: Rowman and Littlefield, 2014), 93.

2. D. H. Lawrence, *Studies in Classic American Literature: The Cambridge Edition of the Works of D. H. Lawrence*. Vol. 2. Ed. Ezra Greenspan, Lindeth Vasey, and John Worthen (Cambridge, UK: Cambridge University Press, 2003), 1–63.

3. Robert Penn Warren, "Why Do We Read Fiction?" *Saturday Evening Post*, July 1986, p. 62.

4. Louis Kantor, "Why Novels?" *New York Tribune*, April 22, 1922, p. 11.

5. D. H. Lawrence, "Why the Novel Matters" *Selected Criticism*, 1956. Available online at http://individual.utoronto.ca/amlit/why_the_novel_matters.htm (accessed December 3, 2014).

6. Gordon Hunter, quoted in Elizabeth Long, *Book Clubs: Women and the Uses of Reading in Everyday Life* (Chicago: University of Chicago Press, 2003), 25–26.

7. Long, *Book Clubs*, 70.

8. Tim Parks, "Do We Need Stories?" *New York Review of Books Blog*, March 26, 2013, 1–2.

9. Michael J. Sandel, *Democracy's Discontent* (1986; reprint, Cambridge, UK: Belknap, Harvard University Press, 1998).

10. Susan Shillinglaw, *On Reading* The Grapes of Wrath (New York: Penguin, 2014), 33–34.

INTRODUCTION

1. Frederick Lewis Allen, *Only Yesterday* (New York: Harper's, 1931), 81.

2. Quoted in Allen, *Only Yesterday*, 82.

3. Quoted in Allen, *Only Yesterday*, 207.

4. Malcolm Bradbury, quoted in C. W. E. Bigsby, *Modern American Drama, 1945–2000* (Cambridge, UK: Cambridge University Press, 2000), 208. See Malcolm Bradbury and David Palmer, eds., *The American Novel in the 1920s* (London: Arnold, 1971).

5. Allen, *Only Yesterday*, 94.

6. Allen, *Only Yesterday*, 82, 141.

7. George W. Gray, quoted in Allen, *Only Yesterday*, 68.

8. Quoted in Allen, *Only Yesterday*, 68.

9. Allen, *Only Yesterday*, 20.

10. Allen, *Only Yesterday*, 143.

11. Ann Douglas, *Terrible Honesty: Mongrel Manhattan in the 1920s* (New York: Farrar, Straus and Giroux, 1995), 64.

12. Allen, *Only Yesterday*, 144.

13. Allen, *Only Yesterday*, 148.

14. Douglas, *Terrible Honesty*, 55.

15. Douglas, *Terrible Honesty*, 55.

16. Allen, *Only Yesterday*, 131–32.

17. Allen, *Only Yesterday*, 157.

18. Allen, *Only Yesterday*, 191.

19. Allen, *Only Yesterday*, 206.

20. Allen, *Only Yesterday*, 170.

21. *New York Times*, October 19, 1924.

22. Allen, *Only Yesterday*, 151.

23. Allen, *Only Yesterday*, 198.

24. Bob Batchelor, *Gatsby: The Cultural History of the Great American Novel* (Lanham, MD: Rowman and Littlefield, 2014), 40.

25. Malcolm Cowley, *Exile's Return: A Literary Odyssey of the 1920s* (1934; reprint, New York: Viking, 1951), 23.

26. Cowley, *Exile's Return*, 3.

27. Cowley, *Exile's Return*, 4.

28. Cowley, *Exile's Return*, 6.

29. Quoted in Cowley, *Exile's Return*, 5.

30. Cowley, *Exile's Return*, 18.

31. Cowley, *Exile's Return*, 25.

32. Cowley, *Exile's Return*, 47.

33. Cowley, *Exile's Return*, 201.

34. Cowley, *Exile's Return*, 58.

35. Cowley, *Exile's Return*, 60.

36. Cowley, *Exile's Return*, 42.

37. Cowley, *Exile's Return*, 175.

38. Cowley, *Exile's Return*, 202.

39. Cowley, *Exile's Return*, 225.

40. Edmund Wilson, *The Shores of Light: A Literary Chronicle of the Twenties and Thirties* (New York: Farrar, Straus, and Young, 1952), 400.

41. Wilson, *The Shores of Light*, 139, 147.

42. Wilson, *The Shores of Light*, 405.

43. Wilson, *The Shores of Light*, 86.

44. Wilson, *The Shores of Light*, 82.

45. Wilson, *The Shores of Light*, 83.

46. Wilson, *The Shores of Light*, 41.

47. Wilson, *The Shores of Light*, 193.

48. Wilson writes, "As for the dramatists, there is still only O'Neill, who, for all his efforts to break away from naturalism, remains a typical naturalistic dramatist of something under the first rank." *The Shores of Light*, 195.

49. Wilson, *The Shores of Light*, 90.

50. Wilson, *The Shores of Light*, 91.

51. Wilson, *The Shores of Light*, 48–50.

52. Wilson, *The Dial*, October 1924, quoted in *The Shores of Light*, 105.

53. Wilson, *The Shores of Light*, 103.

54. Wilson, *The Shores of Light*, 191–92.

55. Wilson, *The Shores of Light*, 193.

56. Wilson, *The Shores of Light*, 193.

57. Wilson, *The Shores of Light*, 193.

58. Wilson, *The Shores of Light*, 194.

59. Wilson, *The Shores of Light*, 195.

60. Joseph Wood Krutch, quoted in Wilson, *The Shores of Light*, 278.

61. Wilson, *The Shores of Light*, 279.

62. Wilson, *The Shores of Light*, 280.

63. Wilson, *The Shores of Light*, 281.

64. Wilson, *The Shores of Light*, 282.

65. Wilson, *The Shores of Light*, 353.

66. Wilson, *The Shores of Light*, 353.

67. Wilson, *The Shores of Light*, 354.

68. Wilson, *The Shores of Light*, 351.

69. Wilson, *The Shores of Light*, 364.

70. Wilson, *The Shores of Light*, 364.

71. Travis Bogards, "The Comedy of Thornton Wilder," Introduction to *Three Plays by Thornton Wilder* (New York: Harper, 1963), 61.

72. Wilson, *The Shores of Light*, 321.

73. Wilson, *The Shores of Light*, 363.

74. Wilson, *The Shores of Light*, 408.

75. Wilson, *The Shores of Light*, 408.

76. Wilson, *The Shores of Light*, 438.

77. Wilson, *The Shores of Light*, 477.

78. Wilson, *The Shores of Light*, 480.

79. Wilson, *The Shores of Light*, 477.

1. BEYOND THE WASTELAND

1. Ann Douglas, *Terrible Honesty: Mongrel Manhattan in the 1920s* (New York: Farrar, Straus, and Giroux, 1995), 208.

2. Jonathan Rose, *The Edwardian Temperament, 1895–1919* (Athens: Ohio University Press, 1986).

3. T. Austin Graham, *The Great American Songbook* (Oxford, UK, and New York: Oxford University Press, 2012), 59.

4. Frank Kermode has observed that the "O" and "Shakespeherian" locates this music within one's mind, creating a musical effect. Perhaps this syncopated rhythm is also a form of scat-singing or piano line, as suggested by Graham, or a way of covering for forgotten lyrics. See Graham, *The Great American Songbook*, 215.

5. David Chinitz, *T. S. Eliot and the Cultural Divide* (Chicago: University of Chicago Press, 2003); Douglas, *Terrible Honesty*, 112–13; Graham, *The Great American Songbook*, 214–18.

6. Graham, *The Great American Songbook*, 65.

7. Graham, *The Great American Songbook*, 69.

8. Quoted in Graham, *The Great American Songbook*, 159–60.

9. Douglas, *Terrible Honesty*, 216.

10. Quoted in T. E. Hulme, "Crites, a Commentary," *Criterion* 2 (April 1924): 23.

11. Hulme, "Crites, a Commentary," 229.

12. Hulme, "Crites, a Commentary," 62–63.

13. Hulme, "Crites, a Commentary," 63.

14. John Dos Passos, *The Fourteenth Chronicle: Letters and Diaries of John Dos Passos*, ed. Townsend Ludington (New York: Gambit, 1973), 69.

15. Fussell writes that this was "not with some Hegelian hope of synthesis involving the dissolution of both extremes (that would suggest a negotiated

peace, which was anathema) but with a sense that one of the poles embodies so wicked a deficiency or flaw or perversion that its total submission is called for." Paul Fussell, *The Great War and Modern Memory* (Oxford, UK, and New York: Oxford University Press, 1975), 127.

16. Gertrude Stein, "Composition as Explanation" (London: Hogarth Press, 1926).

17. Douglas, *Terrible Honesty*, 176.

18. Douglas, *Terrible Honesty*, 179–216.

19. John Dos Passos, *Three Soldiers* (1921; reprint, New York: Library of America, 2003), 10.

20. John Dos Passos, *One Man's Initiation* (1917; reprint, Ithaca, NY: Cornell University Press, 1969), 2.

21. Dos Passos, *One Man's Initiation*, 20.

22. Edgar Jones, "Shell Shock," *American Psychological Association* 46, no. 12 (June 2012): 18.

23. Harry Crosby, *War Letters*, November 14, 1917 (Paris: Black Sun Press, 1932).

24. Crosby, *War Letters*, August 16, 1917.

25. Crosby, *War Letters*, November 23, 1917. Letter to his sister.

26. Harry Crosby, *Shadows of the Sun* (Paris: Black Sun Press, 1925), 1.

27. Lisa Nanney, *John Dos Passos Revisited* (New York: Twayne, 1998), 127.

28. Dos Passos, *Three Soldiers*, 87.

29. Fussell, *The Great War and Modern Memory*, 79.

30. Gertrude Stein, "Memories of Picasso," *Writings, 1932–1946*. Vol. 2 (New York: Library of America, 1998).

31. Frederick J. Hoffmann, *The Twenties: American Writing in the Postwar Decade* (New York: Viking, 1955), 48.

32. Hoffmann, *The Twenties*, 49.

33. Hoffmann, *The Twenties*, 50.

34. Edmund Wilson, *Shores of Light: A Literary Chronicle of the Twenties and Thirties* (New York: Farrar, Straus, and Young, 1952), 118.

35. Gene Ruoff, quoted in *William Faulkner: New Perspectives*, ed. Richard Brodhead (Englewood Cliffs, NJ: Prentice-Hall, 1983), 239; "All the Dead Pilots," *The Collected Short Stories of William Faulkner* (New York: Random House/Vintage, 2012).

36. William Faulkner, *Soldiers' Pay* (New York: Library of America, 1990), 25.

2. ERNEST HEMINGWAY AND F. SCOTT FITZGERALD

1. Malcolm Cowley, *Exile's Return: A Literary Odyssey of the 1920s* (1934; reprint, New York: Viking, 1951), 6; F. Scott Fitzgerald, "The Scandal Detectives," *The Collected Short Stories of F. Scott Fitzgerald*, ed. Matthew Bruccoli (New York: Charles Scribner's Sons, 1989).

2. Sherwood Anderson, *Sherwood Anderson's Notebook* (New York: Liveright, 1926).

3. Edmund Wilson, *The Shores of Light: A Literary Chronicle of the Twenties and Thirties* (New York: Farrar, Straus, and Young, 1952), 468.

4. Gertrude Stein, quoted in Wilson, *The Shores of Light*, 468.

5. Wilson, *The Shores of Light*, 468.

6. Ernest Hemingway, *A Moveable Feast* (1954; reprint, New York: Charles Scribner's Sons, 1963), 13.

7. Ernest Hemingway, *The Sun Also Rises* (New York: Charles Scribner's Sons, 1926), 74; Frederick J. Hoffmann, *The Twenties: American Writing in the Postwar Decade* (New York: Viking, 1955), 81.

8. Hoffmann, *The Twenties*, 81.

9. Wilson, *The Shores of Light*, 281.

10. Alfred R. McIntyre, "Little Brown and Company," in *Publishers and Publishing*, ed. Gerald Gross (New York: Grosset and Dunlap, 1961), 113. Alfred McIntyre of Little Brown and Company saw a gain in sales each year from 1927 to 1929. He points out that the book clubs had "given a tremendous amount of publicity" and "directed public attention to a few titles" (114).

11. Malcolm Cowley, *The Portable Hemingway* (New York: Viking, 1944), vii.

12. Malcolm Cowley, *Exile's Return: A Literary Odyssey of the 1920s* (1934; reprint, New York: Viking, 1951), 50.

13. See Carlos Baker, *Hemingway: A Life Story* (New York: Charles Scribner's Sons, 1969); Jeffrey Meyers, *Hemingway: A Biography* (New York: HarperCollins, 1985).

14. The original letter is in the Scribner's archives in the Firestone Library, Princeton University.

15. F. Scott Fitzgerald, *This Side of Paradise* (New York: Charles Scribner's Sons, 1920), 35.

16. T. Austin Graham, *The Great American Songbook* (Oxford, UK, and New York: Oxford University Press, 2012), 84. Graham compares the novel with musical theater of the 1920s, which is viewed as discontinuous. "Broadway's relative lack of concern with causality, psychological motivation, plot structure, and dramatic unity all find analogues in the abstract associativeness

of *This Side of Paradise*" (87). Musical theater matters in *This Side of Paradise* (89).

17. Fitzgerald, *This Side of Paradise*, 82.

18. Graham, *The Great American Songbook*, 25. We may ask what social role music plays in the novel. Yet, it is difficult to know what Fitzgerald's contemporary audience "heard" and responded to when they read his fiction. For this, we would have to find some comment from their letters, journals, or autobiographies that indicates their reading of Fitzgerald's story (82). Why does a story, play, or song mean one thing to one person and something different to someone else? (90). "Kiss Me Again" illustrates this. As the song is heard from another room, Amory interprets the lyrics in one way and Rosalind interprets them in another. See *This Side of Paradise*, 173, and Graham's discussion in *The Great American Songbook*, 90.

19. Graham, *The Great American Songbook*, 85.

20. Fitzgerald. *This Side of Paradise*, 24.

21. F. Scott Fitzgerald, *F. Scott Fitzgerald: A Life in Letters*, ed. Matthew Bruccoli and Judith S. Baughman (New York: Touchstone, 1995), 61.

22. Matthew Bruccoli, *Some Sort of Epic Grandeur: The Life of F. Scott Fitzgerald* (New York: Harcourt Brace, 1981), 182–83.

23. Hoffmann, *The Twenties*, 106.

24. Kirk Curnutt, *Cambridge Companion to F. Scott Fitzgerald* (Cambridge, UK: Cambridge University Press, 2002), 95.

25. Curnutt, *Cambridge Companion to F. Scott Fitzgerald*, 112.

26. Curnutt, *Cambridge Companion to F. Scott Fitzgerald*, 29.

27. Wilson, *The Shores of Light*, 33.

28. Thomas Woodward, *In His Own Time* (Minneapolis, MN: Privately printed), 245–54. Woodward was a reporter for a St. Paul, Minnesota, daily newspaper.

29. Quoted in Curnutt, *Cambridge Companion to F. Scott Fitzgerald*, 115.

30. Curnutt, *Cambridge Companion to F. Scott Fitzgerald*, 115–16.

31. H. L. Mencken, "Review of *Flappers and Philosophers*," *Smart Set*, 1920.

32. Bruccoli, *Some Sort of Epic Grandeur*, 168.

33. F. Scott Fitzgerald, *The Beautiful and Damned* (New York: Charles Scribner's Sons, 1922), 79.

34. F. Scott Fitzgerald, *The Great Gatsby* (New York: Charles Scribner's Sons, 1925), 34.

35. Fitzgerald, *The Great Gatsby*, 85.

36. Fitzgerald, *F. Scott Fitzgerald: A Life in Letters*, 65.

37. Fitzgerald, *F. Scott Fitzgerald: A Life in Letters*, 75, 78.

38. Fitzgerald, *F. Scott Fitzgerald: A Life in Letters*, 78.

39. Fitzgerald, *F. Scott Fitzgerald: A Life in Letters*, 82.

40. Fitzgerald, *F. Scott Fitzgerald: A Life in Letters*, 86.

41. Ernest Hemingway, *A Moveable Feast* (1954; reprint, New York: Charles Scribner's Sons, 1963), 90.

42. Fitzgerald, *F. Scott Fitzgerald: A Life in Letters*, 109–10.

43. Fitzgerald, *F. Scott Fitzgerald: A Life in Letters*, 100.

44. Fitzgerald, *F. Scott Fitzgerald: A Life in Letters*, 102. Fitzgerald was clearly familiar with the work of his contemporaries, for instance, Willa Cather, Sinclair Lewis, and Gertrude Stein. He admired the lesser-known Hemingway as the model of a fine writer. In a letter to Perkins, Fitzgerald recognizes that Hemingway's *Torrents of Spring* was a parody of Sherwood Anderson. He comments that people were "let down" by Anderson's recent work (133). He calls John Dos Passos "astonishingly good," yet, in a letter of December 30, 1925, he comments that he had "lost faith" in his work (134).

45. Fitzgerald, *F. Scott Fitzgerald: A Life in Letters*, 129. Fitzgerald's insight that his female readers of *The Great Gatsby* "haven't cared for it" because he provided no strong female characters was echoed by one of my female students, who insisted that she did not really like the novel because she believed that the women in Fitzgerald's story were too passive.

46. Hazel McCormack, Letters to F. Scott Fitzgerald, September 1924. Firestone Library, Princeton University.

47. Hazel McCormack, Letters to F. Scott Fitzgerald, May 15, 1925. Firestone Library, Princeton University.

48. Fitzgerald, *F. Scott Fitzgerald: A Life in Letters*, 124.

49. Fitzgerald, *F. Scott Fitzgerald: A Life in Letters*, 128.

50. Jeffrey Meyers, *Hemingway: A Biography* (New York: HarperCollins, 1985), 159.

51. William Rose Benet, *F. Scott Fitzgerald: The Critical Heritage* (New York: Routledge, 1925), 220.

52. Quoted in Curnutt, *Cambridge Companion to F. Scott Fitzgerald*, 116; Benet, *F. Scott Fitzgerald: The Critical Heritage*, 195.

53. Fitzgerald, *The Great Gatsby*, 46; F. Scott Fitzgerald, *Tender Is the Night*, ed. Matthew Bruccoli (1934; reprint, New York: Cambridge University Press, 1991), 76–77.

54. Fitzgerald, *F. Scott Fitzgerald: A Life in Letters*.

55. Curnutt, *Cambridge Companion to F. Scott Fitzgerald*, 35.

56. William Rose Benet, "Review of *All the Sad Young Men*," *Saturday Review*, 1926; Benet, *F. Scott Fitzgerald: The Critical Heritage*, 220.

57. Fitzgerald, *F. Scott Fitzgerald: A Life in Letters*, 169.

58. F. Scott Fitzgerald, "Echoes of the Jazz Age," *New Statesman*, 1931. All quotations that follow are from this essay.

59. Frederick Lewis Allen, *Only Yesterday* (New York: Harper's, 1931), 2–3.

60. Fitzgerald, *This Side of Paradise.*

61. Allen, *Only Yesterday*, 1.

62. See Allen, *Only Yesterday*, 1–25.

63. Mencken, "Review of *Flappers and Philosophers.*" See Benet, *F. Scott Fitzgerald: The Critical Heritage.*

64. The Cornell University student's quip appeared in the university's newspaper.

65. This and the following quotations appear in Fitzgerald's *The Great Gatsby.*

66. Walter Lippmann, quoted in Allen, *Only Yesterday*, 20.

67. F. Scott Fitzgerald, "Dice, Brassknuckles, and Guitar," *The Collected Short Stories of F. Scott Fitzgerald*, ed. Matthew Bruccoli (New York: Charles Scribner's Sons, 1989).

68. F. Scott Fitzgerald, "The Lost Decade," *The Collected Short Stories of F. Scott Fitzgerald*, ed. Matthew Bruccoli (New York: Charles Scribner's Sons, 1989), 749.

69. F. Scott Fitzgerald, "The Lost Decade," 749.

70. Lionel Trilling, *The Liberal Imagination: Essays on Literature and Society* (New York: Viking, 1950).

71. Curnutt, *Cambridge Companion to F. Scott Fitzgerald*, 118–19; Benet, *F. Scott Fitzgerald: The Critical Heritage*, 368–69, 375–76.

72. Curnutt, *Cambridge Companion to F. Scott Fitzgerald*, 121.

3. WILLIAM FAULKNER

1. Richard H. Brodhead, ed., "Introduction," *William Faulkner: New Perspectives* (Englewood Cliffs, NJ: Prentice-Hall, 1983), 3.

2. Eric J. Sundquist, *To Wake the Nations: Race in the Making of American Literature* (Cambridge, MA: Harvard University Press, 1993), 8.

3. Sundquist, *To Wake the Nations*, 8–10.

4. Irving Howe, "The Culture of Modernism," *Commentary* (November 1967): 61.

5. Joseph Blotner, *William Faulkner: A Biography* (New York: Random House, 1974), 251.

6. Blotner, *William Faulkner: A Biography*, 396.

7. Blotner, *William Faulkner: A Biography*, 401.

8. Blotner, *William Faulkner: A Biography*, 392.

9. Blotner, *William Faulkner: A Biography*, 395.

10. Blotner, *William Faulkner: A Biography*, 412.

11. Blotner, *William Faulkner: A Biography*, 413.

12. Blotner, *William Faulkner: A Biography*, 415.

13. Blotner, *William Faulkner: A Biography*, 500.

14. Blotner, *William Faulkner: A Biography*, 501.

15. Blotner, *William Faulkner: A Biography*, 505–6.

16. Blotner, *William Faulkner: A Biography*, 325.

17. Blotner, *William Faulkner: A Biography*, 532.

18. Blotner, *William Faulkner: A Biography*, 459.

19. Blotner, *William Faulkner: A Biography*, 460.

20. Blotner, *William Faulkner: A Biography*, 471.

21. Blotner, *William Faulkner: A Biography*, 490.

22. Blotner, *William Faulkner: A Biography*, 523.

23. Blotner, *William Faulkner: A Biography*, 545.

24. Blotner, *William Faulkner: A Biography*, 548. Photographs of the devastation from the flood are available for viewing online at the Mississippi Archives site.

25. Horace Liveright, quoted in Blotner, *William Faulkner: A Biography*, 560.

26. Sundquist, *To Wake the Nations*, 13.

27. David Minter, in Brodhead, *William Faulkner: New Perspectives*, 121. See also Minter's biography, *William Faulkner: His Life and Work* (Baltimore, MD: Johns Hopkins University Press, 1997).

28. Blotner, *William Faulkner: A Biography*, 584.

29. Quoted in Blotner, *William Faulkner: A Biography*, 225. There is often a difference between the relative importance and longevity of a book and popular sales. The first printing of *The Sound and the Fury* was 1,789. The publisher expected a small, "serious" readership. The sales of *Sanctuary*, which was something of a violent "potboiler," helped the sales of *The Sound and the Fury*; however, for about fifteen years the sales of that classic novel totaled only about 3,000 copies.

30. Blotner, *William Faulkner: A Biography*, 626.

31. Sundquist, *To Wake the Nations*, 9.

32. Howe, "The Culture of Modernism," 48.

33. Howe, "The Culture of Modernism," 53–54.

34. Howe, "The Culture of Modernism," 42.

35. Blotner, *William Faulkner: A Biography*, 339.

36. Robert Penn Warren, in Brodhead, *William Faulkner: New Perspectives*, 20.

37. Brodhead, *William Faulkner: New Perspectives*, 8.

38. Howe, "The Culture of Modernism," 57.

39. Quoted in Brodhead, *William Faulkner: New Perspectives*, 41.

40. Cleanth Brooks, quoted in Brodhead, *William Faulkner: New Perspectives*, 40–41.

41. Quoted in Brodhead, *William Faulkner: New Perspectives*, 35.

42. Brooks, quoted in Brodhead, *William Faulkner: New Perspectives*, 35.

43. Quoted from Robert Fagles's translation of *The Odyssey* (New York: Penguin, 1996), 188.

44. Blotner, *William Faulkner: A Biography*, 607. Blotner notes that there was a New Orleans–St. Louis mob connected with Al Capone (608).

45. Blotner lists the readers as Louise Bonino, Evelyn Harter, Leonore Marshall, and Hal Smith. *William Faulkner: New Perspectives*, 618.

46. Hugh Kenner, *The Pound Era* (Berkeley: University of California Press, 1971), 186.

47. Kenner, *The Pound Era*, 22.

48. Ilse Dusoir Lind, quoted in Daniel J. Singal, *William Faulkner: The Making of a Modernist* (Chapel Hill: University of North Carolina Press, 1999), 141–42.

49. Lind, quoted in Singal, *William Faulkner: The Making of a Modernist*, 141–42.

50. R. G. Collins, "Light in August: Faulkner's Stained Glass Tryptich," *Mosaic* (Fall 1973): 97–153.

4. MODERNISM AND POPULAR
CULTURE IN THE AGE OF EZRA POUND AND JAMES JOYCE

1. Louis Menand, *Discovering Modernism: T. S. Eliot and His Context* (Oxford, UK: Oxford University Press, 1987), 116–17.

2. Pierre Bourdieu, *Distinction: A Social Critique of the Judgment of Taste* (Cambridge, MA: Harvard University Press, 1984).

3. Irving Howe, "The Culture of Modernism," *Commentary* (November 1967): 65.

4. Q. D. Leavis, *Fiction and the Reading Public* (London: Chatto, 1932), 47.

5. Quoted in T. Austin Graham, *The Great American Songbook* (Oxford, UK, and New York: Oxford University Press, 2012), 27.

6. Theodor Adorno, "On Popular Music," *Studies in Philosophy and Social Sciences* 9, no. 1 (1941): 17–48.

7. T. S. Eliot, *The Use of Poetry and the Use of Criticism: Studies in the Relation of Criticism to Poetry in England* (1933; reprint, Cambridge, UK: Cambridge University Press, 1986), 152–54.

8. James Joyce, *Selected Letters*, ed. Richard Ellmann (London: Faber and Faber, 1976), 292.

9. Joyce, *Selected Letters*, 288.

10. Alisdair McCleery, "Changing Audiences: The Case of the Penguin Ulysses," in *Readings on Audience and Textual Materiality*, ed. Graham Allen, Carrie Griffin, and Mary O'Donnell (London: Pickering and Chatto, 2011), 133.

11. McCleery, "Changing Audiences," 32.

12. Joyce, *Selected Letters*, 204.

13. James Joyce, *A Portrait of the Artist as a Young Man* (1916; reprint, New York: Penguin, 2003), 253.

14. Joyce, *Selected Letters*, 85.

15. Joyce, *Selected Letters*, 90.

16. Joyce, *Selected Letters*, 99, 121.

17. Joyce, *Selected Letters*, 106.

18. Richard Ellmann, *James Joyce* (Oxford, UK, and New York: Oxford University Press, 1983), 354.

19. Hugh Kenner, *Joyce's Voices* (London: Faber and Faber, 1978).

20. Lewis Mumford, *Freeman*, April 18, 1923.

21. Nicola Humble, *The Feminine Middlebrow 1920s to 1930s: Class, Domesticity, and Bohemianism* (Oxford, UK, and New York: Oxford University Press, 2001).

22. *Observer*, July 10, 1927, p. 10.

23. See George Orwell, *Bookshop Memories: Collected Essays, Journalism, and Letters*, ed. Sonia Orwell and Ian Ayres (London: Secker and Warburg, 1968). See also "Boy's Weeklies." Orwell's 1944 25,000-word essay in the French journal *Fontaine* discusses crime fiction.

24. Roger Chartier, *The Order of Books* (Cambridge, UK: Polity, 1994), 22–23.

25. Anthony Grafton, "Is the History of Reading a Marginal Enterprise? Guillame Budé and His Books," *Papers of the Bibliographical Society of America* 91 (1997): 141.

26. Barbara Sicherman, *Well-Read Lives: How Books Inspired a Generation of Women* (Chapel Hill: University of North Carolina Press, 2012). See also Simon Eliot and Jonathan Rose, eds., *A Companion to the History of the Book* (Malden, MA, and Oxford, UK: Wiley-Blackwell, 2009).

27. Alexis de Tocqueville, *Democracy in America* (1836; reprint, New York: Penguin, 2003).

28. Robert Bellah et al., *Habits of the Heart: Individualism and Community in American Life* (New York: Harper and Row, 1986); Robert Putnam, *Bowling Alone: The Collapse and Revival of American Community* (New York:

Simon and Schuster, 2001); Elizabeth Long, *Book Clubs: Women and the Uses of Reading in Everyday Life* (Chicago: University of Chicago Press, 2003), 20.

29. *Women's Enterprise*, Baton Rouge, Louisiana, June 1, 1922, p. 9.

30. *Winsboro Record*, Winsboro, South Carolina, October 27, 1922, p. 5.

31. *Madison Journal*, Madison, Louisiana, April 30, 1921, p. 2.

32. Janice Radway, "Reading Is Not Eating: Mass-Produced Literature and the Theoretical, Methodological, and Political Consequences of a Metaphor," *Book Research Quarterly* 2, no. 3 (Fall 1986): 29.

33. Tania Modleski, *Loving with a Vengeance: Mass-Produced Fantasies for Women* (1982; reprint, London: Routledge, 2007), 38, 57.

34. Kay Mussell, *Fantasy and Reconciliation: Contemporary Formulas in Women's Romance Fiction* (Santa Barbara, CA: ABC-CLIO, 1984); Laura Struve, "Sisters of Sorts: Reading Romantic Fiction and the Bonds among Female Readers," *Journal of Popular Culture* 44, no. 6 (December 2011): 1,293.

35. Elizabeth McHenry, *Forgotten Readers: Recovering the Lost History of African American Literary Societies* (Durham, NC: Duke University Press, 2002), 300.

36. Marianne Moore is mentioned in the New York Public Library Minutes, Committee on Circulation, Volume 21, 1921 RG5 on pages 12 and 14, and Larsen on page 378. See also page 207.

37. Ann Douglas, *Terrible Honesty: Mongrel Manhattan in the 1920s* (New York: Farrar, Straus, and Giroux, 1995), 60.

38. Douglas, *Terrible Honesty*, 87.

39. Arthur Miller, *Modern Drama: Twentieth Century Perspectives* (Englewood Cliffs, NJ: Prentice-Hall, 1969), 34.

40. Beth Luey, "Modernity and Print III: The United States, 1890–1970," in *A Companion to the History of the Book*, ed. Simon Eliot and Jonathan Rose (Malden, MA, and Oxford, UK: Wiley-Blackwell, 2009), 371.

41. Luey, "Modernity and Print III," 371.

42. Charles Scribner's Sons Records, Princeton University; Luey, "Modernity and Print III," 371.

43. Alfred Harcourt, "Publishing in New York," in *Publishers on Publishing*, ed. Gerald Gross (New York: Grosset and Dunlap, 1961), 255.

44. Harcourt, "Publishing in New York," 255.

45. Harcourt, "Publishing in New York," 256.

46. Harcourt, "Publishing in New York," 259.

47. Harcourt, "Publishing in New York," 169.

48. Harcourt, "Publishing in New York," 330. Bennett Cerf encouraged the publication of Anita Loos's *Gentlemen Prefer Blondes*, which became a Boni and Liveright best seller. The book's price was set at two dollars, decreased to a

dollar seventy-five, and then returned to the two-dollar mark. Meanwhile, Cerf was able to get Horace Liveright to sell him the Modern Library imprint.

49. Harcourt, "Publishing in New York," 334.

50. Harcourt, "Publishing in New York," 334.

5. MIDWESTERN VISION AND VALUES

1. Frederick Hoffmann, *The Twenties: American Writing in the Postwar Decade* (New York: Viking, 1955), 331.

2. Glenway Wescott, *The Grandmothers* (New York: Harper's, 1927).

3. Zona Gale, "Friendship Village," 1908. *Friendship Village Love Stories* (New York: Macmillan, 2009).

4. Edna Ferber, *Dawn O'Hara: The Girl Who Laughed* (New York: Frederick Stokes, 1911), 50–53.

5. Ferber, *Dawn O'Hara*, 53.

6. Louis Kronenberger, "Review of *Showboat*," *New York Times*, August 22, 1926, p. 12.

7. Quoted in Christine Pawley, *Reading Places: Literacy, Democracy, and the Public Library in the Cold War* (Amherst: University of Massachusetts Press, 2010), 69.

8. Pawley, *Reading Places*, 69–70.

9. Pawley, *Reading Places*, 75.

10. Pawley, *Reading Places*, 34.

11. Wayne A. Wiegand, *Main Street Public Library: Community Places in the Rural Heartland, 1876–1956* (Ames: University of Iowa Press, 2011). See also Wiegand, "Community Places and Reading Spaces: Main Street and Public Libraries in the Rural Heartland, 1876–1956," in *Libraries and the Reading Public in Twentieth-Century America*, ed. Christine Pawley and Louise S. Robbins, 23–39 (Madison: University of Wisconsin Press, 2013).

12. Hoffmann, *The Twenties*, 237.

13. Sherwood Anderson Collection, Newberry Library, Chicago, Illinois.

14. Hoffmann, *The Twenties*, 238.

15. Sherwood Anderson Collection. See also Frederick Hoffmann, "The Voices of Sherwood Anderson," *Shenandoah* (1968) in *The Achievement of Sherwood Anderson*, ed. R.L. White. Chapel Hill: University of North Carolina, 1966, 243.

16. Irving Howe, *Sherwood Anderson* (New York: William Sloane Associates, 1951), 95.

17. Quoted in Howe, *Sherwood Anderson*, 117.

18. Edwin Fussell, quoted in Howe, *Sherwood Anderson*, 105.

19. Hoffmann, *The Twenties*, 107.

20. Howe, *Sherwood Anderson*, 90.

21. David D. Anderson, "Sherwood Anderson after Twenty Years," *Midwest Quarterly* 3 (January 1962): 119–21.

22. Hoffmann, *The Twenties*, 233.

23. Hoffmann, *The Twenties*, 233.

24. Hoffmann, *The Twenties*, 234.

25. Hoffmann, *The Twenties*, 232.

26. Hoffmann, *The Twenties*, 232.

27. Mark Schorer, *Sinclair Lewis: An American Life* (New York: McGraw-Hill, 1961), 250.

28. Schorer, *Sinclair Lewis: An American Life*, 251.

29. Schorer, *Sinclair Lewis: An American Life*, 259.

30. Schorer, *Sinclair Lewis: An American Life*, 262.

31. Schorer, *Sinclair Lewis: An American Life*, 289.

32. Schorer, *Sinclair Lewis: An American Life*, 289.

33. Schorer, *Sinclair Lewis: An American Life*, 289.

34. This idea is echoed by Schorer, *Sinclair Lewis: An American Life*, 295.

35. Signed C. W., "Review of *Zell*," *New York Tribune*, February 9, 1921.

36. Schorer, *Sinclair Lewis: An American Life*, 288.

37. Schorer, *Sinclair Lewis: An American Life*, 294.

38. Hoffmann, *The Twenties*.

39. Schorer, *Sinclair Lewis: An American Life*, 295.

40. Schorer, *Sinclair Lewis: An American Life*, 264.

41. Sinclair Lewis Letters, University of Virginia, Charlottesville, Virginia.

42. Sinclair Lewis Letters.

43. Schorer, *Sinclair Lewis: An American Life*, 268–69.

44. Schorer, *Sinclair Lewis: An American Life*, 264.

45. *Bismarck Tribune*, April 27, 1921, p. 3.

46. This is Schorer's observation, although he provides no direct evidence of this.

47. "Letters of Note: Mrs. Sinclair Lewis to You." Available online at www.lettersofnote.com/2012/05/mrs-sinclair (accessed December 10, 2014).

48. Schorer, *Sinclair Lewis: An American Life*, 269.

49. "Review of *Main Street*," *New York Tribune*, November 27, 1921, p. 9.

50. Schorer, *Sinclair Lewis: An American Life*, 270.

51. *Columbia Evening Missourian*, May 3, 1921, p. 1, middle column.

52. Floyd Dell, quoted in Schorer, *Sinclair Lewis: An American Life*, 277.

53. Thomas J. McCarthy, "Letter" and "Missing Links," *Bismarck Tribune*, March 21, 1921, p. 3.

54. Haywood Broun, *New York Tribune*, October 27, 1920, p. 10.

55. William Allen White, *Emporia Gazette*, 1921; *Bismarck Tribune*, April 27, 1921.

56. Quoted in Schorer, *Sinclair Lewis: An American Life*, 278.

57. Quoted in Schorer, *Sinclair Lewis: An American Life*, 278.

58. Schorer, *Sinclair Lewis: An American Life*, 279.

59. "Lewis Reads Work of Nebraska Authors," *Red Cloud Chief*, April 14, 1921.

60. Schorer, *Sinclair Lewis: An American Life*, 274.

61. Schorer, *Sinclair Lewis: An American Life*, 275. Carl Van Doren noted that people at Columbia University were reading the book.

62. Ames Kendrick, "Lewis's *Babbitt* Is an Even Better Novel Than *Main Street*: Sinclair Lewis Picks on U.S. Americans Again," *Washington Times*, September 17, 1922.

63. *New York Tribune*, September 17, 1922.

64. *Philadelphia Evening Public Ledger*, October 3, 1922, p. 22.

65. Sinclair Lewis, quoted in Schorer, *Sinclair Lewis: An American Life*, 302.

66. Schorer, *Sinclair Lewis: An American Life*, 252.

67. Schorer, *Sinclair Lewis: An American Life*, 356.

68. Schorer, *Sinclair Lewis: An American Life*, 355.

69. Schorer, *Sinclair Lewis: An American Life*, 345.

70. Schorer, *Sinclair Lewis: An American Life*, 345.

71. Schorer, *Sinclair Lewis: An American Life*, 370.

72. Schorer, *Sinclair Lewis: An American Life*, 303.

73. Sinclair Lewis, quoted in Schorer, *Sinclair Lewis: An American Life*, 333.

74. Schorer, *Sinclair Lewis: An American Life*, 318.

75. Schorer, *Sinclair Lewis: An American Life*, 325.

76. Schorer, *Sinclair Lewis: An American Life*, 381.

77. Schorer, *Sinclair Lewis: An American Life*, 381.

78. Quoted in Schorer, *Sinclair Lewis: An American Life*, 415.

79. Schorer, *Sinclair Lewis: An American Life*, 455.

80. Schorer, *Sinclair Lewis: An American Life*, 473.

81. Kurt A. Edwards, "Billy Graham, Elmer Gantry, and the Performance of a New American Revivalism," PhD dissertation, Bowling Green State University, Bowling Green, Ohio, 2008, note 68.

82. Gore Vidal, "The Romance of Sinclair Lewis," *New York Review of Books*, October 8, 1992. Available online at http://www.nybooks.com/articles/archives/1992/oct/08/the-romance-of-sinclair-lewis/ (accessed December 10, 2014).

83. Harry E. Maule and Melville E. Cane, quoted in Elin Arnestrand, "Sinclair Lewis and the American 1920s," master's thesis, Oslo University, Oslo, Norway, 2007.

84. Arnestrand, "Sinclair Lewis and the American 1920s."

85. John Updike, "No Brakes: A New Biography of Sinclair Lewis," *New Yorker*, February 4, 2002. Available online at http://www.newyorker.com/magazine/2002/02/04/no-brakes (accessed December 10, 2014).

86. This is a remarkable comment by Schorer, *Sinclair Lewis: An American Life*.

87. Mark Schorer, quoted in Vidal, "The Romance of Sinclair Lewis."

88. Vidal, "The Romance of Sinclair Lewis."

89. Vidal, "The Romance of Sinclair Lewis."

90. The Willa Cather archive at Drew University includes manuscripts and first editions in the Caspersen collection and letters to musician Yehudi Mehunin. Merrill Skaggs was instrumental in creating a conference on the Cather collection and "Cather in New York." The University of Nebraska archive contains numerous resources, including many of Cather's personal papers.

91. Walter Tittle, "Glimpses of Interesting Americans," *Century*, July 1925, p. 312. Cather's comment that the world broke in two in 1922 or thereabouts may be compared with Virginia Woolf's similar statement in 1910.

92. Willa Cather, interview in *New York World*, April 1925. Cather's interviews and speeches appear in Willa Cather, *Willa Cather in Person: Interviews, Speeches, and Letters*, ed. L. Brent Bohlke (Lincoln: University of Nebraska Press, 1986).

93. Bernice Slote, "The House of Willa Cather," in *The Art of Willa Cather*, ed. Bernice Slote and Virginia Faulkner (Lincoln: University of Nebraska Press, 1974), 47–48.

94. *Washington Herald*, September 23, 1922.

95. Edmund Wilson, *Shores of Light: A Literary Chronicle of the Twenties and Thirties* (New York: Farrar, Straus, and Young, 1952), 118.

96. JoAnn Middleton, *Willa Cather's Modernism: A Study of Style and Technique* (Madison, NJ: Fairleigh Dickinson University Press, 1990), 84.

97. Eva Mahoney, "How Willa Cather Found Herself," *Omaha World-Herald*, November 27, 1921.

98. James Woodress, *Willa Cather: A Literary Life* (Lincoln: University of Nebraska Press, 1987). See also Middleton, *Willa Cather's Modernism*, 60.

99. Quoted in Middleton, *Willa Cather's Modernism*, 88; Joseph Wood Krutch, "Reviews of Four Novels: The Lady as Artist," in *Willa Cather and Her Critics*, ed. James Schroeter (Ithaca, NY: Cornell University Press, 1967), 53. In contrast, Krutch found Cather's next novel, *A Professor's House*, "fragmentary and inconclusive." See Joseph Wood Krutch, "Professor's House: Second

Best" in *Willa Cather and Her Critics*. Ithaca: Cornell University Press, 1967. 369–70.

100. Middleton, *Willa Cather's Modernism*, 94.

101. Fitzgerald wrote a letter to Cather in which he says that he had written *Gatsby* before reading *A Lost Lady*. See Matthew Bruccoli, "An Instance of Apparent Plagiarism: F. Scott Fitzgerald, Willa Cather, and the First *Gatsby* Manuscript," *Princeton University Library Chronicle* 39 (1978): 171–76. On April 28, 1925, Cather cordially replied, adding that the best way to describe beauty was to "describe its effect and not the person." See F. Scott Fitzgerald, *F. Scott Fitzgerald: A Life in Letters*, ed. Matthew Bruccoli and Judith S. Baughman (New York: Touchstone, 1995). James E. Miller considers Cather a likely influence on Fitzgerald. See James E. Miller, *F. Scott Fitzgerald: His Art and His Technique* (New York: New York University Press, 1964). Tom Quirk writes about an influence on "incident and story" in his essay "Fitzgerald and Cather: The Great Gatsby," *American Literature* 54 (December 1978): 576. Quirk documents Fitzgerald's appreciation of Cather's style and techniques (576–91).

102. Hoffmann, *The Twenties*, 155.

103. Eudora Welty, *The Eye of the Story* (New York: Random House, 1977), 53.

104. As Wolfgang Iser points out, a text allows for blanks from "dense, interweaving of perceptions" toward a "horizon." *The Act of Reading* (London: Routledge/Kegan Paul, 1979), 121.

105. Willa Cather, "On the Art of Fiction" in *On Writing*. New York: Alfred A. Knopf, 1950, rpt. Lincoln: University of Nebraska Press, 1988.

106. Middleton, *Willa Cather's Modernism*, 130–32.

107. Middleton, *Willa Cather's Modernism*, 67.

108. Middleton, *Willa Cather's Modernism*, 67.

109. Edward Bloom and Lillian Bloom, *Willa Cather's Gift of Sympathy* (Carbondale: Southern Illinois University Press, 1962), 133.

110. Middleton, *Willa Cather's Modernism*, 79.

111. Middleton, *Willa Cather's Modernism*, 66.

112. Wayne Booth, *The Company We Keep: An Ethics of Fiction* (Berkeley: University of California Press, 1988).

113. Willa Cather, *Not under Forty* (1936; reprint, New York: Alfred A. Knopf, 1964), 43–44.

114. Cather, *Not under Forty*, 92.

115. Middleton, *Willa Cather's Modernism*, 88.

116. Middleton, *Willa Cather's Modernism*, 88–90. Cather, of course, recognized that Henry James usually focused his attention on the study of European societies, not American society.

117. Wayne Booth calls this third-person point of view that of a "reflector." See Wayne Booth, "Distance and Point of View: An Essay in Classification," in *Theory of the Novel*, ed. Philip Stevick (New York: Free Press, 1967), 98–99.

118. Sinclair Lewis, quoted in "Lewis Reads Work of Nebraska Authors," *Red Cloud Chief*, April 14, 1921.

119. *Alliance Herald*, November 8, 1921, p. 3.

120. Robert Darnton, *The Great Cat Massacre* (London: Allen Lane, 1984), 222.

6. SOUNDS OF THE CITY

1. Theodore Dreiser, *An American Tragedy* (1925; reprint, New York: New American Library, 1964), 65.

2. Dreiser, *An American Tragedy*, 160.

3. Dreiser, *An American Tragedy*, 67.

4. Dreiser, *An American Tragedy*, 169.

5. Dreiser, *An American Tragedy*, 161–62.

6. Dreiser, *An American Tragedy*, 350.

7. Lionel Trilling, *The Liberal Imagination: Essays on Literature and Society* (New York: Viking, 1950).

8. John Dos Passos, *Manhattan Transfer* (New York: Harper and Brothers, 1925), 120.

9. Dos Passos, *Manhattan Transfer*, 261.

10. Dos Passos, *Manhattan Transfer*, 320.

11. Dos Passos, *Manhattan Transfer*, 344.

12. Dos Passos, *Manhattan Transfer*, 365–66.

13. Dos Passos, *Manhattan Transfer*, 156.

14. Dos Passos, *Manhattan Transfer*, 4.

15. Dos Passos, *Manhattan Transfer*, 124.

16. D. H. Lawrence, "Review of *Manhattan Transfer* and *In Our Time*," (1927), 364.

17. T. Austin Graham, *The Great American Songbook* (Oxford, UK, and New York: Oxford University Press, 2012), 187.

18. Graham, *The Great American Songbook*, 188.

19. Graham, *The Great American Songbook*, 188.

20. Graham, *The Great American Songbook*, 188.

21. Dos Passos, *Manhattan Transfer*, 616.

22. Graham, *The Great American Songbook*, 192.

23. Dos Passos, *Manhattan Transfer*, 678.

24. Graham, *The Great American Songbook*, 197.

25. Sinclair Lewis, *Main Street* (1920; reprint, New York: Library of America, 1992), 304,

26. John Dos Passos, *Three Soldiers* (1921; reprint, New York: Library of America, 2003), 316–17.

27. John Dos Passos, quoted in Alfred Kazin, "Introduction," *Manhattan Transfer*, vii.

28. Kazin, "Introduction," *Manhattan Transfer*, vii.

29. Edmund Wilson and Lewis M. Dabney, *Edmund Wilson: Literary Essays and Reviews of the 1920s and 1930s* (New York: Library of America, 2007).

30. John Dos Passos, *The Fourteenth Chronicle: Letters and Diaries of John Dos Passos*, ed. Townsend Ludington (New York: Gambit, 1973).

31. Dos Passos, *Manhattan Transfer*, 20.

32. John Dos Passos, *The 42nd Parallel, U.S.A.* trilogy, vol. 1 (1930; reprint, New York: Library of America, 1996), 237.

33. Louise Levitas Henriksen, *Anzia Yezierska: A Writer's Life* (New Brunswick, NJ: Rutgers University Press, 1988), 14.

34. Henriksen, *Anzia Yezierska: A Writer's Life*, 37.

35. *New York American*, May 23, 1911; Henriksen, *Anzia Yezierska: A Writer's Life*, 38.

36. Quoted in Henriksen, *Anzia Yezierska: A Writer's Life*, 91.

37. Quoted in Henriksen, *Anzia Yezierska: A Writer's Life*, 92.

38. Henriksen, *Anzia Yezierska: A Writer's Life*, 128.

39. Quoted in Henriksen, *Anzia Yezierska: A Writer's Life*, 148–49.

40. Henriksen, *Anzia Yezierska: A Writer's Life*, 161.

41. Henriksen, *Anzia Yezierska: A Writer's Life*, 164.

42. Henriksen, *Anzia Yezierska: A Writer's Life*, 156.

43. Henriksen, *Anzia Yezierska: A Writer's Life*, 162.

44. Henriksen, *Anzia Yezierska: A Writer's Life*, 169.

45. Henriksen, *Anzia Yezierska: A Writer's Life*, 183.

46. Quoted in Henriksen, *Anzia Yezierska: A Writer's Life*, 217.

47. Edward D'Alessandro, *The Ginney Block: Reminiscences of an Italian American Dead-End-Street Kid* (Baltimore, MD: Gateway, 1988), 57.

48. D'Alessandro, *The Ginney Block*, 32.

49. Kenneth L. Kusmer, *Black Cleveland, 1870–1930* (Urbana: University of Illinois Press, 1976), 206.

50. Kusmer, *Black Cleveland*, 234.

51. John J. Grabowski, Judith Zielinski-Zak, Alice Boberg, and Ralph Wroblewski, "Polish Americans and Their Communities of Cleveland," *Cleveland Memory Project*, Michael Swartz Library, Cleveland State University (2007),

164. Available online at http://clevelandmemory.org/ebooks/Polish/ (accessed December 12, 2014).

52. Gene P. Veronesi, "Italian Americans and Their Communities in Cleveland," *Cleveland Memory Project*, Michael Swartz Library, Cleveland State University (2007), 233. Available online at http://www.clevelandmemory.org/italians/ (accessed December 12, 2014).

53. Veronesi, "Italian Americans and Their Communities in Cleveland," 239.

54. Louis B. Seltzer, "The Years Were Good," *Cleveland Memory Project*, Michael Swartz Library, Cleveland State University (1956), 57. Available online at http://www.clevelandmemory.org/ebooks/tywg/ (accessed December 12, 2014).

55. Seltzer, "The Years Were Good," 45.

56. Seltzer, "The Years Were Good," 28.

57. Seltzer, "The Years Were Good," 46.

58. Langston Hughes, *My Early Days in Harlem* (New York: Random House, 1963), 312.

59. Quoted in Ann Douglas, *Terrible Honesty: Mongrel Manhattan in the 1920s* (New York: Farrar, Straus, and Giroux, 1995), 313.

60. Hughes, *My Early Days in Harlem*, 312.

61. Langston Hughes, *Not without Laughter* (New York: Alfred A. Knopf, 1930), 259.

62. Douglas puts the figure at 87,417 in *Terrible Honesty*, 312.

63. Douglas, *Terrible Honesty*, 308.

64. Quoted in Douglas, *Terrible Honesty*, 303.

65. Langston Hughes, *The Big Sea: An Autobiography* (New York: Random House, 1940), 72.

66. *Chicago Tribune*, November 20, 1927; *Amsterdam News*, November 1927.

67. William H. Ferris, "Individuality Is Race's Greatest Need," *Pittsburgh Courier*, November 27, 1926.

68. Benjamin Brawley, *Negro Genius: An Appraisal of the American Negro in Literature and the Fine Arts* (New York: Dodd, Mead, 1937), 13.

69. "American Art or Negro Art," *Nation* 122 (August 18, 1927): 743; "These Bad New Negroes: A Critique on Critics," *Pittsburgh Courier*, April 7, 1927.

70. James Weldon Johnson, *Black Manhattan* (1930; reprint, New York: Arno Press, 1968).

71. Sterling Brown, "Our Literary Audience," *Opportunity*, February 1930, p. 42.

72. Brown, "Our Literary Audience," 77.

73. Quoted in Douglas, *Terrible Honesty*, 79.

74. Douglas, *Terrible Honesty*, 81.

75. Leon Coleman, *Carl Van Vechten and the Harlem Renaissance: A Critical Assessment* (New York: Garland, 1998).

76. William Rose Benet, "Cursive and Discursive," *Saturday Review II*, January 26, 1926, pp. 505–07. See also Coleman, *Carl Van Vechten and the Harlem Renaissance*, 99. Hughes notes that the parties were reported on in the Negro newspapers. *The Big Sea*, 251.

77. Carl Van Vechten, quoted in Douglas, *Terrible Honesty*, 83.

78. Carl Van Vechten, "Folk Songs of the American Negro," *New York Herald Tribune Books*, October 25, 1928, 52.

79. Carl Van Vechten, "All God's Chillun Got Songs," *Nation* 62 (August 1925): 63.

80. Van Vechten, "Folksongs of the American Negro," 2.

81. Van Vechten, "Folk Songs of American Negro," 52; Van Vechten, "All God's Chillun Got Songs," 24, 63.

82. The original letter is in the James Weldon Johnson Collection, Beinecke Library, Yale University, New Haven, Connecticut. See Michael Kardos, "Musical and Ideological Synthesis in James Weldon Johnson's *Autobiography of an Ex-Colored Man*," in *Music and Literary Modernism*, ed. Robert McParland (Newcastle upon Tyne, UK: Cambridge Scholars Publishing, 2007), 126–35.

83. James Weldon Johnson Collection; cited in Coleman, *Carl Van Vechten and the Harlem Renaissance*, 87–88.

84. Coleman, *Carl Van Vechten and the Harlem Renaissance*, 84. See also "A Triumphant Negro Heroine," *New York Herald Tribune Books*, April 11, 1928, p. 3.

85. Langston Hughes, Letter to Carl Van Vechten, James Weldon Johnson Collection.

86. "Downhearted Blues" was written by Alberta Hunter and Lovie Houston.

87. Langston Hughes, "The Negro Artist and the Racial Mountain," *Langston Hughes Reader* (New York: George Braziller, 1981), 31–36. Langston Hughes and Arnold Rampersad, *The Collected Works of Langston Hughes* (Columbia: University of Missouri Press, 2002), 31.

88. Quoted in Douglas, *Terrible Honesty*, 101.

89. Douglas, *Terrible Honesty*, 310.

90. See James Weldon Johnson, "Preface to *The Book of Negro American Poetry*," *James Weldon Johnson: Writings* (New York: Library of America, 2004), 688–719; James Weldon Johnson, "Preface to *The Second Book of Ne-*

gro Spirituals," *James Weldon Johnson: Writings* (New York: Library of America, 2004), 730–43.

91. Mark Tucker, *The Duke Ellington Reader* (Oxford, UK, and New York: Oxford University Press, 1995), 218.

7. HISTORY AND MYTHMAKERS

1. Frederick Hoffmann, *The Twenties: American Writing in the Postwar Decade* (New York: Viking, 1955), 156–57 (note 43), 183.

2. F. Scott Fitzgerald, *F. Scott Fitzgerald: A Life in Letters*, ed. Matthew Bruccoli and Judith S. Baughman (New York: Touchstone, 1995), 115.

3. Fitzgerald, *A Life in Letters*.

4. Fitzgerald, *A Life in Letters*, 68.

5. Charles Beard, December 1, 1920. See R. H. Tawney, *Religion and the Rise of Capitalism* (New York: Harcourt Brace, 1926).

6. Kenneth Burke, "Heaven's First Law," *Dial* (February 1922): 197.

7. William Carlos Williams, *In the American Grain* (1925, 1956; reprint, New York: New Directions, 2009).

8. William Carlos Williams, *Spring and All* (Paris: Contact Publishing, 1923).

9. Williams, *In the American Grain*, 178.

10. Paul Mariani, *William Carlos Williams: A New World Naked* (New York: W. W. Norton, 1990), 207.

11. Mariani, *William Carlos Williams: A New World Naked*, 214.

12. William Carlos Williams, letter to Kenneth Burke, Monday, November 1923; see Mariani, *William Carlos Williams: A New World Naked*, 214.

13. Charles Fenton, *Stephen Vincent Benet: The Life and Times of an American Man of Letters, 1808–1943* (New Haven, CT: Yale University Press, 1958), 81.

14. Stephen Vincent Benet, "Elemental," *Cosmopolitan* 72 (April 1922): 17.

15. Elinor Wylie, "Review of *Young People's Pride*," *New Republic* 32 (October 25, 1922): 22.

16. Quoted in Fenton, *Stephen Vincent Benet: The Life and Times of an American Man of Letters*, 127.

17. Fenton, *Stephen Vincent Benet: The Life and Times of an American Man of Letters*, 147.

18. Fenton, *Stephen Vincent Benet: The Life and Times of an American Man of Letters*, 169.

19. Quoted in Harry Salpeter, "The First Reader," *New York World*, August 16, 1927.

20. Quoted in Fenton, *Stephen Vincent Benet: The Life and Times of an American Man of Letters*, 215.

21. Fenton attests to a southern response to the poem, which is borne out by sales figures.

22. Hoffmann, *The Twenties*, 145.

23. Fenton, *Stephen Vincent Benet: The Life and Times of an American Man of Letters*, 17.

24. Susan Shillinglaw, *On Reading* The Grapes of Wrath (New York: Penguin, 2014), xi.

25. John Steinbeck, *Cup of Gold* (New York: McBride, 1929), 187, 262.

26. Shillinglaw, *On Reading* The Grapes of Wrath, 163.

27. Quoted in Shillinglaw, *On Reading* The Grapes of Wrath, 176.

28. John Steinbeck, *America and Americans and Selected Nonfiction*, ed. Susan Shillinglaw and Jackson J. Benson (New York: Viking, 2002), 388.

29. Steinbeck, *America and Americans and Selected Nonfiction*, 404.

30. Steinbeck, *America and Americans and Selected Nonfiction*, 401.

31. Steinbeck, *America and Americans and Selected Nonfiction*, 319.

32. Steinbeck, *America and Americans and Selected Nonfiction*, 330–32.

33. Steinbeck, *America and Americans and Selected Nonfiction*, 335.

34. Steinbeck, *America and Americans and Selected Nonfiction*, 335.

BIBLIOGRAPHY

Ackroyd, Peter. *Notes for a New Culture: An Essay on Modernism*. New York: Barnes and Noble, 1976.

———. *T. S. Eliot: A Life*. New York: Simon and Schuster, 1984.

Adorno, Theodor. "On Popular Music." *Studies in Philosophy and Social Sciences* 9, no. 1 (1941): 17–48.

Allen, Frederick Lewis. *Only Yesterday*. New York: Harper's, 1931.

Anderson, David D. "Sherwood Anderson after Twenty Years." *Midwest Quarterly* 3 (January 1962): 119–32.

Anderson, Paul Allen. *Deep River: Music and Memory in Harlem Renaissance Thought*. Durham, NC: Duke University Press, 2001.

Anderson, Sherwood. *Dark Laughter*. New York: B. W. Heubsch, 1925.

———. *Horses and Men*. New York: B. W. Heubsch, 1923.

———. *The Letters*. Boston: Little Brown, 1953.

———. *Many Marriages*. New York: B. W. Heubsch, 1923.

———. *Poor White*. New York: B. W. Heubsch, 1920.

———. *Sherwood Anderson's Notebook*. New York: Liveright, 1926.

———. *A Story Teller's Story*. New York: B. W. Heubsch, 1924.

———. *Tar: A Midwest Childhood*. New York: Liveright, 1926.

———. *The Triumph of the Egg*. New York: B. W. Heubsch, 1921.

———. *Windy McPherson's Son*. 1916. Reprint, New York: B. W. Heubsch, 1921.

———. *Winesberg, Ohio*. New York: B. W. Heubsch, 1919.

Arnestrand, Elin. *Sinclair Lewis and the American 1920s*. Master's thesis, Oslo University, Oslo, Norway, 2007.

Arnold, M. *Willa Cather's Short Fiction*. Athens: Ohio University Press, 1969.

Auerbach, Erich. *Hemingway: A Life Story*. New York: Charles Scribner's Sons, 1969.

———. *Hemingway: The Writer as Artist*, 4th ed. Princeton, NJ: Princeton University Press, 1972.

———. *Mimesis*. Princeton, NJ: Princeton University Press, 1958.

———. "The Mountain and the Plain." In *Critical Essays on Ernest Hemingway's* A Farewell to Arms. Ed. George Monteiro, 97–103. Boston: G. K. Hall, 1984.

Baker, Houston A. *Blues, Ideology, and Afro-American Literature: A Vernacular Theory*. Chicago: University of Chicago Press, 1984.

———. *Modernism and the Harlem Renaissance*. Chicago: University of Chicago Press, 1987.

Bakhtin, Mikhail. *The Dialogic Imagination*. Ed. Michael Holquist. Trans. Caryl Emerson and Michael Holquist. Austin: University of Texas Press, 1981.

Baldick, Chris. *Literature of the 1920s: Writers among the Ruins*. Edinburgh, UK: Edinburgh University Press, 2012.

Baraka, Amiri. *Black Music*. New York: William Morrow, 1967.

Barnouw, Eric. *A Tower of Babel: A History of Broadcasting in the United States*. 2 vols. New York: Oxford University Press, 1966.

Batchelor, Bob. *Gatsby: The Cultural History of an American Novel*. Lanham, MD: Rowman and Littlefield, 2014.

Beach, Joseph Warren. "*Manhattan Transfer*: Collectivism and Abstract Composition." In *Dos Passos, the Critics, and the Writer's Intention*. Ed. Allen Belkind, 54–69. Carbondale: Southern Illinois University Press, 1971.

Beard, Charles A., and Mary R. Beard. *The Rise of American Civilization*. New York: Macmillan, 1927.

Beegel, Susan F. "'That Always Absent Something Else': 'A Natural History of the Dead' and Its Discarded Coda." In *Critical Approaches to the Short Stories of Ernest Hemingway*. Ed. Jackson J. Benson, 73–95. Durham, NC: Duke University Press, 1990.

Belkind, Allen, ed. *Dos Passos, the Critics, and the Writer's Intentions*. Carbondale: Southern Illinois University Press, 1971.

Bell, Millicent, "Pseudoautobiography and Personal Metaphor." In *Critical Essays on Ernest Hemingway's* A Farewell to Arms. Ed. George Monteiro, 145–60. Boston: G. K. Hall, 1984.

Bellah, Robert, et al. *Habits of the Heart: Individualism and Community in American Life*. New York: Harper and Row, 1986.

Benet, Stephen Vincent. *The Ballad of William Sycamore*. New York: G. H. Doran Co., 1923.

———. *The Beginning of Wisdom*. New York: Henry Holt, 1921.

———. *The Devil and Daniel Webster*. New York: Farrar and Rinehart, 1937.

———. "Elemental." *Cosmopolitan* 72 (April 1922): 17.

———. *John Brown's Body*. New York: Doubleday, 1928.

———. *Spanish Bayonet*. New York: G. H. Doran Co., 1926.

———. *Tales before Midnight*. New York: G. H. Doran Co., 1939.

———. *Thirteen O'Clock*. New York: G. H. Doran Co., 1937.

———. *Western Star*. New York: G. H. Doran Co., 1943.

———. *Young People's Pride*. New York: G. H. Doran Co., 1922.

Benet, William Rose. "Cursive and Discursive." *Saturday Review II*, January 26, 1926, pp. 505–7.

———. *F. Scott Fitzgerald: The Critical Heritage*. New York: Routledge, 1925.

Benson, Jackson J., ed. *Critical Approaches to the Short Stories of Ernest Hemingway*. Durham, NC: Duke University Press, 1990.

Berman, Ronald. *The Great Gatsby and Fitzgerald's World of Ideas*. Tuscaloosa: University of Alabama Press, 1997.

———. *The Great Gatsby and Modern Times*. Urbana: University of Illinois Press, 1994.

Berry, Faith. *Langston Hughes: Before and Beyond Harlem*. New York: Citadel, 1983.

Bewley, Marius. "Scott Fitzgerald's Criticism of America." In *F. Scott Fitzgerald: A Collection of Critical Essays*. Ed. Arthur Mizener, 124–41. Englewood Cliffs, NJ: Prentice-Hall, 1963.

Bigsby, C. W. E. *Modern American Drama, 1945–2000*. Cambridge, UK: Cambridge University Press, 2000.

Blair, Amy L. *Reading Up: Middle-Class Readers and the Culture of Success in the United States in the Early Twentieth Century*. Philadelphia, PA: Temple University Press, 2011.

Bliven, Bruce. "Jane's a Flapper." *New Republic*, September 9, 1925.

Bloom, Edward, and Lilian Bloom. *Willa Cather's Gift of Sympathy*. Carbondale: Southern Illinois University Press, 1962.

Blotner, Joseph. *William Faulkner: A Biography*. New York: Random House, 1974.

Bochner, Jay, and Justin D. Edwards. *American Modernism across the Arts*. New York: Peter Lang, 1999.

Bogards, Travis. "The Comedy of Thornton Wilder." Introduction to *Three Plays by Thornton Wilder*. New York: Harper, 1963.

Booth, Wayne. *The Company We Keep: An Ethics of Fiction*. Berkeley: University of California Press, 1988.

———. "Distance and Point of View: An Essay in Classification." In *Theory of the Novel*. Ed. Philip Stevick. New York: Free Press, 1967.

Borshuk, Michael. *Swinging the Vernacular: Jazz and African American Modernist Literature*. New York: Routledge, 2006.

Botshon, Lisa, and Meredith Goldsmith, eds. *Middlebrow Moderns: Popular American Women Writers of the 1920s*. Boston: Northeastern University Press, 2003.

Bourdieu, Pierre. *Distinction: A Social Critique of the Judgment of Taste*. Cambridge, MA: Harvard University Press, 1984.

Boyum, Joy Gould. *Double Exposure: Film into Fiction*. New York: Universe, 1985.

Bradbury, Malcolm, and David Palmer, eds. *The American Novel in the 1920s*. London: Arnold, 1971.

Brantley, John. *The Fiction of John Dos Passos*. The Hague, Netherlands: Mouton, 1968.

Brawley, Benjamin. *Negro Genius: An Appraisal of the American Negro in Literature and the Fine Arts*. New York: Dodd, Mead, 1937.

Brenner, Gerry. "A Hospitalized World." In *Critical Essays on Ernest Hemingway's* A Farewell to Arms. Ed. George Monteiro, 130–44. New York: G. K. Hall, 1984.

Brodhead, Richard, ed. *William Faulkner: New Perspectives*. Englewood Cliffs, NJ: Prentice-Hall, 1983.

Brooker, Jewel Spears, and Joseph Bentley. *Reading the Wasteland: Modernism and the Limits of Interpretation*. Amherst: University of Massachusetts Press, 1990.

Brooks, Van Wyck. *America's Coming of Age*. New York: B. H. Heubsch, 1915.

———. *The Confident Years, 1885–1915*. New York: E. P. Dutton, 1952.

———. *The Ordeal of Mark Twain*. New York: E. P. Dutton, 1920.

———. *The Wine of the Puritans*. London: Sisley, 1909.

Brown, Kathleen L. *Teaching Literary Theory Using Film Adaptations*. Jefferson, NC: McFarland, 2009.

Brown, Marion Marsh, and Ruth Crone. *Willa Cather: The Woman and Her Works*. New York: Charles Scribner's Sons, 1970.

Brown, Sterling. *The Negro in American Fiction*. Washington, DC: Associates in Negro Folk Education, 1937.

———. "Our Literary Audience." *Opportunity*, February 1930.

Bruccoli, Matthew. *The Composition of* Tender Is the Night: *A Study of the Manuscripts*. Pittsburgh, PA: University of Pittsburgh Press, 1963.

———. "An Instance of Apparent Plagiarism: F. Scott Fitzgerald, Willa Cather, and the First *Gatsby* Manuscript." *Princeton University Library Chronicle* 39 (1978): 171–76.

———. *The Notebooks of F. Scott Fitzgerald*. New York: Harcourt Brace, 1978.

——— *Some Sort of Epic Grandeur: The Life of F. Scott Fitzgerald*. New York: Harcourt Brace, 1981.

———, ed. *New Essays on* The Great Gatsby. Cambridge, UK: Cambridge University Press, 1985.

Bruccoli, Matthew J., and Jackson R. Bryer. *F. Scott Fitzgerald in His Own Time*. New York: Popular Library, 1971.

Bruccoli, Matthew J., and Margaret M. Duggan. *The Correspondence of F. Scott Fitzgerald*. New York: Random House, 1980.

Burke, Kenneth. "Heaven's First Law." *Dial* (February 1922): 197–200.

Cabell, James Branch. *Jurgen: A Comedy of Taste*. New York: Robert M. McBride, 1919.

Carr, Virginia Spencer. *Dos Passos: A Life*. Garden City, NY: Doubleday, 1984.

Carter, John F. "The Young Generation." *Atlantic Monthly*, September 1920.

Carter, Paul. *Another Part of the Twenties*. New York: Columbia University Press, 1977.

Cassuto, Leonard, Clare Virginia Eby, and Benjamin Reiss. *Cambridge History of the American Novel*. Cambridge, UK, and New York: Cambridge University Press, 2011.

Cather, Willa. *A Lost Lady*. 1923. Reprint, New York: Vintage, 1972.

————. "On the Art of Fiction" in *On Writing*. New York: Alfred A. Knopf, 1950, rpt. Lincoln: University of Nebraska Press, 1988.

————. *Collected Short Fiction*. Lincoln: University of Nebraska Press, 1965.

————. *Death Comes for the Archbishop*. 1927. Reprint, New York: Vintage, 1971.

————. *My Antonia*. 1918, 1926. Reprint, Boston: Houghton Mifflin, 1954.

————. *Not under Forty*. 1936. Reprint, New York: Alfred A. Knopf, 1964.

————. *O Pioneers!* 1913. Reprint, Boston: Houghton Mifflin, 1941.

————. *One of Ours*. 1922. Reprint, New York: Vintage, 1950.

————. *The Professor's House*. 1925. Reprint, New York: Vintage, 1973.

————. *The Song of the Lark*. 1915, Reprint, Boston: Houghton Mifflin, 1965.

————. *Willa Cather in Person: Interviews, Speeches, and Letters*. Ed. L. Brent Bohlke. Lincoln: University of Nebraska Press, 1986.

Chartier, Roger. *The Order of Books*. Cambridge, UK: Polity, 1994.

Chinitz, David. "Dance, Little Lady: Poets, Flappers, and the Gendering of Jazz." In *Modernism, Gender, and Culture: A Cultural Studies Approach*. Ed. Lisa Rado, 319–35. New York: Garland, 1987.

————. *T. S. Eliot and the Cultural Divide*. Chicago: University of Chicago Press, 2003.

Clark, Michael. *Dos Passos's Early Fiction, 1912–1938*. London: Associated University Presses, 1987.

Colclough, Stephen. "Readers: Books and Bibliography." In *A Companion to the History of the Book*. Ed. Simon Eliot and Jonathan Rose, 50–62. Malden, MA, and Oxford, UK: Wiley-Blackwell, 2009.

Coleman, Leon. *Carl Van Vechten and the Harlem Renaissance: A Critical Assessment*. New York: Garland, 1998.

Collins, R. G. "Light in August: Faulkner's Stained Glass Tryptich." *Mosaic* (Fall 1973): 97–153.

Commager, Henry Steele, ed. *The American Mind*. New Haven, CT: Yale University Press, 1950.

————. *The Story of America: The Twenties*. New York: Toronto Star, 1975.

Cooper, John Xiros. *T. S. Eliot's Orchestra: Critical Essays on Poetry and Music*. New York: Garland, 2000.

Cooper, Wayne F. *Claude McKay: Rebel Sojourner in the Harlem Renaissance*. New York: Schocken, 1987.

Cooperman, Stanley. *World War I and the American Novel*. Baltimore, MD: Johns Hopkins University Press, 1967.

Cowley, Malcolm. *After the Genteel Tradition: American Writers since 1910*. New York: W. W. Norton, 1936.

————. *Exile's Return: A Literary Odyssey of the 1920s*. 1934. Reprint, New York: Viking, 1951.

————. "Hemingway's Wound." *Georgia Review* 38 (Summer 1984): 229–30.

————. *The Portable Hemingway*. New York: Viking, 1944.

Crosby, Harry. *Shadows of the Sun*. Paris: Black Sun Press, 1925.

————. *War Letters*. Paris: Black Sun Press, 1932.

cummings, e. e. *The Enormous Room*. 1929. Reprint, New York: Liveright 2014.

Curnutt, Kirk. *Cambridge Companion to F. Scott Fitzgerald*. Cambridge, UK: Cambridge University Press, 2002.

C. W. "Review of *Zell*." *New York Tribune*, February 9, 1921.

Daisches, David. *Willa Cather: A Critical Introduction*. Ithaca, NY: Cornell University Press, 1951.

D'Alessandro, Edward. *The Ginney Block: Reminiscences of an Italian American Dead-End-Street Kid*. Baltimore, MD: Gateway, 1988.

Darnton, Robert. *The Great Cat Massacre*. London: Allen Lane, 1984.

De Koven, Marianne. *Rich and Strange: Gender, History, Modernism*. Princeton, NJ: Princeton University Press, 1991.

de Tocqueville, Alexis. *Democracy in America*. 1836. Reprint, New York: Penguin, 2003.

Dettmar, Kevin, and Stephen Watt. *Marketing Modernism: Self-Promotion, Canonization, Rereading.* Ann Arbor: University of Michigan Press, 1996.

Deveaux, Scott Knowles. *The Birth of Bebop.* Berkeley: University of California Press, 1997.

Di Battista, Maria, and Lucy Mc Dairmid. *High and Low Moderns: Literature and Culture, 1889–1939.* Oxford, UK: Oxford University Press, 1996.

Dickstein, Morris. *Critical Insights: The Great Catsby.* Pasadena, CA: Salem Press, 2010.

Donaldson, Scott. *Fool for Love: F. Scott Fitzgerald.* New York: Congdon and Weed, 1983.

Dos Passos, John. *1919. U.S.A.* trilogy, vol. 2. 1932. Reprint, New York: Library of America, 1996.

———. *The 42nd Parallel. U.S.A.* trilogy, vol. 1. 1930. Reprint, New York: Library of America, 1996.

———. *The Big Money. U.S.A.* trilogy, vol. 3. 1934. Reprint, New York: Library of America, 1996.

———. *The Fourteenth Chronicle: Letters and Diaries of John Dos Passos.* Ed. Townsend Ludington. New York: Gambit, 1973.

———. *John Dos Passos: The Major Nonfictional Prose.* Ed. Donald Pizer. Detroit: Wayne University Press, 1988.

———. *Manhattan Transfer.* New York: Harper and Brothers, 1925.

———. *One Man's Initiation.* 1917. Reprint, Ithaca, NY: Cornell University Press, 1969.

———. *Streets of Night.* New York: George Doran, 1923.

———. *Three Soldiers.* 1921. Reprint, New York: Library of America, 2003.

Douglas, Ann. *Terrible Honesty: Mongrel Manhattan in the 1920s.* New York: Farrar, Straus and Giroux, 1995.

Dowd, Jerome. *Negro in American Life.* New York: Century Company, 1926.

Dreiser, Theodore. *An American Tragedy.* 1925. Reprint, New York: New American Library, 1964.

Du Bois, W. E. B. *Essays and Articles.* New York: Library of America, 1987.

Ebel, Jonathan. *Faith in the Fight. Religion and the American Soldier in the Great War.* Champaign: University of Illinois Press, 2010.

Edwards, Kurt A. "Billy Graham, Elmer Gantry, and the Performance of a New American Revivalism." PhD dissertation, Bowling Green State University, Bowling Green, Ohio, 2008.

Eliot, T. S. *Complete Poems and Plays, 1909–1950.* New York: Harcourt Brace, 1980.

———. *Selected Prose.* Ed. Frank Kermode. New York: Harcourt Brace Jovanovich, 1975.

———. *The Use of Poetry and the Use of Criticism: Studies in the Relation of Criticism to Poetry in England.* 1933. Reprint, Cambridge, UK: Cambridge University Press, 1986.

———. *The Waste Land. A Facsimile and Transcript of the Original Drafts, Including the Annotations of Ezra Pound.* Ed. Valerie Eliot. New York: Harcourt Brace Jovanovich, 1971.

Ellis, Steve. "The Wasteland and the Reader's Response." In *The Waste Land.* Ed. Tony Davies and Nigel Wood, 83–104. Buckingham, UK: Open University Press, 1994.

Ellison, Ralph. *Shadow and Act.* 1964. Reprint, New York: Vintage, 1995.

Ellmann, Richard. *James Joyce.* Oxford, UK, and New York: Oxford University Press, 1983.

Evans, David. *Big Road Blues.* Berkeley: University of California Press, 1982.

Fabre, Genevieve. *Jean Toomer and the Harlem Renaissance.* New Brunswick, NJ: Rutgers University Press, 2001.

———. *Temples for Tomorrow: Looking Back at the Harlem Renaissance.* Bloomington: Indiana University Press, 2001.

Fagles, Robert, trans. *The Odyssey.* New York: Penguin, 1996.

Farrar, John. *Nerves.* New York: Samuel French, 1922.

Farrell, Walter, Jr., and Patricia A. Johnson. "Poetic Interpretations of Black Urban Folk Culture: Langston Hughes and the Bebop Era." *MELUS: The Journal for the Study of Multi-Ethnic Literature of the United States* 8, no. 3 (Fall 1981): 51–72.

Faulkner, William. "All the Dead Pilots." *The Collected Stories of William Faulkner.* New York: Random House/Vintage, 2012.

————. *Light in August*. Novels 1930–1935. Ed. Joseph Blotner and Noel Polk. New York: Library of America.

————. *Mosquitoes*. Novels, 1926–1929. Ed. Joseph Blotner and Noel Polk. New York: Library of America.

————. *Sanctuary*. Novels 1930–1935. Ed. Joseph Blotner and Noel Polk. New York: Library of America.

————. "Sherwood Anderson: An Appreciation." *Atlantic* 191 (June 1953): 27–29.

————. *Soldiers' Pay*. Novels, 1926–1929. Ed. Joseph Blotner and Noel Polk. New York: Library of America, 1990.

————. *The Sound and the Fury*. Ed. Noel Polk and Stephen M. Ross. London: Folio, 2012.

————. *The Sound and the Fury*. Novels, 1926–1929. Ed. Joseph Blotner and Noel Polk. New York: Library of America, 1999.

————. *The Uncollected Stories of William Faulkner*. New York: Random House/Vintage, 1987.

Fenton, Charles. *Stephen Vincent Benet: The Life and Times of an American Man of Letters, 1898–1943*. New Haven, CT: Yale University Press, 1958.

Ferber, Edna. *Cimarron*. Garden City, NY: Doubleday/Doran, 1929.

————. *Dawn O'Hara: The Girl Who Laughed*. New York: Frederick Stokes, 1911.

————. *Show Boat*. Garden City, NY: Doubleday, 1926.

————. *So Big*. Garden City, NY: Doubleday/Page, 1924.

Ferris, William H. *Blues from the Delta*. Garden City, NY: Doubleday, 1978.

————. "Individuality Is Race's Greatest Need." *Pittsburgh Courier*, November 27, 1926.

Fitzgerald, F. Scott. *All the Sad Young Men*. New York: Charles Scribner's Sons, 1926.

————. *The Beautiful and Damned*. New York: Charles Scribner's Sons, 1922.

————. *The Collected Short Stories of F. Scott Fitzgerald*. Ed. Matthew Bruccoli. New York: Charles Scribner's Sons, 1989.

————. *Correspondence of F. Scott Fitzgerald*. Ed. Matthew Bruccoli and Margaret M. Duggan. New York: Random House, 1980.

————. "Echoes of the Jazz Age." *New Statesman*, 1931.

————. *F. Scott Fitzgerald: A Life in Letters*. Ed. Matthew Bruccoli and Judith S. Baughman. New York: Touchstone, 1995.

————. *Flappers and Philosophers*. New York: Charles Scribner's Sons, 1920.

————. *The Great Gatsby*. New York: Charles Scribner's Sons, 1925.

————. *The Notebooks of F. Scott Fitzgerald*. Ed. Matthew Bruccoli. New York: Harcourt Brace Jovanovich, 1978.

————. *Tales of the Jazz Age*. New York: Charles Scribner's Sons, 1922.

————. *Tender Is the Night*. Ed. Matthew Bruccoli. 1934. Reprint, New York: Cambridge University Press, 1991.

————. *This Side of Paradise*. New York: Charles Scribner's Sons, 1920.

Fitzgerald, Zelda. *Zelda Fitzgerald: The Collected Writings*. Ed. Matthew Bruccoli. New York: Charles Scribner's Sons, 1991.

Fleming, Robert E. *James Weldon Johnson*. New York: Twayne, 1987.

Foley, Barbara. "From *U.S.A.* to Ragtime: Notes on the Forms of Historical Consciousness in Modern Fiction." *American Literature* 50 (March 1978): 85–105.

Ford, Ford Madox. *The Good Soldier*. 1915. Reprint, London: Folio, 2008.

————. *Women and Men*. Paris: Three Mountains Press, 1928.

Frank, Waldo. Foreword to *Cane*. 1923. Reprint, New York: Norton, 1988.

————. *The Re-Discovery of America: An Introduction to a Philosophy of American Life*. New York: Charles Scribner's Sons, 1929.

————. "Winesberg, Ohio after Twenty Years." *Story* 19 (September/October 1949): 29–33.

French, Warren, ed. *The Twenties: Fiction, Poetry, Drama*. Deland, FL: Everett Edwards, 1975.

Freud, Sigmund. *The Standard Edition of the Complete Psychological Works of Sigmund Freud*. 24 vols. Ed. James Strachey. London: Hogarth Press, 1953–1974.

Fussell, Edwin. "Winesberg, Ohio: Art and Isolation." *Modern Fiction Studies* 6, no.1 (Spring 1960): 106–14.

Fussell, Paul. *The Great War and Modern Memory*. Oxford, UK, and New York: Oxford University Press, 1975.

Gabbin, Joann V. *Sterling A. Brown: Building the Black Aesthetic Tradition*. Charlottesville: University of Virginia Press, 1994.

Gale, Zona. "Friendship Village," 1908. *Friendship Village Love Stories*. New York: Macmillan, 2009.

———. *Miss Lulu Bett*. New York: Appleton, 1920.

Gans, Herbert G. *Popular Culture and High Culture: An Analysis and Evaluation of Taste*. New York: Basic, 1974.

Gay, Peter. *Freud: A Life for Our Time*. New York: W. W. Norton, 1988.

Geismar, Maxwell. *The Last of the Provincials: The American Novel between the Two Wars*. Boston: Houghton Mifflin, 1948.

———. *Writers in Crisis: The American Novel between Two Wars*. Boston: Houghton Mifflin, 1942.

Gelfant, Blanche. *The American City Novel*. Norman: University of Oklahoma Press, 1954.

Gerber, Philip. *Willa Cather*. Boston: Twayne, 1975.

Giannone, Richard. *Music in Willa Cather's Fiction*. Lincoln: University of Nebraska Press, 1968.

Gibbs, Janet Frances. "Zona Gale: Pulitzer Playwright, Social Activist, 20th-Century Literary Comet." Unpublished PhD dissertation, Drew University, Madison, New Jersey.

Gilmer, Walker. *Horace Liveright: Publisher of the Twenties*. New York: David Lewis, 1970.

Goffmann, Erving. *The Presentation of Self in Everyday Life*. New York: Anchor, 1959.

Grabowski, John J., Judith Zielinski-Zak, Alice Boberg, and Ralph Wroblewski. "Polish Americans and Their Communities of Cleveland." *Cleveland Memory Project*, Michael Swartz Library, Cleveland State University (2007), 164. Available online at http://clevelandmemory.org/ebooks/Polish/ (accessed December 12, 2014).

Grafton, Anthony. "Is the History of Reading a Marginal Enterprise? Guillaume Budé and His Books." *Papers of the Bibliographical Society of America* 91 (1997): 137–57.

Graham, T. Austin. *The Great American Songbook*. Oxford, UK, and New York: Oxford University Press, 2012.

Habermas, Jurgen. *The Structural Transformation of the Public Sphere: An Inquiry into a Category of Bourgeois Society*. Boston: MIT Press, 1991.

Harcourt, Alfred. "Publishing in New York." In *Publishers on Publishing*. Ed. Gerald Gross, 245–232. New York: Grosset and Dunlap, 1961.

Harker, Jaime. *America the Middlebrow: Women's Novels, Progressivism, and Middlebrow Authorship between the Wars*. Amherst: University of Massachusetts Press, 2007.

Hart, James D. *The Popular Book: A History of America's Literary Taste*. New York: Oxford University Press, 1950.

Hazard, Lucy L. *The Frontier in American Literature*. New York: Thomas Crowell, 1927.

Hemingway, Ernest. "Big Two-Hearted River." *The Collected Short Stories of Ernest Hemingway*. Finca Vigia Edition. New York: Charles Scribner's Sons, 1987.

———. *A Farewell to Arms*. 1929. Reprint, New York: Charles Scribner's Sons, 1957.

———. *For Whom the Bell Tolls*. New York: Charles Scribner's Sons, 1940.

———. *In Our Time*. 1925. Reprint, New York: Charles Scribner's Sons, 1958.

———. *The Letters of Ernest Hemingway*. Vol. 1, 1901–1922. Ed. Sandra Spanier and Robert W. Trogden. Cambridge, UK: Cambridge University Press, 2011.

———. *The Letters of Ernest Hemingway*. Vol 2, 1923–1925. Ed. Sandra Spanier and Albert J. De Fazio III. Cambridge, UK: Cambridge University Press, 2013.

———. *A Moveable Feast*. 1954. Reprint, New York: Charles Scribner's Sons, 1963.

———. "Soldier's Home." *The Collected Short Stories of Ernest Hemingway*. Finca Vigia Edition. New York: Charles Scribner's Sons, 1987.

———. *The Sun Also Rises*. New York: Charles Scribner's Sons, 1926.

———. *The Torrents of Spring*. New York: Charles Scribner's Sons, 1925.

Henriksen, Louise Levitas. *Anzia Yezierska: A Writer's Life*. New Brunswick, NJ: Rutgers University Press, 1988.

Hoffman, Frederick. *Freudianism and the Literary Mind*. 1945. Reprint, Baton Rouge: Louisiana State University Press, 1957.

———. *The Twenties: American Writing in the Postwar Decade*. New York: Viking, 1955.

Hoffman, Frederick, Charles Allen, and Carolyn Ulrich. *The Little Magazine: A History and a Bibliography*. Princeton, NJ: Princeton University Press, 1946, 1947.

———. "The Voices of Sherwood Anderson." *Shenandoah* 13 (Spring 1962): 15–19.

Frederick Hoffmann "The Voices of Sherwood Anderson" *Shenandoah* (1968) in *The Achievement of Sherwood Anderson*, ed. R.L. White. Chapel Hill: University of North Carolina, 1966, 243.

Homestead, Melissa. "Middlebrow Readers and Pioneer Heroines: Willa Cather's *My Antonia*." In *Crisscrossing Borders in the Literature of the American West*. Ed. Reginald Dyck and Cheil Reuter, 75–94. New York: Palgrave Macmillan, 2009.

Hook, Andrew, ed. *Dos Passos: A Collection of Critical Essays*. Englewood Cliffs, NJ: Prentice-Hall, 1974.

Howe, Irving. "The Culture of Modernism." *Commentary* (November 1967): 48–65.

———. *Sherwood Anderson*. New York: William Sloane Associates, 1951.

Huggins, Nathan. *Harlem Renaissance*. 1971. Reprint, Oxford, UK: Oxford University Press, 2007.

Hughes, Langston. "American Art or Negro Art." *Nation* 122 (August 18, 1927): 743.

———. *The Big Sea: An Autobiography*. New York: Random House, 1940.

———. *The Collected Works of Langston Hughes*. Columbia: University of Missouri Press, 2001, 2002.

———. *My Early Days in Harlem*. New York: Random House, 1963.

———. "The Negro Artist and the Racial Mountain." *Langston Hughes Reader*. New York: George Braziller, 1981.

———. *Not without Laughter*. New York: Alfred A. Knopf, 1930.

Hughes, Langston, and Arnold Rampersad. *The Collected Works of Langston Hughes*. Columbia: University of Missouri Press, 2002.

Hulme, T. E. "Crites, a Commentary." *Criterion* 2 (April 1924): 23.

Humble, Nicola. *The Feminine Middlebrow 1920s to 1930s: Class, Domesticity, and Bohemianism*. Oxford, UK, and New York: Oxford University Press, 2001.

Hurston, Zora Neale. *Dust Tracks on a Road: An Autobiography*. New York: J. B. Lippincott, 1942.

———. *Their Eyes Were Watching God*. 1937. Reprint, New York: Fawcett, 1969.

———. *A Zora Neale Hurston Reader*. Ed. Alice Walker. Old Westbury, NY: Feminist Press, 1979.

Huxley, Aldous. *Brave New World*. 1932. Reprint, New York: HarperCollins, 2006.

Iser, Wolfgang. *The Act of Reading*. London: Routledge/Kegan Paul, 1979.

———. *The Implied Reader*. Baltimore, MD: Johns Hopkins University Press, 1974.

Izzo, David, and Lincoln Konkle, eds. *Stephen Vincent Benet: Essays on His Life and Work*. Jefferson, NC: McFarland, 2002.

"Jefferson Mother's Club." *Columbia Evening Missourian*, May 3, 1921.

Johnson, James Weldon. *Autobiography of an Ex-Colored Man*. 1912, 1927. Reprint, New York: Library of America, 2004.

———. *Black Manhattan*. 1930. Reprint, New York: Arno Press, 1968.

———. *James Weldon Johnson: Writings*. New York: Library of America, 2004.

———. *The Negro in New York: An Informal History. 1626–1940*. Ed. Roy Ottley and William Wetherby. New York: Praeger, 1969.

Jones, Edgar. "Shell Shock." *American Psychological Association* 46, no. 12 (June 2012): 18.

Joseph, Michael. *The Adventure of Publishing*. London: Allen Wingate, New York: R. R. Bowker, 1949. Reprinted in *Publishers on Publishing*. Ed. Gerald Gross. New York: Grosset and Dunlap, 1961.

Joyce, James. *A Portrait of the Artist as a Young Man*. 1916. Reprint, New York: Penguin, 2003.

———. *Selected Letters*. Ed. Richard Ellmann. London: Faber and Faber, 1976.

———. *Ulysses*. Gabler Edition. New York: Vintage/Random House, 1986.

Kalaidjian, Walter, ed. *Cambridge Companion to American Modernism*. Cambridge, UK: Cambridge University Press, 2005.

Kantor, Louis. "Why Novels?" *New York Tribune*, April 22, 1922, p. 11.

Kardos, Michael. "Musical and Ideological Synthesis in James Weldon Johnson's *Autobiography of an Ex-Colored Man*." In *Music and Literary Modernism*. Ed. Robert McParland, 126–35. Newcastle upon Tyne, UK: Cambridge Scholars Publishing, 2007.

Kazin, Alfred. *On Native Grounds: An Interpretation of Modern American Prose Literature*. New York: Reynal and Hitchcock, 1942.

Kazin, Alfred, and Ted Solataroff. *Alfred Kazin's America: Critical and Personal Writings*. New York: Harper Perennial, 2004.

Kendrick, Ames. "Lewis's *Babbitt* Is an Even Better Novel Than *Main Street*: Sinclair Lewis Picks on U.S. Americans Again." *Washington Times*, September 17, 1922.

Kenner, Hugh. *Joyce's Voices*. London: Faber and Faber, 1978.

———. *The Pound Era*. Berkeley: University of California Press, 1971.

Kerman, Cynthia Earle, and Richard Eldridge. *The Lives of Jean Toomer: A Hunger for Wholeness*. Baton Rouge: Louisiana State University Press, 1987.

Kidd, David Comer, and Emanuele Castano. "Reading Literary Fiction Improves Theory of Mind." *Science* 342, no. 6 (October 2013): 377–80.

Kofsky, Frank. *Black Music, White Business: Illuminating the History and Political Economy of Jazz*. New York: Pathfinder, 1998.

Kronenberger, Louis. "Review of *Showboat*." *New York Times*, August 22, 1926, p. 12.

Krutch, Joseph Wood. *American Drama since 1918: An Informal History*. New York: Random House, 1929.

———. *The Modern Temper*. New York: Random House, 1929.

———. "Professor's House: Second Best" in *Willa Cather and Her Critics*. Ithaca: Cornell University Press, 1967. 369–70.

———. "Reviews of Four Novels: The Lady as Artist." In *Willa Cather and Her Critics*, ed. James Schroeter, 52–54. Ithaca, NY: Cornell University Press, 1967.

Kusmer, Kenneth L. *Black Cleveland, 1870–1930*. Urbana: University of Illinois Press, 1976.

Landsberg, Melvin. *Dos Passos's Path to U.S.A.: A Political Biography, 1912–1936*. Boulder, CO: Associated University Press, 1972.

Laurance, Frank M. *Hemingway and the Movies*. Jackson: University Press of Mississippi, 1981.

Lawrence, D. H. *Phoenix: The Posthumous Papers of D. H. Lawrence*. Ed. Edward McDonald. London: Heinemann, 1936.

———. "Review of *Manhattan Transfer* and *In Our Time*" (1927), 364.

———. *Studies in Classic American Literature: The Cambridge Edition of the Works of D. H. Lawrence*. Vol. 2. Ed. Ezra Greenspan, Lindeth Vasey, John Worthen. Cambridge, UK: Cambridge University Press, 2003.

———. "Why the Novel Matters." *Selected Criticism*, 1956. Available online at http://individual.utoronto.ca/amlit/why_the_novel_matters.htm (accessed December 3, 2014).

Leavis, Q. D. *Fiction and the Reading Public*. London: Chatto, 1932.

Lehan, Richard. *Theodore Dreiser: His World and His Novels*. Carbondale: Southern Illinois University Press, 1969.

Levine, Lawrence. *Highbrow/Lowbrow: The Emergence of Cultural Hierarchy in America*. Cambridge: Harvard University Press, 1988.

Levy, Eugene. *James Weldon Johnson: Black Leader, Black Voice*. Chicago: University of Chicago Press, 1973.

Lewis, David Levering. *W. E. B. Du Bois: Biography of a Race*. New York: Henry Holt, 1993.

———. *When Harlem Was in Vogue*. 1979. rpt. New York: Vintage, 1982.

"Lewis Reads Work of Nebraska Authors." *Red Cloud Chief*, April 14, 1921.

Lewis, Sinclair. *Arrowsmith*. New York: Harcourt Brace, 1925.

———. *Babbitt*. 1922. Reprint, New York: Library of America, 1992.

———. *Dodsworth*. New York: Harcourt Brace, 1929.

———. *Elmer Gantry*. New York: Harcourt Brace, 1927.

————. *Main Street*. 1920. Reprint, New York: Library of America, 1992.

————. *The Man from Main Street: Selected Essays and Other Writings of Sinclair Lewis. A Sinclair Lewis Reader, 1909–1950*. Ed. Harry E. Maule and Melville E. Cane. 1963. Reprint, London: Heinemann, 1964.

————. *The Man Who Knew Coolidge*. New York: Harcourt Brace, 1928.

————. "Manhattan at Last!" *Saturday Review of Literature* 2 (December 1925): 361.

Richard Lingeman. *Sinclair Lewis: Rebel from Main Street*. St. Paul Borealis Books: Minnesota Historical Society Press, 2002. p. 552.

Lippmann, Walter. *A Preface to Morals*. New Brunswick, NJ: Transaction, 1982.

Locke, Alaine. *The New Negro*. 1925. Reprint, New York: Simon and Schuster, 1992.

Lomax, Alan. *The Land Where the Blues Began*. New York: Pantheon, 1993.

Long, Elizabeth. *Book Clubs: Women and the Uses of Reading in Everyday Life*. Chicago: University of Chicago Press, 2003.

Lott, Eric. *Theft and Love: Blackface Minstrelsy and the American Working Class*. New York: Oxford University Press, 1993.

Lowenthal, Leo. *Literature, Popular Culture, and Society*. Palo Alto: University of California Press, 1961.

Lowry, E. D. "*Manhattan Transfer*: Dos Passos's Wasteland." In *Dos Passos: A Collection of Critical Essays*. Ed. Andrew Hook, 53–60. Englewood Cliffs, NJ: Prentice-Hall, 1974.

Ludington, Townsend. *John Dos Passos: A Twentieth-Century Odyssey*. New York: E. P. Dutton, 1980.

Luey, Beth. "Modernity and Print III: The United States, 1890–1970." In *A Companion to the History of the Book*. Ed. Simon Eliot and Jonathan Rose, 368–80. Malden, MA, and Oxford, UK: Wiley-Blackwell, 2009.

Lynn, Kenneth S. "The Troubled Fisherman, Big Two-Hearted River." In *Critical Approaches to the Short Stories of Ernest Hemingway*. Ed. Jackson J. Benson, 149–55. Durham, NC: Duke University Press, 1990.

Madden, David. "The Necessity for an Aesthetic of Popular Culture," *Journal of Popular Culture* 7 (1973): 1–13.

Magill, Frank, ed. *Cinema: The Novel into Film*. Magill Surveys. Pasadena, CA: Salem, 1980.

Mahoney, Eva. "How Willa Cather Found Herself." *Omaha World-Herald*, November 27, 1921.

Mailloux, Stephen. *Interpretive Conventions: The Reader in the Study of American Fiction*. Ithaca, NY: Cornell University Press, 1982.

Maine, Barry. *Dos Passos: The Critical Heritage*. London: Routledge, 1988.

Mariani, Paul. *Theodore Dreiser*. New York: William Sloane Associates, 1951.

————. *William Carlos Williams: A New World Naked*. New York: W. W. Norton, 1990.

Matthiessen, F. O. *The Achievement of T. S. Eliot*. New York: Houghton Mifflin, 1935.

Mayfield, Sara. *Exile from Paradise: Zelda and Scott Fitzgerald*. New York: Delacorte, 1971.

McCarthy, Thomas J. "Letter." *Bismarck Tribune*, March 21, 1921.

McCleery, Alisdair. "Changing Audiences: The Case of the Penguin Ulysses." In *Readings on Audience and Textual Materiality*. Ed. Graham Allen, Carrie Griffin, and Mary O'Donnell, 131–142. London: Pickering and Chatto, 2011.

McCormack, Hazel. Letters to F. Scott Fitzgerald. September 1924, May 15, 1925. Firestone Library, Princeton University.

McDonald, Gail. *American Literature and Culture, 1900–1960*. Malden, MA: Blackwell, 2007.

McHenry, Elizabeth. "An Association of Kindred Spirits: Black Readers and Their Reading Rooms." In *Institutions of Reading: The Social Life of Libraries in the United States*. Ed. Thomas Augst and Kenneth Carpenter, 99–110. Amherst: University of Massachusetts Press, 2007.

————. *Forgotten Readers: Recovering the Lost History of African American Literary Societies*. Durham, NC: Duke University Press, 2002.

McIntyre, Alfred R. "Little Brown and Company." In *Publishers on Publishing*. Ed. Gerald Gross, 111–127. New York: Grosset and Dunlap, 1961.

McKay, Claude. *Banjo: A Story without a Plot*. New York: Harper and Brothers, 1929.

Menand, Louis. *Discovering Modernism: T. S. Eliot and His Context*. Oxford, UK: Oxford University Press, 1987.

Mencken, H. L. "Review of *Flappers and Philosophers*." *Smart Set*, 1920.

———. "Review of *The Great Gatsby*." *Chicago Daily Tribune*, May 3, 1925.

Meyers, Jeffrey. *Hemingway: A Biography*. New York: HarperCollins, 1985.

———. *Scott Fitzgerald: A Biography*. New York: HarperCollins, 1994.

Middleton, JoAnn. *Willa Cather's Modernism: A Study of Style and Technique*. Madison, NJ: Fairleigh Dickinson University Press, 1990.

Miller, Arthur. *Modern Drama: Twentieth Century Perspectives*. Englewood Cliffs, NJ: Prentice-Hall, 1969.

Miller, Gabriel. *Screening the Novel: Rediscovered American Fiction in Film*. New York: Frederick Unger, 1980.

Miller, James E. *F. Scott Fitzgerald: His Art and His Technique*. New York: New York University Press, 1964.

Millett, Fred B. *Contemporary American Authors*. New York: Harcourt Brace, 1940.

Minter, David. *A Cultural History of the American Novel: Henry James to William Faulkner*. New York: Cambridge University Press, 1994.

———. "Pride and Nakedness, As I Lay Dying." *William Faulkner: New Perspectives*. Ed. Richard Brodhead. Englewood Cliffs, NJ: Prentice-Hall, 1983.

———. "The Strange Career of Joe Christmas," Ed. Harold Bloom. New York: Chelsea House, 2008.

———. *William Faulkner: His Life and Work*. Baltimore, MD: Johns Hopkins University Press, 1997.

Mitchell, Angelyn, ed. *Within the Circle: An Anthology of African American Criticism from the Harlem Renaissance*. Durham, NC: Duke University Press, 1994.

Mizener, Arthur. *The Far Side of Paradise*. Boston: Houghton Mifflin, 1951.

Modleski, Tania. *Loving with a Vengeance: Mass-Produced Fantasies for Women*. 1982. Reprint, London: Routledge, 2007.

Molesworth, Charles. *Marianne Moore: A Literary Life*. New York: Atheneum, 1990.

Morrison, Mark S. *The Public Face of Modernism: Little Magazines, Audiences, and Reception, 1905–1920*. Madison: University of Wisconsin Press, 2001.

Mumford, Lewis. *Freeman*, April 18, 1923.

———. *Melville*. New York: Harcourt Brace, 1929.

Murphy, John J. *Critical Essays on Willa Cather*. Boston: G. K. Hall, 1984.

Mussell, Kay. *Fantasy and Reconciliation: Contemporary Formulas in Women's Romance Fiction*. Santa Barbara, CA: ABC-CLIO, 1984.

Nanney, Lisa. *John Dos Passos Revisited*. New York: Twayne, 1998.

Noggle, Burt. *Into the 1920s: The United States from Armistice to Normalcy*. Urbana: University of Illinois Press, 1974.

North, Michael J. *The Dialect of Modernism: Language and Twentieth-Century Literature*. New York: Oxford University Press, 1994.

———. *Reading 1922: A Return to the Scene of the Modern*. Oxford, UK: Oxford University Press, 1999.

O'Brien, Sharon. *Willa Cather: The Emerging Voice*. New York: Oxford University Press, 1987.

O'Daniel, Thurman, ed. *Jean Toomer: A Critical Evaluation*. Washington, DC: Howard University Press, 1988.

Ogren, Kathy J. *The Jazz Revolution: Twenties America and the Meaning of Jazz*. Oxford, UK: Oxford University Press, 1989.

Oliver, Paul. *Aspects of the Blues Tradition*. 1968. Reprint, New York: Oak Publications, 1970.

Ong, Walter J. *Orality and Literacy: The Technologizing of the Word*. 1982. Reprint, New York: Methuen, 1988.

Orwell, George. *Bookshop Memories: Collected Essays, Journalism, and Letters*. Ed. Sonia Orwell and Ian Ayres. London: Secker and Warburg, 1968.

Ostransky, Leroy. *The Anatomy of Jazz*. Seattle: University of Washington Press, 1964.

Parker, Dorothy. *The Portable Dorothy Parker*. New York: Viking, 1973.

Parks, Tim. "Do We Need Stories?" *New York Review of Books Blog*, March 26, 2013, 1–2.

Parrington, Vernon. *Main Currents of American Thought*. New York: n.p., 1927–1930.

Paulson, Daryl S., and Stanley C. Krippner. *Haunted by Combat: Understanding PTSD in War Veterans, Reservists, and Troops Coming Back from Iraq*. Santa Barbara, CA: Greenwood, 2007.

Pavlic, Edward M. *Crossroads Modernism: Descent and Emergence in African American Literary Culture*. Minneapolis: University of Minnesota Press, 2002.

Pawley, Christine. *Reading Places: Literacy, Democracy, and the Public Library in the Cold War*. Amherst: University of Massachusetts Press, 2010.

Phillips, Gene D. *Hemingway and Film*. New York: Frederick Ungar, 1980.

Phillips, William L. "How Sherwood Anderson Wrote *Winesberg, Ohio*." *American Literature* 23 (March 1951): 7–30.

———. "Sherwood Anderson's Two Prize Pupils." *University of Chicago Magazine* 47 (January 1955): 9–12. Reprinted in *The Achievement of Sherwood Anderson*. Ed. Tray Lewis White. Chapel Hill, NC: University of North Carolina Press, 1996.

Pizer, Donald. *John Dos Passos: A Critical Study*. Charlottesville: University of Virginia Press, 1988.

Pound, Ezra. *Literary Essays*. Ed. T. S. Eliot. 1918. Reprint, New York: New Directions, 1968.

Prigozy, Ruth. *The Cambridge Companion to F. Scott Fitzgerald*. Cambridge, UK, and New York: Cambridge University Press, 2001.

———. "Poor Butterfly: F. Scott Fitzgerald and Popular Music." *Prospects* 2 (1976): 41–8.

Putnam, Robert. *Bowling Alone: The Collapse and Revival of American Community*. New York: Simon and Schuster, 2001.

Quirk, Tom. "Fitzgerald and Cather: The Great Gatsby." *American Literature* 54 (December 1978): 576–91.

Radway, Janice. "Reading Is Not Eating: Mass-Produced Literature and the Theoretical, Methodological, and Political Consequences of a Metaphor." *Book Research Quarterly* 2, no. 3 (Fall 1986): 7–29.

Rainey, Lawrence. *Institutions of Modernism: Literary Elites and Public Culture*. New Haven, CT: Yale University Press, 1998.

Rampersad, Arnold. *The Art and Imagination of W. E. B. Du Bois*. New York: Schocken, 1989.

———. *The Life of Langston Hughes*. New York: Oxford University Press, 1986.

———. "W. E. B. DuBois as a Man of Literature." *American Literature* 51 (March 1979): 50–68.

Ransom, John Crowe. *The New Criticism*. Norfolk, VA: New Directions, 1941.

Reynolds, Michael. *The Young Hemingway*. Oxford, UK: Blackwell, 1986.

Rhodes, Chip. *Structures of the Jazz Age: Mass Culture, Progressive Education, and Racial Discourse in American Modernism*. New York: Verso, 1998.

Rieff, Philip. *Freud: The Mind of the Moralist*. 1959. Reprint, Chicago: University of Chicago Press, 1979.

Robinson, Phyllis. *The Life of Willa Cather*. Garden City, NY: Doubleday, 1983.

Rose, Jonathan. *The Edwardian Temperament, 1895–1919*. Athens: Ohio University Press, 1986.

Rosenfeld, Paul. *Men Seen: Twenty-Four Modern Authors*. New York: Dial, 1925.

Rosowski, Susan. *The Voyage Perilous: Willa Cather's Romanticism*. Lincoln: University of Nebraska Press, 1986.

Salpeter, Harry. "The First Reader." *New York World*, August 16, 1927.

Sandel, Michael J. *Democracy's Discontent*. 1986. Reprint, Cambridge, UK: Belknap, Harvard University Press, 1998.

Sanders, David. *John Dos Passos: A Comprehensive Bibliography*. New York: Garland, 1983.

Sartre, Jean-Paul. "John Dos Passos and 1919." In *Literary and Philosophical Essays*. Trans. Annette Michelson, 88–96. London: Rider, 1955.

Schlesinger, Arthur M., Jr. *The Age of Roosevelt: The Crisis of the Old Order, 1919–1933*. Boston: Houghton Mifflin, 1957.

Schorer, Mark. "Ernest Hemingway." In *Major Writers of America*. Ed. Perry Miller, 675. New York: Harcourt Brace Jovanovich, 1962.

———. *Sinclair Lewis: An American Life*. New York: McGraw-Hill, 1961.

Schuller, Gunther. *Early Jazz: Its Roots and Musical Development*. New York: Oxford University Press, 1968.

Scott, Bonnie Kime, ed. *Gender in Modernism: New Geographies, Complex Intersections*. Urbana: University of Illinois Press, 2007.

Seldes, Gilbert. *The Seven Lively Arts*. New York: Harper and Brothers, 1924.

Seltzer, Louis B. "The Years Were Good." *Cleveland Memory Project*, Michael Swartz Library, Cleveland State University (1956), 57. Available online at http://www.clevelandmemory.org/ebooks/tywg/ (accessed December 12, 2014).

Shillinglaw, Susan. *On Reading* The Grapes of Wrath. New York: Penguin, 2014.

Sicherman, Barbara. *Well-Read Lives: How Books Inspired A Generation of Women*. Chapel Hill: University of North Carolina Press, 2012.

Singal, Daniel J. *William Faulkner: The Making of a Modernist*. Chapel Hill: University of North Carolina Press, 1999.

Sklar, Robert. *Movie Made America: A Social History of American Movies*. New York: Random House, 1975.

Slote, Bernice. "The House of Willa Cather." In *The Art of Willa Cather*. Ed. Bernice Slote and Virginia Faulkner, 31–48. Lincoln: University of Nebraska Press, 1974.

Soto, Michael. *The Modernist Nation: Generation, Renaissance, and Twentieth-Century American Literature*. Tuscaloosa: University of Alabama Press, 2004.

Soule, George. *Prosperity Decade, 1917–1929*. New York: Rinehart, 1947.

Spengler, Oswald. *The Decline of the West*. London: Allen and Unwin, 1926.

Spiller, Robert, et al. *Literary History of the United States*. Vol. 3. New York: Macmillan, 1948.

St. Pierre, Roger. *The Best of the Blues: The Essential CD Guide*. San Francisco, CA: Collins, 1993.

Stearns, Marshall. *The Story of Jazz*. Oxford, UK, and New York: Oxford University Press, 1956.

Stein, Gertrude. *The Autobiography of Alice B. Toklas*. New York: Vintage, 1990.

———. "Composition as Explanation." London: Hogarth Press, 1926.

———. "Memories of Picasso." *Writings, 1932–1946*. Vol. 2. New York: Library of America, 1998.

Steinbeck, John. *America and Americans and Selected Nonfiction*. Ed. Susan Shillinglaw and Jackson J. Benson. New York: Viking, 2002.

———. *Cup of Gold*. New York: McBride, 1929.

———. *The Grapes of Wrath*. New York: Viking, 1939.

———. *A Life in Letters*. Ed. Elaine Steinbeck and Robert Wallston. New York: Viking, 1975.

Stephens, Robert O. *Hemingway's Nonfiction: The Public Voice*. Chapel Hill: University of North Carolina Press, 1968.

Stepto, Robert. *From Beyond the Veil: A Study of Afro-American Narrative*. Urbana: University of Illinois Press, 1979.

Stewart-Baxter, Derrick. *Ma Rainey and the Classic Blues Singers*. New York: Stein and Day, 1970.

Stouck, David. *Willa Cather's Imagination*. Lincoln: University of Nebraska Press, 1975.

Strachey, Lytton. *Eminent Victorians*. 1918. Reprint, New York: Penguin, 1990.

Stroud, Parry. *Stephen Vincent Benet*. New York: Twayne, 1962.

Struve, Laura. "Sisters of Sorts: Reading Romantic Fiction and the Bonds among Female Readers." *Journal of Popular Culture* 44, no. 6 (December 2011): 1,289–1,306.

Sundquist, Eric J. *To Wake the Nations: Race in the Making of American Literature*. Cambridge, MA: Harvard University Press, 1993.

Susman, Warren I. *Culture as History: The Transformation of American Society in the Twentieth Century.* New York: Pantheon, 1984.

Sylvander, Carolyn Weedon. *Jessie Redmon Fauset.* Troy: Whitson, 1981.

Tanksley, William. "Frederick Hoffmann." PhD dissertation, University of Illinois, Chicago, Illinois, 1969.

Tawney, R. H. *Religion and the Rise of Capitalism.* New York: Harcourt Brace, 1926.

"These Bad New Negroes: A Critique on Critics." *Pittsburgh Courier,* April 7, 1927.

Thurman, Wallace. *The Collected Writings of Wallace Thurman.* Ed. Amritjit and Daniel Scott III. New Brunswick, NJ: Rutgers University Press, 2003.

Tichi, Cecelia. *Shifting Gears: Technology, Literature, Culture in Modernist America.* Chapel Hill: University of North Carolina Press, 1987.

Tick, Edward. *War and the Soul: Healing Our Nation's Veterans from PTSD.* Wheaton, IL: Quest, 2005.

Tittle, Walter. "Glimpses of Interesting Americans." *Century,* July 1925, p. 312.

Toomer, Jean. *Cane.* 1923. Reprint, New York: Norton, 1988.

———. *A Jean Toomer Reader.* Ed. Frederick L. Rusch. New York: Oxford University Press, 1993.

———. *The Letters of Jean Toomer, 1919–1924.* Ed. Mark Whalan. Knoxville: University of Tennessee Press, 1996.

Trilling, Lionel. "Hemingway and His Critics," *Partisan Review* 6 (Winter 1939).

———. *The Liberal Imagination: Essays on Literature and Society.* New York: Viking, 1950.

"A Triumphant Negro Heroine." *New York Herald Tribune Books,* April 11, 1928, p. 3.

Tucker, Mark. *The Duke Ellington Reader.* Oxford, UK, and New York: Oxford University Press, 1995.

Updike, John. "No Brakes: A New Biography of Sinclair Lewis." *New Yorker,* February 4, 2002. Available online at http://www.newyorker.com/magazine/2002/02/04/no-brakes (accessed December 10, 2014).

Van Doren, Carl. "Lucifer from Nantucket: An Introduction to Moby Dick." *Century,* August 1925, pp. 495–501.

Van Vechten, Carl. "All God's Children Got Songs." *Nation* 62 (August 1925): 63.

———. *Excavations: A Book of Advocacies.* 1926. Reprint, New York: Books for Libraries Press, 1971.

———. "Folk Songs of the American Negro." *New York Herald Tribune Books,* October 25, 1928, 52

———. *Keep A-Inchin' Along: Selected Writings of Carl Van Vechten about Black Art and Letters.* Ed. D. Bruce Kellner. Westport, CT: Greenwood, 1979.

Veronesi, Gene P. "Italian Americans and Their Communities in Cleveland." *Cleveland Memory Project,* Michael Swartz Library, Cleveland State University (2007), 233. Available online at http://www.clevelandmemory.org/italians/ (accessed December 12, 2014).

Vidal, Gore. "The Romance of Sinclair Lewis." *New York Review of Books,* October 8, 1992. Available online at http://www.nybooks.com/articles/archives/1992/oct/08/the-romance-of-sinclair-lewis/ (accessed December 10, 2014).

Wagner, Linda W. *Dos Passos: Artist as American.* Austin: University of Texas Press, 1979.

Walcutt, Charles. *American Literary Naturalism: A Divided Stream.* Minneapolis: University of Minnesota Press, 1956.

Warren, Robert Penn. "Why Do We Read Fiction?" *Saturday Evening Post,* July 1986, pp. 62–65.

Way, Brian. *F. Scott Fitzgerald and the Art of Social Fiction.* New York: St. Martin's Press, 1980.

Weaver, Raymond M. *Herman Melville: Mariner and Mystic.* 1921. Reprint, New York: Pageant, 1961.

Wells, H. G. *Outline of History.* New York and London: Macmillan, 1920.

Welty, Eudora. *The Eye of the Story.* New York: Random House, 1977.

Wescott, Glenway. *The Apple of the Eye.* New York: Dial, 1924.

———. *Goodbye Wisconsin.* New York: Harper's, 1928.

———. *The Grandmothers.* New York: Harper's, 1927.

Wexler, Joyce Piell. *Who Paid for Modernism? Art, Money, and the Fiction of Conrad, Joyce, and Lawrence*. Fayetteville: University of Arkansas Press, 1997.

Wharton, Edith. *The Age of Innocence*. New York: Appleton, 1920.

———. *Fighting France: From Dunkerque to Belfort*. New York: Charles Scribner's Sons, 1915.

———. *The House of Mirth.* New York: Charles Scribner's Sons, 1905.

———. *Old New York*. New York: Appleton, 1924.

———. *A Son at the Front*. New York: Charles Scribner's Sons, 1923.

———. *The Writing of Fiction*. New York: Charles Scribner's Sons, 1925.

White, Ray Lewis, ed. *The Achievement of Sherwood Anderson: Essays in Criticism*. Chapel Hill: University of North Carolina Press, 1966.

Wiegand, Wayne A. "Community Places and Reading Spaces: Main Street and Public Libraries in the Rural Heartland, 1876–1956." In *Libraries and the Reading Public in Twentieth-Century America*. Ed. Christine Pawley and Louise S. Robbins, 23–39. Madison: University of Wisconsin Press, 2013.

———. *Main Street Public Library: Community Places in the Rural Heartland, 1876–1956*. Ames: University of Iowa Press, 2011.

Wilder, Thornton. *The Bridge of San Luis Rey*, 1927.

———. *The Cabala*. New York: Boni and Liveright, 1926.

———. *Our Town*. 1938. *Three Plays by Thornton Wilder*. New York: Harper Perennial, 2007.

———. *The Skin of Our Teeth*. 1942. *Three Plays by Thornton Wilder*. New York: Harper Perennial, 2007.

———. *The Woman of Andros*. 1930.

Williams, Raymond. *Culture and Society, 1780–1950.* New York: Harper and Row, 1966.

Williams, William Carlos. *The Autobiography of William Carlos Williams*. New York: New Directions, 1967.

———. *The Build Up*. New York: Random House, 1952.

———. *The Great American Novel*. New York: Three Mountains Press, 1923.

———. *Imaginations. The Great American Novel*. Ed. Webster Scott. New York: New Directions, 1970.

———. *In the American Grain*. 1925, 1956. Reprint, New York: New Directions, 2009.

———. *In the Money*. Norfolk, CT: New Directions, 1940.

———. *Paterson*. Norfolk, CT: New Directions, 1946, 1948. 1949, 1951, 1958.

———. *Spring and All*. Paris: Contact Publishing, 1923.

———. *A Voyage to Pagany*. New York: Macaulay, 1928.

———. *White Mule*. Norfolk, CT: New Directions, 1937.

Williams, Wirt. *The Tragic Art of Ernest Hemingway*. Baton Rouge: Louisiana State University Press, 1982.

Wilson, Edmund. *Edmund Wilson: Literary Essays and Reviews, 1920s and 30s*. New York: Library of America, 2007.

———. *The Portable Edmund Wilson*. Ed. Lewis M. Dabney. New York: Viking, 1983.

———. *The Shores of Light: A Literary Chronicle of the Twenties and Thirties*. New York: Farrar, Straus, and Young, 1952.

Wilson, Edmund, and Lewis M. Dabney. *Edmund Wilson: Literary Essays and Reviews of the 1920s and 1930s*. New York: Library of America, 2007.

Wilson, Elena, ed. *Edmund Wilson: Letters on Literature and Politics, 1912–1972*. New York: Farrar, Straus and Giroux, 1977.

Wintz, Cary D. *Black Culture and the Harlem Renaissance*. Houston, TX: Rice University Press, 1988.

Wiser, William. *The Crazy Years: A Hectic Scrapbook of the Jazz Age*. London: Thames and Hudson, 1983.

Wolfe, Thomas. *Look Homeward Angel*. New York: Charles Scribner's Sons, 1929.

Women's Enterprise. Baton Rouge, Louisiana, June 1, 1922, p. 9.

Woodress, James. *Willa Cather: A Literary Life*. Lincoln: University of Nebraska Press, 1987.

Woodward, Thomas. *In His Own Time*. Minneapolis, MN: Privately printed.

Wrenn, John. *John Dos Passos*. New York: Twayne, 1961.

Wylie, Elinor. "Review of *Young People's Pride*." *New Republic* 32 (October 25, 1922): 22–24.

Yeats, William Butler. *Collected Poems*. New York: Macmillan, 1974.

Yezierska, Anzia. *Arrogant Beggar*. New York: Doubleday, 1927.

———. *The Bread Givers*. New York: Doubleday.Page, 1925.

———. *Children of Loneliness*. New York: Funk and Wagnalls, 1923.

———. *Hungry Hearts*. Boston: Houghton Mifflin, 1920.

———. *Salome of the Tenements*. New York: Boni and Liveright, 1922.

Zimmerman, Michael P. "Herman Melville in the 1920s: A Study of the Origins of the Melville Revival with Annotated Bibliography." PhD dissertation. Columbia University, New York, 1963.

INDEX

ABOUT THE AUTHOR

Robert McParland is associate professor of English and chair of the Department of English at Felician College. He has published numerous book chapters and articles, including essays on Herman Melville, Ernest Hemingway, and Robert Penn Warren, amongst others. McParland is editor of *Music and Literary Modernism* (2008) and *Film and Literary Modernism* (2013), as well as author of *Charles Dickens's American Audience* (Lexington, 2010), *How to Write about Joseph Conrad* (2011), and *Mark Twain's Audience: A Critical Analysis of Reader Responses to the Writings of Mark Twain* (Lexington, 2014).